MAMA PAYS THE GROCERY BILL

❀

ROSEMARY DUFF WILLIAMSON

MILLENNIA BOOKS

Ida Mobberly Duff as a beautiful young matron. It is thought that the dress in which she posed displays "shadow embroidery," a popular fashion of the day.

I finished writing this book about my mother in 1987, for the enjoyment and remembrance of my family. When my sister, Beryl Barnett, died in 1987, I had six copies duplicated and spiral bound for my surviving siblings and my three children to enjoy while they were still with us.

Some of these copies have been given away and all of them have been lent out so much that they are becoming pretty beat-up. When excerpts have appeared in other publications, I have received requests from strangers asking for a copy of my "book," and that is the reason I finally decided to have it published.

As I reread it before sending it to the publisher, I realized how many people I mention have died in the last ten years, and I hope their families will see their part in our life in the first half of the twentieth century.

The book was written with the encouragement and forbearance of my husband, Henry (Hank) Williamson, who died in 1993. It is dedicated to his memory.

> Rosemary Duff Williamson
> Riverton, Wyoming
> 1996

Copyright ©1996 by Rosemary Duff Williamson

All rights reserved. No part of this publication may be reproduced or transmitted in any form or by any means, electronic or mechanical, including photocopy, recording, or any information storage or retrieval system, or otherwise, without the written permission of the author, except by a reviewer, who may wish to quote passages in a review for a newspaper, magazine, radio, or television.

ISBN 1-887150-08-0

Millennia Books
2120 70th Street
Lubbock, Texas 79412

Printed and bound in the United States of America

CONTENTS

Foreword
   Why Am I Writing About Mama?   *(1)*
Chapter 1
   Mama's Family   *(4)*
Chapter 2
   YaPapa   *(10)*
Chapter 3
   What Makes Mama Tick?   *(23)*
Chapter 4
   What Did Mama Look Like?   *(29)*
Chapter 5
   The First Thirteen Years   *(35)*
Chapter 6
   The House in the Country   *(49)*
Chapter 7
   More Country Life   *(66)*
Chapter 8
   It Was the Best of Times   *(74)*
Chapter 9
   It Was Still the Best of Times   *(87)*
Chapter 10
   It Was the Worst of Times   *(99)*
Chapter 11
   It Was Still the Worst of Times   *(110)*
Chapter 12
   Across from East Ward   *(125)*
Chapter 13
   Missionary Boxes from Heaven   *(136)*
Chapter 14
   The Hamburger Store   *(150)*
Chapter 15
   Big Spring Boarding House   *(159)*

Contents

Chapter 16
  Mama Never Sang in Church Again   *(170)*
Chapter 17
  Miss Ida Again   *(176)*
Chapter 18
  Mrs. Duff Took Care of Her Own   *(185)*
Chapter 19
  We Need to Move   *(201)*
Chapter 20
  Tech Tavern   *(211)*
Chapter 21
  More Crises for Mama   *(222)*
Chapter 22
  Oh, I Missed the Mountains   *(233)*
Chapter 23
  Life at 2118   *(244)*
Chapter 24
  Those Boarders at 2118   *(258)*
Chapter 25
  I Wish I'd Taught You to Cook   *(269)*
Chapter 26
  Grandma, We Didn't Hardly Have to Beg You   *(290)*
Afterword
  The Gospel According to Mama   *(313)*

MAMA PAYS THE GROCERY BILL

Ida Mobberly Duff: Her later years.

FOREWORD

What Am I Doing Writing a Book About Mama?

Any one of my siblings could have written (and may yet write) his or her version of this book about Mama. From their viewpoints, it might be an entirely different book because when we are together, we are amazed at the differences in what we remember. Even when we have recollections of the same incident, we remember completely different details, timing, individuals involved, and the outcome.

I have written several essays about Mama for writing classes and as entries in literary contests. A professor reminded me of other books that were collections of separate reminiscences, and several judges have expressed interest in knowing more about Mama. What did she look like? What motivated her? These were some of the questions they asked.

Friends say, "Your mother must have been quite a character—I'd like to have known her."

The last literary contest judge, in awarding me first place for my short essay, "Mama Pays the Grocery Bill," encouraged me with, "I'd like to see this made into a book." That's one of the reasons I'm the one of Mama's children who is writing this book.

Another reason is that when I was nineteen I was quite ill in the hospital for several weeks, unable to have visitors, and Mama was at my bed day and night for most of that time. She read to me, but I preferred hearing her talk about the olden days. Never again did we have that much uninterrupted time together, and she seemed to enjoy talking of her mother and of her own girlhood and early married life. As sick as I was, I remember wishing I could take this down in shorthand.

What Am I Doing Writing a Book About Mama? 2

I couldn't, of course, but her words must have been programmed deep in my memory, because as I write these reminiscences years later, many of the tales she told, the philosophies she expressed, and her feelings about different persons, have come back to me loud and clear. As she would say, "The Lord do provide."

I also want to leave to my grandchildren, who will spend more of their lives in the twenty-first century than in the twentieth century (if they live and nothing happens, as Mama might say, invariably adding, "How can you live and nothin' happen?") a little record of what life was like for their ancestors in the first half of the twentieth century. I hope they enjoy reading it when they're on a space station some day.

In addition to those reasons, I'm the middle child. Mama had four boys and a girl before she had me and three girls and a boy after me. Fred, the oldest, was nine years older than I, and I was ten years and a day when Mama's last baby was born. I have a soft spot in my heart for middle children—they're too young to do the things the big kids do and too old to be treated like little children. They are more closely connected with both ends of a family's life, however, and being the middle child comes in handy for the purpose of writing this book.

My knowledge of Mama and Papa and their life before my memory began retaining large chunks of facts is based on what Mama told me through the years and on the reminiscences of my brothers Berry and Howard. I have waited too late to benefit specifically from the memories of Fred and our sisters Elsie and Ida Rule. All are dead.

Mama lived sixteen years after I left home, but Ann lived in Mama's home until she, Ann, married and then she continued to live in the same Texas city—Lubbock—that Mama lived in the last twenty-five years of her life. Beryl lived in Plainview, a nearby town, and I have relied heavily on the reminiscences of those sisters. Although I was in pretty close touch with Mama during that time and saw her frequently through visits together in our respective homes, most of my memories of Mama and Papa are of the middle years of their lives.

I have encouraged my brothers and sisters and the grandchildren who remember Mama and Papa to share their memories with me, and the story would be missing many details without their contributions.

Rosemary Duff Williamson
Riverton, Wyoming
1987

CHAPTER 1

MAMA'S FAMILY

Mama would never have considered herself a career woman. All she wanted to do was earn enough money to help pay the grocery bill.

I never tried to analyze what motivated Mama. When Mama married him, Papa already owned a set of heavy, dark oak dining room furniture with a table that could extend to seat sixteen people.

"We'll just have to get busy and fill it up," Mama told him. And fill it she did—with their ten children and assorted visiting kinfolks and boarders. I suppose she thought if she wanted a big family, the least she could do was help pay the grocery bill.

The old Bible that was in the antique walnut dresser when it came to me after Mama's death has a full page covered with Papa's ornate handwriting, enumerating the family members and listing important days in the family's history.

B N Duff July 20 1873. That's Papa. B. N. stood for Berry Napoleon. Although Papa's maternal grandfather, Louis Paillet, had been born in Illinois in 1804, Papa's mother, Roseaner Paillet, had the blood of French patriots running in her veins and named her other son Lafayette. Papa was born in Alto, a small town near Monroe, Louisiana.

Ida Aug 15 1885. That's all Papa had written for Mama. She was Ida Belle Mobberly, born in Longview, Texas. Her mother was from a proud family of Kentucky and her father was another Kentuckian who was quite an entrepreneur in

post-Civil War East Texas. Mama was visiting her oldest sister in Monroe, Lousiana, when she met Papa.
Married Oct 10 1904. They were married at her parents' home in Longview and immediately went to Monroe to live.
Frederick M Nov 7 1905. The *M* was for Morton. Mama was thinking of her future daughter-in-law when she named her first-born Frederick Morton. Remember that Berry Napoleon name mentioned above? Mama was married in a time and society when it was absolutely essential for a proper young married woman to have engraved calling cards, and, for those cards to be socially correct, the husband's first two names must be used.

"There was no way I'd use a card with 'Mrs. Berry Napoleon Duff' engraved on it, so I had mine made with 'Mrs. Berry N. Duff' and always felt that I was out of step, socially speaking. That's why I gave that first baby a name I thought would look perfectly elegant on his wife's calling cards: 'Mrs. Frederick Morton Duff.'"

I believe he was through school and working before we called him Fred all the time. Before that he was called Frederick. My second son is named Fred.
Berry N Duff Aug 1 1908. The *N* is for Noel, a well-used family name on Mama's side of the house. He was called Berry Noel until he was nearly grown and since that time it has just been Berry. His oldest son is Berry Noel, Jr.
Howard C June 7 1910. The *C* is for Carlton, the name of a boarder and friend at the time. Mama warned us about naming a child after a living person, as Cap'n Carlton fell into disfavor with Mama and Papa for some reason unknown to me.
Gordon M Aug 10 1911.
Died 22 1911.

The *M* is for Mobberly. This was a blue baby who lived such a little while. Mama was told he could never have lived to adulthood. It would be 1944 before the operation that corrected the condition that caused the lack of oxygen in certain newborns—blue babies—was performed.

Elsie Mob. Duff Dec 27 1912. Mob. was Papa's abbreviation for Mobberly. Elsie was never particularly happy with her name or her birth date. She didn't care for the name Elsie; Mobberly certainly isn't conducive to shortening into a nickname, and the Christmas season did not lend itself to a personal birthday party nor more gifts for her birthday. Mama's next-to-the-youngest sister was Elsie Mobberly Standley, and Elsie, her namesake, was very fond of Aunt Elsie.

Rosemary Duff Oct 30 1914. That's me. They wanted to name me after my two grandmothers, and Mama chose the name Rosemary. Someone reminded her there was a movie actress of the time named Rosemary Lamar and she surely didn't want to name a child after her. Mama then changed the name to Mary Rose, until she very sensibly decided the world would not long remember the scandalous movie star and that I might as well have that pretty name. So back to Rosemary it was—all through school, graduation, Social Security, marriage—and then I got my birth certificate so I could get a pass to go on Army posts and found that I was legally Mary Rose. Evidently Mama forgot to tell the doctor she'd changed her mind.

Mama was still alive; Dr. Robert W. Faulk, the doctor who delivered me, was still alive, and I was working in a law office, so I came up with a long, convoluted affidavit to the effect that the baby registered as Mary Rose was the same person as the one who had gone through life as Rosemary.

Both Mama and the doctor signed it and I attached it to the copy of the birth certificate. Twenty-five years later, when I needed a passport, I could find neither the certificate nor the affidavit, and I traveled under the name of Mary Rose.

For the first dozen or so years of my life I was called "Manie" by my family (seems "Manie" was baby Elsie's pronunciation of Rosemary) and I've been called "Rosie" by about half of my friends since then.

I have been well-pleased with the name Rosemary; it was the only thing about me that the teachers always reacted to favorably and immediately. And I passed it on to my first-born.

Beryl Cath D Dec 17 1917. Beryl Catherine is named for Papa and for Papa's stepmother, whom we children called "Grandma," and Papa called "Aunt Kate." Although Beryl and I don't remember the same things at all, and she sometimes drives the rest of us up the wall with her peripatetic energy, her love of travel, and her interest in people—all so similar to Mama's characteristics—she has done more than any of the rest of us to keep the family in close contact since Mamas's death.

Ida Rule Duff Sep 16 1919. She was named after Mama, of course, and a friend of Mama's, Miss Effie Rule. All friends of Mama's were called "Miss" whatever their first name was. If they had married names or last names, they were of no consequence to us as children. There was a woman in town named Ida Rule Shaw who always claimed Ida Rule was named for her. Mama let her think that—said it made the woman feel better.

See that September 16th birth date? By this time Mama had learned that a child had to be seven years old by September 15 to be admitted to first grade, so she pragmatically instructed the doctor to date Ida Rule's birth certificate September 15, and he did.

Lydia Ann July 16 1923. Ann is named for Mama's sister Lydia and Papa's sister, Aunt Annie. She has been called Ann since she has been an adult. Mama wouldn't let us make Ann wash dishes when she was young.

"She'll be at home long after the rest of you are off on your own, and she'll be looking after us when we're old," Mama reasoned. As usual, Mama was right. Ann did look after Mama and helped Mama look after Papa in their last illnesses.

Lawrence M D Nov 1 1924. This last baby was born in Longview after Papa left for West Texas. They hadn't decided on a name before Papa left, and he wasn't named for several weeks. We youngsters called him "Little Boy Baby" because Lydia Ann, then only fifteen months old, was "the baby." By the time Papa wrote that he'd like to name him Lawrence Markham after their good friends, the H. M. Lawrences and Dr. Louis Markham, the name Little Boy had stuck, and we girls called him that until the time of his death. The big brothers called him "Mac."

Howard's younger son is named Lawrence Gordon, after Mama's two boys who died.

Well, there we are. Eight of us grew to become adults. I wish I could say that it's true that if you give children love, discipline, exemplary home life, a firm religious background, a sense of humor, a pride in family—all those things the experts recommend, and all of which Mama and Papa gave us —raising a family is a piece of cake. It doesn't work that way.

We were eight rugged individualists. Some of us had bad tempers; some of us were easy going. Some of us were stubborn, sarcastic, or sharp of tongue; some of us were the opposite. Some of us were too interested in worldly comforts; some of us rebelled from our parents' lifestyle and values.

The few times I saw mama cry were nearly always caused by her children. The first time, Howard and Berry were fighting and really going at it. A few years later, Elsie ran away from home and got married before she finished high school. Then I once thought it was a matter of life and death that I have something that cost two dollars and fifty cents when I was in college during the worst of the Depression years. Mama cried when she had to tell me that we couldn't afford it. Now I can't even remember what it was that I wanted.

The last time I saw her cry, Fred was in financial trouble. Mama, anxious to share the blame, said it was because he had helped the family so generously.

I know there must have been other times, because she often said, "I wouldn't take a million dollars for any one of my children, but there are times I'd give you the whole kit'n'caboodle for nothin."

Mama once gave Hank, my husband, a thumbnail character sketch of each of her children. The longer we live the more we see how accurate and incisive each sketch was. She recognized and encouraged what assets each of us had, but she also knew our faults and foibles and loved us anyway.

While the brothers and sisters are similar, yet different, and while we do not see those family years exactly alike, there are two immutable facts upon which we all agree. First, there was a very small supply of money, and second, but more important, there was a very large supply of love. We all knew that we were loved—loved completely and unequivocally. We were not an outwardly affectionate family, and I doubt that Mama and Papa ever put their love for us into words. They just lived it.

Mama wanted a big family and it never occurred to her to worry about whether they could afford it. "I reckon some people would say havin' four boys was enough family, but I wouldn't have missed havin' my five girls for anything in the world. I reckon I didn't have any more sense than to believe that the good Lord wouldn't send more children than we could handle. Although it's been quite a hojang at times, I reckon I can still say—and every day that I live I say it over and over again—"The Lord do provide."

CHAPTER 2

YAPAPA

Mama, of course, didn't have all those children right off the bat, at the very beginning of her marriage. But she did start off at the very beginning of her marriage trying to help pay the grocery bill by taking in boarders. One or two elderly gentlemen at a time were settled into the front room—not always a spare room, because Papa's father and stepmother lived with them in the early years when those boarders took their meals with the family. It was not a necessity that she help with the grocery bill at that time because, as she told us in later years, they were considered quite a prosperous young couple.

"YaPapa (Mama always called him "YaPapa" when she was speaking to us children) was the catch of Monroe when I married him. He was thirty-two years old and the handsomest man in town. He didn't smoke, drink, or gamble—he was a Baptist! When I told my own Papa all of that, when he asked about this young man I'd met in Monroe and wanted to marry, my own Papa said, 'I reckon he sounds like he just might be too good for you.' Not only that, YaPapa was makin' about a hundred dollars a month, about twice as much, maybe three times as much, as most other young men made in those days. Oh, I was lucky as all git out."

Mama had been visiting her oldest sister, Daisy, whose husband, W. T. Tardy, was pastor of the First Baptist Church in Monroe, Louisiana, when Mama met Papa at church. For the rest of their days, church was an important part of their lives, Papa being a deacon and sometimes Sunday School superintendent and Mama often teaching women's classes and at one time serving as treasurer of the church. We have an old clipping from a Monroe newspaper, which tells the story well:

> "Mr. B. N. Duff will leave tomorrow morning for Long View, Texas, where he will be married to Miss Ida Mobberly, a charming young lady of that place, Monday morning. Miss Mobberly is a sister of Mrs. W. T. Tardy of this city, and made many friends during a recent visit here. Mr. Duff is one of Monroe's most promising young business men, being a stockholder in the large wholesale house of the Keller Grocer company. The Star is pleased to extend its congratulations."

Until I found this clipping in recent years, I thought he had worked for Kelley Grocery Company. That was because of Mama's southern accent, which she passed on to most of her children. In our family there were very few *R* sounds, particularly at the end of a word, no final *G's* comin' or goin', and most words that should have ended in an *O* sound ended with an *A*: *tomorra* for *tomorrow,* for instance, and *Negra* for *Negro.* Somehow, *wasn't* came out *wadden,* and *isn't* came out *idden,* but we understood one another. Of course, *y'all* was the plural form of *you.* We were one of those families who thought President Jimmy Carter was the first president who didn't have an accent.

The photograph made of Papa about the time of the clipping shows a solemn, handsome young man with deep brown eyes and black hair. Beryl's son Robert strongly resembles that picture.

All of his life, Papa always dressed completely upon arising each morning—shirt, tie, the whole works. He was a tall man, probably overweight in his middle years, but we thought all papas were that way. When he was in his seventies, Papa got into a fight with a young man who called him an old man and accused Papa of stealing money from the ice house where they worked. Ann said he came in from work and cooked supper for her (Mama was gone on some of her travels at the time.), and it was only when she saw blood on his shirt that she realized he'd had troubles. She was able to get few of the details out of him, but he repeated several times, "He had no business sayin' that about me."

Papa's mother had died when Papa was about eighteen months old. The family story is that her last words were, "Get the baby, he's about to fall."

They found the baby—Papa—just about to fall from a high, outside porch (which Papa always called a *gallery*). Papa and his siblings were placed in an orphanage for some time until his father married his late wife's sister, Catherine—Papa's Aunt Kate and our Grandma.

Papa had no more than a grammar school education (I thought he went only through third grade.). I recently saw on Ann's bookshelf a Revised Edition of *The Elementary Spelling Book* by Noah Webster, L.L.D., published in 1857. On the inside of the front cover is written: "Berry Napoleon Duff's book, Jan. 22, 1887."

Howard tells me that Papa went through a "Business School" in Atlanta, Georgia. He could certainly read well, and he did read the Bible and Bible study helps, and many newspapers, but he didn't particularly enjoy reading books. When I began making a little money after my graduation from college, however, I bought, at the forceful suggestion of Mama, a set of *Encyclopaedia Britannica* ("YaPapa has always wanted a set of encyclopedia.") and Papa, in the leisure of his senior years, read all twenty-four volumes of it.

His was that large, fancy Spencerian handwriting, and could he figure! Calculate, he called it. How impatient he got with us children when we needed a pencil and paper to figure out an arithmetic problem. He could work percentages in his head, but he never could explain to us how to do it.

Howard: Papa was very sharp with mathematics. When I got into high school and started algebra, I tried to stump him with what I thought were tough problems. He quickly solved in his head what I had to solve on paper with a formula.

Papa's most frequent admonitions to us were, "Show a little gumption. Use some common sense." Not bad advice for anyone.

All through his life as new inventions came on the market, he'd say, "Well, I'll be jiggered! I thought of that thingamajig years ago—just couldn't figure how to get it made and on the market."

Long before he met Mama he had been desperately ill with spinal meningitis, and it was one of his favorite tales to say, "They were so sure I was going to die, they'd bought my coffin and they'd hired *two* men to fill my job. You just remember that—it took two men to fill my job!" I believe him. In all the jobs he had during the years, I cannot remember his having a paid vacation.

To us children, Papa called her "YaMama" ("Go help YaMama." "Take this to YaMama."); to most others he called her "Mrs. (pronounced 'Miz') Duff," but to Mama, he addressed her as "Sweetheart."

We were not an outwardly affectionate family, but all my life I could remember his putting his arm across her shoulders and addressing her as "Sweetheart." Nevertheless, he had a disconcerting habit of doing this in the crowded kitchen while

Mama was busy with a thousand and one things.

Beryl: Mama said if a couple reached their fiftieth wedding anniversary, it was sure proof that neither one kept a loaded gun around the house.

Mama told us that we didn't realize how lucky we were to have parents who cared about each other and showed it. The older I get, the more I realize that, as usual, Mama was right.

With a repertoire of finger games and nonsense rhymes, Papa was affectionate and playful with very little children. My granddaughter Christa told me recently of a new song she'd learned at day care: *"Chickey ma chickey ma craney crow, went to the well to wash my toe,"* etc. I told her my daddy had taught that to me when I was younger than she is. She was surprised to learn we used language in those dark ages, but she didn't know what a well was. When the novel *One Flew Over the Cuckoo's Nest* was published, I was the only one of my acquaintances who knew the old children's rhyme—often recited by Papa as he played a finger game with us—from which the title had been taken.

Papa delighted in letting little children crawl over him. He pretended to snap at and bite their fingers if they got those fingers too close to his mouth, and they, in turn, delighted in seeing how close they could get without getting caught.

In general, he was a fond and loving Papa, and later, Grandpa—until the children were about two years old, when he expected them to straighten up suddenly and fly right. Just as a little earlier, he'd spoiled them to pieces and ignored their table manners, suddenly they could clean their plates, behave themselves, and forget about passing through the terrible twos.

I don't remember Papa ever spanking me, but I certainly knew he could and he would. I do remember his spanking Ida Rule once—she must have been in the terrible twos. He spanked her so that it was another one of the few times I ever saw Mama cry. I don't know if he ever spanked one of us after that, but, as I said, we knew he could.

When I was about twelve years old, my friend Beth Patterson and I spent a long Sunday afternoon just goofing off. We were returning from a walk when our imaginations got the best of us, and we thought we saw something or someone peering out of a window in Beth's house. We hid in a hedge for such a long time—until Beth's folks drove up and I could go on home, because, of course, there was no one in her house—that Papa stood me up against a door, put one hand on the door by my head, and shook his other hand in my face until I thought I was a goner.

"Young lady," he said, "don't you ever stay out 'till dark again. You had YaMama worried ta death. If that ever happens again, you'll get the spankin' of your life." It never happened again.

I don't know whether they were really worried or just angry because I was too late to go to BYPU (Baptist Young People's Union).

Papa must have worried about the responsibility of bringing up those five girls, but most of the time he relayed his wishes and laws through Mama. When my future husband and I were going to take a trip (we were taking Ann along for appearances' sake), he told Mama, "I don't think she ought to go on that trip with him. You oughta tell her she can't go."

Mama told him to tell me himself, but he never did.

When Beryl was still a rather small girl, she and one of the neighborhood boys in Big Spring were wrestling. I overheard Papa say to Mama, "You oughta put a stop to that monkey business. They're gettin' too big for such carryin's on."

Beryl: In Lubbock, a boy came over to see me one night and we sat on a blanket on that tiny little front lawn watching the world go by. We weren't doing a thing, but Papa came to the front door and called me in and, shaking his finger in my face, he said, "You just bring that blanket directly in the house. If you're goin to stay out in the yard, you're sure 'nuf not goin' to have that blanket out there." I sure brought the blanket in.

Ann: My date and I were sitting in his car in front of 2118, the house in Lubbock, just sitting there, when Pop came storming out in his split-tail nightshirt and demanded that I come in the house and the date go on his way. Needless to say, I didn't marry that boy—I'm not sure I even saw him again.

Although he could seem aloof and forbidding to youngsters, Papa tried hard to be friends with his children, even before it was the accepted practice to spend time with one's children. Berry recalls a trip he made with Papa in a Model T Ford from Longview to Ore City, Texas. It was one of Papa's one-day trips when he was traveling for the Moore Grocery Company. When Howard was about ten years old, he also took a similar trip with Papa, but they went on the train—a combination passenger and freight train.

One summer when he was an outside salesman for A. G. Winn Produce Company in Sweetwater, Papa took us girls—two at a time—on an overnight trip with him. We stayed for the first time in a hotel and ate our first meal in a cafe.

Ann: Pop took Little Boy and me with him on a day's trip from Big Spring to Forsan. He bought the makings for ham sandwiches, and that was a wonderful trip. I'm sure there was nothing to do but ride along in the car, or sit in the car while he was calling on the store owners, but we thought that was the most wonderful day in the world—just going somewhere by ourselves with Pop.

On a certain Fourth of July, Papa loaded us five girls, Mama and Little Boy in his company coupe. Elsie and I sat under the propped-up lid of the turtle (back end of the coupe, for the benefit of you young persons out on a space station);

Beryl and Ida Rule huddled on the shelf in back of the driver, and Little Boy and Lydia Ann were on the seat with Mama and Papa. Thus we went out to a cow pasture some distance from Sweetwater for a picnic under the mesquite trees. It was a memorable time, because it was an unusual occasion for him to take us on a picnic and because Papa, dressed in his three-piece black wool suit and tie, killed the first tarantula any of us had ever seen.

At Christmastime in Big Spring, Texas, Papa took us five girls out to get a Christmas tree. We girls would be satisfied with nothing but the biggest scrub cedar on the hillside. The lower limbs must have been six feet long, growing right next to the ground, and poor, overweight Papa, in his middle fifties, had to crawl under those limbs and cut down what he called "the consarned thing," fussing all the time. On the cold ride back into town, Elsie and I stood on the running boards and held the tree on the turtle of the company coupe. Papa never again went out to cut down a tree.

My husband's favorite story about Papa takes place in the boarding house at Lubbock—the place we call "2118"—with Papa seated at the head of the table. Jimmy and Barbara Jean, Elsie's two small children, were seated at a small, child-size table right in back of Papa. Jimmy surreptitiously fed the current ever-present family cat, in spite of Papa's telling him repeatedly not to do that. Finally, Papa, without turning his head, and with one swift movement of his arm, knocked the cat winding and Jimmy out of his chair, and Papa never said a word nor missed a bite. A chastened Jimmy put himself back in his chair and finished his meal. I wish I knew whether or not he ever fed the cat from the table again.

There was always a family cat that had to be put out at night. One very cold night in Lubbock, the cat made straight for the kids' sandbox and sat to do its job. Papa said, "When

I wanted to lock the door for the night, she'd look over her shoulder and go 'Meow' so pitiful—like she was sayin' 'wait for me, don't lock the door yet.' When she finally finished, she made straight for the door and said a little 'Mew' as if to say, 'Thanks for waitin'." Papa got a charge out of telling that story.

Speaking of sandboxes, when there were young children around, and that was usually all the time, Papa tried to see that there were swings, perhaps a see-saw, and sometimes a sandbox for their enjoyment.

Papa mellowed somewhat over the years. When Howard and his family were in Lubbock on a short visit, Papa wanted to excuse Karl and Eleanor, Howard's children, from eating all of their meal. I remember hearing Howard mutter, "What happened to the old rule, 'clean your plate or no dessert'?"

None of us children can remember being bribed to eat, but my daughter Rosemary recalls that when she was about four or five years old, she was at the kitchen table at 2118 with Joe, Beryl's second son, who is a couple of years younger than she is. Joe was reluctant to drink his milk and Papa offered him a dime to drink it. When Joe did finish his glass of milk, Papa gave him a nickel. Rosemary, who was indignant because she hadn't been given anything for drinking hers, said, "That's not a dime, that's a nickel."

"Shh!" Papa said. "Don't tell him, he's too little to know the difference."

Ann: My memories of Pop are gentler memories than the rest of you have. In the first place, I called him "Pop" or "Dad." When the boys came along in the early years, Pop thought it would be sissy of them to call him Daddy, and so the term "Papa" was insisted on as it had been used a generation earlier.

By the time I came along he was fifty years old, and I guess the younger children in a family, or the children of older parents are, as a general rule, supposed to have an easier time. Anyway, I was his baby and he tried to see that I got what I wanted, if he could manage it.

In Big Spring, he came home to find me in the back yard crying because all the other kids had stilts and I didn't have any. "You go tell YaMama I'll be in to supper terreckly," he said. And he built a pair of stilts for me before he ate supper. I sure was proud of those stilts.

Another time he knew I wanted a juice harp—French harp, Jew's harp, harmonica—whatever you want to call them. He bought me one for fifty cents, and fifty cents was a lot of money in those days, a whole lot. He could really play that thing—as I remember him now, I think he played as well as anyone we hear on TV now, but I'm probably prejudiced, or recalling through the rosy glow of pleasant memories.

Perhaps the occasion that causes me the most wonder, particularly the older I get, happened the first year in Lubbock. He knew I wanted to go to the South Plains Fair, and he and I walked from 2318 9th Street clear to the fairgrounds. I was ten years old, so he would have been sixty and this was in the days when sixty meant sixty hard years of living and working, and the distance must have been more than two miles, one way. He walked with me over there and stood and watched me ride all the rides I could get for my fifty cents—probably ten rides —and then the two of us walked home.

If that had been me, even in my younger years, I'd have said to that kid, "Oh, you don't want to go some place like that. We don't have a way—we don't have the money"—any reason that would work to keep me from taking that kid. Pop was a pretty special person to me.

Papa had been a bachelor and was ready to settle down and stay at home when he and Mama married. Mama was nineteen years old and had been living at her parents' home, and she was ready to "be up and doin' with a heart for any fate." This was such a favorite saying of Mama's that I was surprised when I got in school and learned that she hadn't made it up. Papa wouldn't go out, so Mama just went without him.

"I didn't go anywhere out of line—just to church and to friends' houses, and places like that. But when he saw that I was goin' anyway, he started goin' with me."

Mama had learned that trick from her mother. When Grandfather Mobberly returned from the Civil War, he had picked up the habit of cussing, as the way of soldiers often has been. Grandmother Mobberly couldn't get him to stop, so she just started saying whatever he said.

"Can you imagine my mother—a proper, genteel, beautiful, great lady—a truly gentle woman as well as a gentlewoman, cussin' like a soldier? But it sure 'nuf stopped my Papa from cussin'."

Grandmother Mobberly also gave Mama some sage advice that was helpful, though trying, through the years: "Don't ever threaten the children with their father, saying that he'll take care of them when he gets home. If something should happen to Berry, then where would you be? You'd have no control over them."

Papa was well-respected in the town. Mama told the story of the Fourth of July when Howard was missing. The message, "Berry Duff's boy is lost" flashed on the screen of the moving picture house. The movie emptied as people came to look for Howard. He last had been seen asleep on a certain bed in the house, but he wasn't to be seen on it or under it, or anywhere in the house or yard, which was only about a block from the Ouachita River. He had rolled over and was wedged between the bed and the wall, so he couldn't be seen from above or below. After friends and neighbors had spent several hours looking for the child, some sort of bug stung the little boy awake and he came up with a loud cry. Everyone was impressed with the way the people of Monroe had turned out to look for Berry Duff's little boy.

When my husband and I and our four children were living in a two-bedroom home, I spent the summer looking for a larger home. I had my list of wants and must-haves and went from one real estate agent to another, trying to find just the right place. Mama came to see me that summer.

"I, too, always wanted a bigger house than whatever we had. One time in Monroe, a big, old, lovely mansion was for sale and I wanted it so very, very much that I went to our banker friend and asked him to try to talk YaPapa into buying that house. He just said, 'Miss Ida, you know Berry Duff can't afford that place.' I felt so foolish."

Maybe Mama wanted to help buy a bigger house as well as help pay the grocery bill.

Perhaps it was in that same conversation that Mama and I were talking about her younger sister, my Aunt Noel.

Aunt Noel had married Uncle Tad, a lawyer, who was doing quite well financially before the oil boom hit East Texas. After that, his fortunes expanded, along with the oil field, so Aunt Noel was known in our family as "the rich aunt." Aunt Noel had her share of money, but she also had her share of worries.

I told Mama of the time I had gone with my cousin Mary Noel and Aunt Noel to the railroad station in Longview to meet Uncle Tad, who was returning from a trip to California for an extended stay in a drying-out spa. He was helped from the train by the porter and staggered up to Aunt Noel. He had stopped in El Paso and had gone to Juarez to hit the booze again. I heard Mary Noel at my side crying as she said, "Oh, poor, poor Mother!"

"I reckon our rich aunt wasn't always so rich, after all, was she?" I said to Mother.

"No, your Uncle Tad has been a bettah providah, but Ya-Papa has been a bettah husband—a much bettah husband," Mama said thoughtfully.

CHAPTER 3

WHAT MAKES MAMA TICK?

If Mama and Papa were such a prosperous young couple, why did Mama feel the need to help pay the grocery bill at such an early date?

As I have mentioned, Mama was nineteen years of age when she married and had been living at her parents' home since her graduation from Longview High School three years earlier. After graduation, Mama studied shorthand and typing with a woman who taught the subjects in a room on the second floor of a business building in Longview.

"I remember climbing those steep stairs every day for months, and I learned shorthand pretty well, too. I was pretty good at it and I could have had a job then, but Mama wouldn't let me take it. She said no daughter of hers was goin' to work in an office where there were men! Said it wasn't proper or ladylike. I reckon I was the first one of her girls who wanted to work, and it seemed to sorta discombobulate her. She didn't mind my studying shorthand—I paid the tuition with money I had made pickin' and sellin' strawberries—but she sure 'nuf wouldn't let me work in an awful ol' office where *men* worked!"

That proud lady changed her mind by the time her youngest child, my Aunt Mary—ten years younger than Mama—finished high school, before World War I started. Aunt Mary went to Washington to work for the government and after the war she lived in New York City, where she had a long and successful career as a secretary and businesswoman.

But that didn't help Mama at the age of about seventeen, sitting on what she always called "the home place," feeling that life was passing her by.

"I never felt that I was a young lady—I went from bein' a school girl to bein' a married woman, and never was a young, independent woman."

Grandmother Mobberly resorted to other devices to shield her seven daughters from the cold, cruel world. They were not allowed to play with the white children in town because it was the theory of my grandmother, born in pre-Civil War Kentucky, that the white children might presume to think they were as good as the Mobberly girls, whereas the little colored children wouldn't dare to make that presumption, audibly, at least.

Grandmother even imported a Yankee schoolteacher, a gentleman—no, a man, because no Yankee was considered a gentleman—from New York State, whose name is not recalled, to tutor the girls at home so they wouldn't have to attend public schools.

The tributes and memorials published at the time of Grandmother Mobberly's death indicate that she was a much loved and respected member of her community, so her highfalutin' notions must have been acceptable to her contemporaries.

Grandmother (Mary Belle Noel Mobberly) had been raised in a manner similar to that in which she raised her own girls. Known as Molly, she was six years of age when the Civil War started. Her father, Charles Todd Noel, was a prosperous planter and doctor who organized and commanded Company A, Kentucky Confederate Cavalry.

He was killed in the second year of the war, leaving his widow, Sarah, and three young children.

My records don't show how Sarah coped with raising her

children in the reconstructed South, but she managed to do that and still maintain her image as a gentlewoman and also retain her place in the society of the South. She did not marry again and spent her final years with her daughter Molly in Longview and is buried there.

Years later, when my sisters or I would do something that exasperated Mama, she would say, "I wonder what my mother would think of you girls today. She was such a lady, and y'all can do such unladylike things."

After a pause, she nearly always added, "But my mother said the same thing about her mother. She even said she was glad her mother didn't live to see us sisters grow up—that her mother would have been so shocked by some of the things we Mobberly girls did. She said if we thought she was persnickety, we should have seen her mother—she was truly a great lady. Oh, my, my, I wonder what my grandmother would have thought of you Duff girls today."

Perhaps Mama inherited her ability to cope with adversity from her grandmother Sarah; perhaps she inherited her determination to help pay the grocery bill from her own father, James Mobberly. Twenty-year-old Jim Mobberly served in Captain Noel's company during the Civil War and after the war he went west to seek his fortune. Mama's tale was that he went out on the Pecos River to search for silver. At the time she told me that, I thought the Pecos River was only that short stretch that passes through the city of Pecos, Texas, but the Pecos is a long river that flows from the mountains of New Mexico through New Mexico and Texas to the Rio Grande. Where he found the little bit of silver he had, I don't know, but I have a small, pure silver teaspoon with an *M* engraved on it that is supposed to be all the silver he found in his search for a fortune. Mother gave me the spoon because, she said, with the name of Williamson, I could imagine that it was a *W* on the handle instead of an *M*.

After trying his hand at several endeavors, Jim Mobberly returned to Kentucky, and he and Mary Belle Noel were married in 1874, when he was thirty-three and she was twenty. They returned to Texas, where Grandfather took his bride to his sawmill on the Sabine River, deep in the piney woods of East Texas.

"Oh, my, yes," Mama told me. "My mama usta talk about how she hated it down there. It was miles from anyone else. There was no other woman to talk to, except the wife of the colored helper at the mill, an' the bugs an' snakes an' mosquitoes nearly drove her crazy. Her first baby was born while they lived out there, with only the colored woman to help her. My mama always thought the reason she had back trouble the rest of her life was because she picked up her older child too soon after the second baby was born. Papa eventually sold the sawmill an' they moved into town—Longview."

In town, Grandfather tried his luck at several businesses. According to Mama, he had the first electric light plant and the first ice-making plant in Longview, and he and his brother Sam built the Mobberly Hotel, located at the junction of the Texas and Pacific and the I&GN Railroads—the finest hotel in the area, with a multitude of rooms, each furnished with a beautiful bedroom set of cherry, walnut, or mahogany. And not a private bathroom in the whole place!

Although the hotel catered to railroad men and traveling men, it was so genteel that men were not allowed to eat in the dining room without a coat. A couple of spare coats were kept hanging on the back of the door for such uncouth and unprepared guests.

Since Grandmother would not have her daughters raised around a hotel, Grandfather built a home on a farm of 120 acres he owned near Longview. The bricks for the house were made at the red clay pit on the place.

Howard: Someone asked him what he would produce on that red clay hill, and Jim Mobberly said, "Bricks and daughters."

Although it looked big, the two-story house was essentially six rooms, plus front stair hall, and was not at all large for a large family home. Mama said it was only the rear wing of a planned colonial mansion, but like many oft-laid plans, they went awry and the mansion was never built, although the structure provided adequate room and a comfortable home for Mama and her sisters.

Howard: May Dee Bruce, the mother of Florine Eddins, a classmate of mine, had known the Mobberly sisters well and often went out there from time to time to spend the night with them. From her I learned that with seven daughters, no sons, and an outside privy, Grandfather used to keep a man's coat and hat for the girls to wear when they had to use the privy at night. Safety first!

There were strawberry beds and blackberry patches on the sandy-land farm, and the year Mama was thirteen she picked strawberries to sell for enough money to buy a wrought iron bed with brass knobs on the corner posts.

"Fancy wrought iron bedsteads were so fashionable that lotsa folks got rid of their beautiful old walnut and mahogany bedsteads and replaced them with iron beds. Times do change." Known as the "strawberry bed," it was used by Mama during all of her homemaking days. Its iron rods are worked into the shape of two *R*s on each end of the bed, and as soon as I learned to recognize letters, I began calling it my bed, because I was the only child whose name began with *R*, and it is a prized heirloom in my home today.

Whether Grandfather wasn't much of a farmer, or whether his other business ventures were not successful, or whether his family was just outgrowing his income—for whatever reason, by the time Mama was thirteen, her folks were running low on funds for the tutor and for the private young ladies' academy back in Bowling Green, Kentucky, to which the three older sisters had been sent as they reached their teens, and so Mama went to public school. The principal took one look at her height and said, "You're big enough to be in the sixth grade" and into the sixth grade she went, without any testing or further preparation.

With her grandmother's gumption, her father's interest in making money, and her mother's determination that her daughter would act like a lady, it's easy to see why Mama may have been restless those two or three years she stayed at home with her mother and father. Mama's mother was blind the latter part of her life, and Mama spent long hours reading to her. Years later Mama said, "Everybody ought to read the great classics at least twice. I read lots of Charles Dickens' stories to my Mama, but now that I'm reading them again in my old age, I get so much more out of them."

Mama had many friends in those years, boys and girls both, who were getting married by this time. Years later she still had a gold locket and a gold pin an old boyfriend or sweetheart, whatever they were called about the turn of the century, had given her. She told Beryl she came awfully close to marrying that young man.

Her three younger sisters were still in school. Going to church could use up only a few hours on Sunday—not counting Wednesday night prayer meeting—so Mama welcomed the opportunity to take her first trip to Monroe, Louisiana, to visit her older sister, Daisy.

This was Mama's first opportunity to get away from home and show the world what Mama was like.

CHAPTER 4

WHAT DID MAMA LOOK LIKE?

She just looked like Mama. When asked what his wife looked like, President Harry Truman is reported to have said, "She looks like any woman who is a mother and has lived a certain number of years ought to look." That was Mama. She looked like a mother ought to look for the age of her children and the years she had lived at any point in her life.

Howard recently sent to the rest of us brothers and sisters a picture of Mama that none of us had seen before. Beryl didn't think it was Mama, because the young subject has on a sheer, almost-off-the-shoulder blouse or dress exposing beautiful shoulders and neckline and "Mama wouldn't wear anything that revealing," according to Beryl.

Although Mama never considered herself beautiful, the young woman in the picture, with heavy, wavy, brown—almost auburn—hair, a slight widow's peak, dark eyebrows, Mobberly nose and full and generous mouth has to be Mama. I think it was probably taken about the time she married, at the age of nineteen.

Saying she wanted to leave each of her girls something pretty, Mama once made a luncheon cloth for me with something she called "shadow embroidery." It is a design embroidered in reverse on the underside of sheer material, in the case of my cloth, organdy, and the handiwork is seen through the outside of the article or garment. I think Mama's daring blouse is made of shadow embroidery, because Mama told me that blouses (waists, they were called then) made with shadow embroidery were very stylish when she was a young woman. Just by the nature of the design, they had to be of sheer material and, although the young woman might have on a brassiere (they were not bras then), a corset cover, camisole, and slip under the blouse, many nasty-nice persons considered them immodest, if not immoral. Mama said so much pulpit time was wasted on preaching against shadow-embroidered garments that many young women felt unwelcome and became very lukewarm in their church life. Mama never did have much patience with preachers who got too worked up over the current fad, whether it was sheer blouses, bobbed hair, or the length of skirts.

Our cousin Catherine Murphy Thomas, who was associated with the photographer's profession for years, says the picture is of Mama. Catherine informs us Mama had asked her to make a copy of the old picture. Mama wanted to hang it above the mantle with pictures of her mother and grandmother as young women, and with pictures of her five girls. Mama never did get that arrangement over the mantel, but today, on the sides of Mama's old walnut-framed mirror, I have pictures of seven generations.

The pictures of Mama's mother and grandmother show beautiful young women in the elaborate hairstyles of the mid- and early nineteenth century. Mama said old Kentucky friends would say, "Miss Mary (that's Mama's mother) has some beautiful daughters, but none of them are as beautiful as Miss Mary was." So Mama had to grow up in the shadow of a great beauty.

We have a picture of an approximately one-year-old Mama with her three older sisters. She is sitting on the lap of her oldest sister, Daisy, who at the age of nine or so already shows signs of becoming the beauty she was as a woman. Mama looks a little like me in a picture made about thirty years later. I am sitting on Frederick's knee with three other solemn siblings with us. Mama said it was one of her hardest days' work to get all five of us clean, dressed and downtown to the photographer's studio on a hot summer afternoon in Louisiana. As I said, in the old picture Mama looks a little like me as a baby, but she looks more like my granddaughter Christa. Maybe all year-old babies in a family look alike even though they're born nearly a hundred years apart.

We have no pictures of Mama as a youngster or as a teenager, so the picture Howard sent is doubly welcome for a glimpse of a beautiful young woman.

We have a yellowed snapshot of Mama, Aunt Elsie, and three-year-old Frederick sitting on the high steps leading to the gallery (front porch) of a house in Monroe. The pompadoured young women are in spotless, white, full-skirted dresses (that had to be meticulously ironed) draped to cover their legs and feet. The high necklines and Gibson girl sleeves emphasize their slim waists.

"Not many women can have ten children and still have a figure." She attributed it to wearing a corset all the time. She was a firm believer in putting on a corset immediately after having a baby (after the prescribed twenty-one day bed rest) and she said that was what kept her waistline visible and her back from hurting. She put on that corset first thing upon arising each morning. I never saw her dressed in a robe to fix breakfast.

One day, when I told her that a teacher said I had pretty hands, she said, rather wistfully, "I used to have pretty hands, too." They still looked okay to me in spite of her having washed hundreds of tubs of clothes and having scrubbed countless floors and kids. In the back yard of the house in Lubbock, she was washing all of our fall clothes in naphtha in order to save dry cleaning charges, and would not let me do anything to help except hang the clothes on the line. "My hands are already a mess. No use you ruinin' your hands by puttin' them in this stuff."

Another time she laughed about how aggravated her sisters got because every hat that came in the house looked good on Mama. "They were all considered beauties, but it was sorta funny—all their hats looked better on me than they did on the beauties."

Mama might have been a little envious of her sisters' beautiful, soft, white complexions. They stayed in East Texas and Louisiana with moist, windless climates and, having plenty of domestic help and laundresses, they probably never hung a freshly laundered garment on a clothesline in the wind and bright sun, whereas Mama lived the last half of her life in West Texas, land of wind and sand.

Another studio portrait is of a sober-faced, maturing young woman, again in what appears to be shadow-embroidery, but with a very high neckline. This portrait seems to emphasize her hair. Mama's hair was beautiful, almost auburn, soft and thick, wavy and long. Before Mama put it into a braid each night, we girls loved to comb or brush it, but she said she was tenderheaded and we were too rough. Over Papa's objections, she had her hair cut when she was in her mid-forties, and soon after that she had a studio portrait made of herself because she regretted not having a picture of her own mother in her middle years.

The only other studio portrait she had made was for job applications when she started her career in hotel housekeeping. She looks just like a well-preserved, fiftyish mother of ten should look. When Mama's weight crowded 200 pounds, she would skip eating supper until it got back to about 180. Her last driver's license gives her weight as 160.

One Christmas I wanted to make a dress for a gift for Mama and asked my neighbor, who I thought was about Mama's size, what size pattern I should buy. I made the dress in my neighbor's size, taking care to follow Mama's likes and dislikes: a waistline, but no belt, loose sleeves neither too short nor too long, a becoming color for Mama's blue eyes, and white around the face ("The Kennadys always need white around the face," she'd say, the Kennadys being some of her ancestors) and all such details. Then I found that the pattern was two sizes smaller than that which Elsie, the expert seamstress in the family, used in making dresses for Mama. I had already mailed it to Texas, and I puzzled over what would happen to the first thing I'd ever made for Mama. Needless to say, I was most gratified to hear from Beryl, "The dress looks so good on Mama, just like she likes. How in the world did you get such a good fit? She wanted to keep as a surprise for you that she's lost twenty pounds this winter!" The Lord do provide, as Mama might have said.

We do have snapshots of Mama through the decades, beginning in the thirties—Mama at a reunion with her five surviving sisters, Mama and Papa and all their living children in Big Spring, Mama at my wedding (professional wedding photographers had not been discovered, at least by our family, at the time) when she had very few gray hairs, Mama and Papa in 1953, shortly before Papa was stricken with his last illness, and through the remaining years of her life as she became grayer and frailer.

In some of those last pictures she looks almost angry. She often told me, "You're like me. When you're not smiling you look mad." All my life older people told me I looked like Mama; I thought it was because I had Mama's blue eyes and Elsie had Papa's brown eyes.

What Did Mama Look Like?

In an anthropology class a professor made the statement that brown eyes would be the dominant gene over blue eyes, or words to that effect. I said, "It wasn't in my family. There are three with Papa's brown eyes and five with Mama's blue eyes."

He said, "That's not a large enough number to test the law accurately."

I replied, "They had ten children, for heaven's sake. How many did you expect them to have?"

Nowadays, especially when I'm tired, when I look in the mirror, I see Mama. The old folks knew what they were talking about.

In the last picture of her at my house in Casper, Wyoming, my youngest child, Lucy, (Mama's next-to-youngest of twenty-one grandchildren) is playing at her feet. Mama loved to travel until the end of her life, but she never rushed up with squeals of joy to frighten her young grandchildren. She not only wasn't the squealing type, but she said many times, "They don't want an ugly old lady grabbing hold of them. Let them take their own good time getting acquainted with this old lady."

She may have been surfeited with grandchildren by the end of her life. While I thought my new baby, Dick, was one of the most beautiful babies ever born, Mama said he was just another baby. And by the time my Lucy was born, she told Pauline, Howard's wife, "When you have twenty grandchildren, they all begin to look alike."

She offered to babysit whenever possible, however, and all of her grandchildren quickly made up to her; none of her children or grandchildren considered her an "ugly old lady." She just looked like Mama—the way a mama who has lived a certain number of years and has middle-aged children and twenty-one grandchildren ought to look.

CHAPTER 5

THE FIRST THIRTEEN YEARS

Mama and Papa were married October 10, 1904, at her parents' home in Longview, Texas. We have no newspaper clipping describing the wedding, perhaps because in my grandmother's standard of behavior for proper young ladies, a lady's name did not appear in the newspapers of the time except, perhaps, at the occasion of her death. Mama wore a dark dress; thirty-seven years later she still had the dark, metal buttons from the dress. Papa gave Mama a ring, a single-carat diamond in a Tiffany setting, the only ring I ever saw Mama wear.

They left immediately after the ceremony and went by train to their new home in Monroe, Louisiana, where they would live for the next thirteen years.

I'm afraid the image of Monroe at the turn of the century, which I hold in my mind, is based upon having read too many novels set in the South, and also upon a couple of visits I made in recent years to see my cousins Dorothy Standley Coons and Mary Jo Standley and her husband, Troy Guillory, in the Guillorys' lovely, modern, air-conditioned home, in a quiet section of the city, with a landscaped lawn extending to the banks of the bayou. My visits were timed for spring and autumn when I didn't experience any of the unpleasant weather I have heard Mama mention.

"You children just don't know what it's like to try to sleep in heat so bad you have to put a wet sheet over you and turn the electric fan on yourself. Or what it's like to have ice on the front porch steps so slick you can't get up or down them. And you've never had to worry about sprinkled clothes mildewin' before they can be ironed, or babies cryin' with the prickly heat. There's something to be said for the weather in dry, sandy West Texas, I reckon."

One ninety-year-old woman still recalls the muddy, unpaved streets and the outdoor toilet in every yard, but in my imagination I picture Mama taking life easy on a shady front porch, with affluent friends and neighbors and perhaps a sister or two to keep her company, with well-behaved little children and with plenty of black help to care for the children as well as with the housework.

Wrong again. One writer, W. T. Tardy, in his autobiography, *Trials and Triumphs*, described Monroe at the turn of the century:

Monroe was a place of glaring contrasts. Ample wealth and dire poverty sat together on almost every block. Virtue and vice looked at each other across every street. Honor and knavery went together in all offices and public places. Since time immemorial the town has been notorious for three things: cotton gambling, poker playing and whiskey drinking. Morally and physically, the atmosphere was heavy. Everywhere, fetid smoke hung low over the green tables. Moral sensibilities were blunted and spiritual discernment was blinded.

How did Mama and Papa manage to make a life for themselves in such an atmosphere? The same writer offers some encouragement:

With all the objections that could be raised against the town, it was in many respects a fascinating place in which to live. Cookery was reduced to a fine art and the pleasures of the table were universal and abundant. The social life of all that section was richer and fuller than anything of the kind I had ever known. Vital religion was just beginning to have its day when I arrived in the city. Hitherto the churches had been tolerated, now they had to be reckoned with. A self-assertiveness, strange and incomprehensible to the old inhabitants, was marking the activities and coloring the work of some of the more virile Christian bodies in the town.

Mama and Papa quickly settled into the church life of the town (Papa had been baptized into the Monroe Baptist Church ten years earlier and he, his father, and his sister Willie had been active in that church since that time), and Mama dragged Papa into the social life of the community as mentioned elsewhere.

It may have been that Mama thought she had to help with the financing of the new furnishings for their home which she felt were needed to enhance their social life in the community. Although Papa had the set of dining room furniture with the extended table that inspired the large family, he also owned a large set of beautiful Limoges china which I believe he had acquired as premiums for being a good tobacco salesman. Mama said, "When he told me he had those dishes down in the warehouse, I was scared to death they'd be tacky or common. It was certainly the relief of my life to see those pretty pink roses all over that fine china."

In addition to those dishes, there were many other pieces of crystal, china, and cut glass, whether gifts or purchased during the prosperous years, I can't say. One gift from the Sunday School class of women taught by Mama was a set of classic, fine crystal goblets that we used for Thanksgiving, Christmas, comp'ny-come-to-Sunday-dinner and other holiday meals. Since they were for adults only—the little children drank from cut glass tumblers until the collection of those was destroyed through carelessness—it was a big day to be grown up enough to be served water in a crystal goblet instead of milk in a cut glass tumbler. The set of goblets was sent to Elsie in Wyoming soon after World War II.

Mama had a fish set—a large china platter and matching plates with jumping fish hand-painted on each piece. They were for serving the fish course at formal dinners, and Mama gave that set to Howard and Pauline when they moved to the Seattle area because "they're more apt to be serving fish dinners than any of the rest of y'all."

Other dessert sets and tea sets, hand-painted with rich, red roses or the heads of elegant, beautiful women, were passed onto other children through the years.

I remember other pieces usually designated by the way they were used: the sweet pickle boat, the cranberry dish, the pickled peach bowl, the celery and jelly dishes, and the large, fluted Waldorf salad bowl of white Bavarian flowers with pale green, gold-trimmed leaves. That salad bowl was sent to me whole and I managed to break it on my first move after I received it.

All of these were in addition to the pink rose-covered Limoges china service for twelve which was also sent to me after Mama's death. The cups and saucers, as well as most of the breakfast plates and salad plates, were all gone the way of fragile dishes in a large family of children. Some of the serving pieces had been glued back together through the years and they're mostly for looking, not eating, but I use the rest frequently, and they bring back memories of happy meals at Mama's house.

When Mama married, brides did not "select a pattern" of china or sterling silver, but well-wishers gave as wedding gifts a piece or pieces from patterns the givers admired. That's why Mama had so many disconnected sets of china and many unrelated pieces of sterling.

When Beryl chose a certain pattern of sterling silver when she married, Mama said, "Why, I believe that old broken sugar shell in the drawer of the stove is that same pattern."

It was, and Mama sent it in to the maker company, who fastened the bowl to the handle, and it is still in service in Beryl's home, together with the other pieces of sterling that survived the years and kids and kids' sandbox digging.

I have the ornate silver ladle that was used for dipping the breakfast cocoa every winter morning, until the last child had left home.

Mama had a tall pitcher and at least two fruit bowls, with assorted other smaller dishes of cut glass. Although we grew up thinking everyone had such a collection of "good dishes," and we children didn't appreciate them when we were young, I do remember one occasion when I had a sudden awareness of what we had. When I was in high school, a group of my fellow students came over to the house and we were goofing off in the big dining room in Big Spring. A couple of ornery boys took the cut glass bowls from their place on the sideboard and began throwing them to each other, the bowls passing in mid-air. When I could imagine those bowls crashing together and then to the floor, the thought of Papa coming from his bedroom in his split-tail nightshirt and getting after us was enough to make me assert myself and put an end to the boys' foolishness.

Since all of these dishes had to be stored somewhere, it's easy to believe that one of the first items Mama and Papa needed to purchase was the china closet with curved glass sides, which ever after held down a corner in our overcrowded houses. Although the advertisements of the period list china closets, or cabinets, at what seem ridiculously low prices, we have to remember it would have been about a third of Papa's monthly salary.

Other purchases during the early years must have been the big oak bedroom set with tall headboard bed and a wide bureau with a big, big mirror. That set also had a clothes wardrobe with mirrored doors hiding shelves on one side and hanging space on the other, plus two drawers at the bottom. Most houses, particularly the older ones, had very little closet space, and wardrobes were a necessity. The folks also had a similar set made of fine cherry wood, but they sold it later, in the move from Longview to Sweetwater, whereas the oak set known as "Mama's bedroom set" stayed with Mama almost to the very end of her life.

Other acquisitions made during those years included the library table as well as the leather-covered davenport (couch or sofa) with each wooden arm carved into a lion's head with an open mouth that both fascinated and frightened small children. Because Mama wanted her children to have the advantage of music in the house, she acquired a table-model Victrola in Monroe for the great sum of fifty dollars. We called all phonographs "Victrolas" until the term almost became a generic word, but ours really was a Victrola with a picture, on the inside of the top, of the white dog listening to his master's voice.

As long as I can remember, Mama had a well-used handy, occasional or lamp table about the size of a card table. The thick oak top would have been square except each corner ballooned out into a circle. The heavy, turned legs angled out to support a shelf a foot or so from the floor, and each leg ended in a metal claw grasping a large, clear glass ball. I don't remember how much she said she paid for it, perhaps about five dollars, a little more or less, but I remember her tale about it. "I was so proud of that table. I thought it was the most elegant and beautiful table in town. And the very week it was delivered from the store, some ladies' magazine had an article on do's and don'ts for decorating your house, and there leading the list of the don'ts was a picture of my beautiful table, with a warning: 'Never buy a table like this. Very common or cheap or tacky.' Whatever they called it, they ruined my table for me for the rest of the time."

Another prominent piece of furniture purchased during the prosperous years, as Mama later called them, was the bookcase of oak, with glass doors protected by decorative oak fretwork. "You children don't know how lucky you are to have books in the house. Some children never have any books at all except what they might bring home from school."

We, however, had books and more books. Some of those Mama bought after her marriage included the complete works of Charles Dickens (in dark red bindings) and a big set of *American Authors* (in beautiful blue bindings). I mention the color of the bindings because, when I was interviewed for a job in the library at college, I remarked that I arranged the books at home according to their colors, the colors I thought looked good together placed next to each other. Needless to say, I didn't get the job.

Mama had a big set of leather-bound volumes of *Stoddard's Library,* with just about all the great literature ever written. With both the *American Authors* and *Stoddard's Library* at our disposal, we seldom had to use the school libraries. In fact, occasionally teachers asked us to bring a certain volume to class to share with the other students. *Stoddard's Lectures* was a large set of fascinating stories and pictures of the author's travels all around the world. Years later, when I planned a trip to Europe, I wished mightily for the familiar volume with the picture of the Castle of Chillon in Switzerland.

Our big, well-used set of children's literature had every myth, legend, fairy tale, story, and poem ever written for children, from the time of Aesop to Robert Louis Stevenson. Some of these volumes had been used so much they were already falling to pieces when I first began reading them.

Mama also bought Hurlbut's *Story of the Bible* when it first came out. Some of the books—the set of Shakespeare's works with notes and helps that served me well as it had served Mama years earlier, the volume of Tennyson's works, the volume of poems by William Cullen Bryant with "Ida Mobberly, Christmas, 1898 written on the flyleaf—were brought by Mama into her new home.

"YaPapa would get so mad when I bought books. He didn't mind spendin' money on necessities, but he sure 'nuf didn't like it when I bought books."

Perhaps the purchase that aggravated him most was *two* sets of books about World War I. One was large with encyclopedic-sized volumes with many scary pictures; the other had smaller volumes of light green with fewer pictures but more personal experiences of wartime.

There was a time between the prosperous years and the time the first children started earning a little money when not many new books were purchased. But Mama instilled in her children a love of books and reading that caused most of us to spend more money on books than was probably good for us.

There were many other reasons Mama might have been interested in having more income, even in the early prosperous years. Her sister Daisy lived in the Baptist parsonage in Monroe which had been built recently for the munificent sum of five thousand dollars, and we can wonder if Mama was envious of Daisy's lovely home.

Daisy and her family moved from Monroe a few years after Mama and Papa were married, but Mama soon saw the crisis that occurred when Daisy's husband was tragically stricken with lateral sclerosis. He became completely incapacitated for some years, then was able to lecture from a wheelchair for a short while before his death. Mama must have seen the struggle her beautiful older sister Daisy had in caring for her husband and earning a living for their family in a time before any means were provided for a pastor's illness or retirement. Before that happened, however, Mama settled into the life of a young matron in Monroe and began that big family she wanted. Frederick was born in 1905, at which time they got a wrought iron baby bed, painted white with little angel heads looking down from each end, and trimmed with brass scrollwork, which Mama eventually painted white also. It was used by all of Mama's babies and by most of her grandchildren, at least for a visit or two, and is still in use in my home for young guests of yet another generation.

Berry Noel was born in 1908, Howard in 1910, the baby who lived twelve days in 1911, and Elsie in 1912. Mama told me that in those days it was not considered proper for an expectant mother to go outside of her own yard after about the fifth month of pregnancy, so she certainly must have been confined close to her own residence for an extended period of years. Her babies were born at home, of course, and usually Mama had a black nurse during her confinement and another helper to care for the baby. Years later she always felt sorry for her children, who had their babies without the benefit of any domestic or nursing help in the home, and if possible, she tried to give us a hand when the babies were very small.

Berry: My earliest memory is of a morning in the house on Pine Street the spring following Elsie's birth in December. Mama was bathing Elsie on the library table and there was a portable kerosene heater lit for warmth. Howard and I (or was it Fred and I?) were chasing each other around the room and knocked over the heater. Mama threw a throw rug around the heater, picked it up and threw it down the back porch steps. It was wrapped in such a way that it stayed wrapped as it rolled down the steps and caught fire only after it was on the sidewalk. The paper reported, "Mrs. Duff's presence of mind and quick thinking perhaps prevented a quite serious fire."

Mama's sister Elsie had visited Mama several times and it was in one of those visits that she met Jim Standley, who courted her on the bottom step of the high front porch because, she told her daughters, "Your dad talked so loud he bothered all the family sittin' up on the front porch." The courtship was successful; they were married in 1912 and Aunt Elsie began her long lifetime in Monroe.

While she was still a single young woman, she had taught baby Howard to take his first steps. When Berry Noel started to kindergarten at the age of four, he wouldn't have given a picayune for all the schools in the country that day, and Aunt Elsie had to follow him to school with a paddle in her hand, giving him step-by-step encouragement from her own special board of education. About twenty-five years later Mama said, "We thought we'd never get him started to school, and now I think he'll nevah stop." This was when he took more than the traditional four years to work his way through college.

I was born in 1914 in the house on Arkansas Avenue.

Berry: I remember the day Rosemary was born. Willis Jackson, the Negro handyman who helped Papa around the grocery store that Papa had at the time, drove all of us kids in the buggy out to Aunt Elsie's place, Bon Air Plantation. I just remember how cold it was as we snuggled down under the lap robe in the buggy, and for a long time after that when I heard the line "early on one frosty morn" in the song "Dixie" I thought about that morning."

When I was a baby (Mama always dated every event—from the 1910 Halley's Comet to the first atomic bomb—by who was the baby at the time) Mama took all the children with her and went by train to Bryan, Texas, to visit Papa's sister, our Aunt Annie Cook. Such a trip must have taxed even Mama's love of travel.

On a cold winter evening when I was about four or five

months old, a small, fourteen-year-old black girl from Arkansas appeared at Mama's back door looking for a place to stay until she could find some of her kinfolks. Her name was Mahaley Jackson. Mama took her in, found her some warm clothes, made a bed for her on the big, old, green velour-covered, overstuffed quilt box until she could arrange for a regular bed, and Mahaley stayed with us for about eight or nine years. I am sure Mahaley earned every cent of the small salary Mama was able to pay her, yet she was a big part of our family life. Because I was the baby when she came to us, I was always her favorite and she defended me from the teasing of the big brothers. Elsie was the favorite of Grandma, and both of us were probably spoiled by our respective guardian angels.

Howard: Mama demanded that we treat Mahaley with respect, and while she discouraged us from ever using the word "nigger" at any time, she absolutely would never allow us to call Mahaley a "nigger." I think Mama would have skinned us if we did.

Mahaley bought a ukelele and accompanied herself as she sang, a hobby she loved. Her favorite songs were *Red Wing* and a parody of *Red Wing* about Charlie Chaplin. Forty years later when Mama visited me in Casper, Wyoming, I told her of hearing the gospel singer Mahalia Jackson on the radio and wondered if it could be our Mahaley. The program had been honoring Mahalia Jackson's birthday. Mama granted that the month was the same as Mahaley's birth month, but Mama insisted, "It couldn't be our Mahaley. That singer is a big woman and Mahaley was thin and wiry."

I replied, "Mama, forty years ago we were all skinny and wiry and look at us now!"

The early beginnings of Mahalia Jackson, the gospel singer, as described in the biographies I read, did not coincide with the beginnings of Mahaley as I remembered Mama telling them, although their ages were very close to the same. I have always regretted that I never wrote the great singer to ask her if she could possibly be "our Mahaley," particularly after I read that children who knew her called her "Miss Mahaley."

Mahaley was an indispensable mother's helper to Mama and moved with us to Longview.

Beryl: When I visited with Aunt Elsie in the last years of her life, she often said in her soft, southern speech, "Ah don' know why on earth Ida and Berry Duff evah left Monroe. It was a terrible mistake. He had a real good business and was makin' money, and they had a whole passel of friends. Ah declare Ah don' know what evah got into them. Berry Duff had the world by the tail and they'd have been a lot bettah off if they'd stayed right heah in Monroe."

Mama always told me they moved because there were so many saloons in Monroe and she didn't want to raise her three boys around that many saloons. W. T. Tardy wrote that one reason he moved from Monroe was "the older children were mature enough to observe the hideous moral conditions."

"I told YaPapa that we'd lived in his hometown for thirteen years and we'd go back to my hometown, which was dry, for thirteen years," Mama told me. "YaPapa's grandfather, Grandpa Duff's father, had a drinkin' problem, and I've always heard that the drinkin' habit will come out in every third generation and I didn't want my boys to be drunkards."

Grandpa (William Hiram) and Grandma Duff had lived with Mama and Papa during much of their time in Monroe. Grandpa Duff was a monomaniac on the subject of the Siege of Jackson, Mississippi, in July of 1863, and he could and did talk of that and nothing else for hours at a time. When she spoke of those trying times, Mama quoted an old maxim: "You can't tell the strength of the tea until it's been tested in boiling water."

In a speech class in college, years later, I referred to that saying and Mama's use of it in trying times, and it really upped my grade with the professor.

Berry: My only memory of Grandpa is of a time I asked to use his knife. He let me, but warned me to be careful. I promptly dropped the open knife and it made a long, fine shallow cut on my arm from which oozed a few scattered drops of blood. Grandpa told me I'd have that scar the rest of my life and I do still have it. Then he gave me "what for" for being careless with his knife.

Grandpa died in 1913 and is buried in Monroe. I remember his funeral. We rode in a cold rain out to the cemetery and I sat in the surrey while the burial took place.

Grandma continued to divide her time between our home and that of her daughter, our Aunt Willie.

In one of my very earliest memories I am making mudpies in front of the house where either Grandma or Mahaley is playing *Poor Butterfly* on the Victrola, and Mama returns from a trip somewhere and brings me a small parasol or umbrella.

When I told Mama of that memory, she remarked, "That would have been when I returned from Longview when my Papa died. YaPapa always wanted me to put off goin' anywhere for another week—'Just wait 'til next week,' he'd say—and I hadn't arrived in Longview before my Mama died. So when I received word that Papa was doin' poorly, I just left y'all with Mahaley and your Grandma, and I did get home before Papa died."

Grandfather Mobberly had died in July of 1917 and the "home place," as Mama called it, was not occupied.

Berry: The folks moved from Monroe to Longview for two reasons. In spite of his five children and another on the way, and in spite of being forty-five years old, Papa was about to get drafted into the army in World War I, and they figured a farmer wouldn't be drafted.

And Papa thought that the 120 acres of half sandy land and half piney woods, with a ravine and a clay pit and a pond, would be an ideal place to raise a family—particularly three rambunctious boys.

So move they did. In August, 1917, their furniture was loaded into a boxcar and the family boarded the passenger train bound for Mama's hometown, Longview, Texas. Berry can remember the train trip and hearing Papa exclaim, "The freight bill was less than we figured, and we saved fifty dollars on the move!"

It was an auspicious beginning for the next chapter in the lives of Mama and Papa.

CHAPTER 6

THE HOUSE IN THE COUNTRY

I have always thought of it as "the house in the country," because to me as a child we seemed to live in the country, certainly not in town. Mama called it "the home place" because it was the place where she had been a girl and a young lady and from which she was married. Berry calls it "out on the hill," because it was on a slight hill, maybe a mile or so south down Mobberly Avenue from the Mobberly Hotel, which was in that part of the town of Longview known as "the Junction."

So all of the names apply. The house sat in the middle of the woods, with cultivated fields out in back of the barn, and we had no very near neighbors. The slight hill on which the house was built ran down to the pond at the front of the property and to the ravine at the back of the property.

Berry: When we arrived by train at the Junction, we spent one night, maybe two, at the Mobberly Hotel, then Aunt Noel came in her big car and drove us all out to the house on the hill.

Mama seemed to limit her money-making endeavors during this time to "the home place" and we have no record of any attempts to make money, although she certainly helped with the grocery bill through her work on the farm.

We don't know when Mama learned to milk, because, according to Berry, the family had not owned milk cows in Monroe, and it doesn't sound like a skill Mama's mother would have let her learn as a proper young lady. But milk she could, and she taught Frederick, who was twelve, and Berry Noel, who just turned nine, to milk as soon as they moved to the farm, and Howard learned to milk soon thereafter. It was a skill she never let us girls learn. She said if we didn't know how to milk, we never would have to milk. We didn't argue with her.

Berry: Mama taught me and Fred to milk on ol' Muley. She was a good cow that Uncle Tad had paid two hundred dollars for. The other cow was Silk. She was just ornery and mean. We had to have two cows because when one of them was dry, we had the other one for milk. We kept the milk down in the well out by the barn to keep it cool. It was in a five gallon milk can with a lid that clamped on, and the rope holding the can had a mark painted on it so you'd know how far to let it down so the milk can would be in the water, yet the water wouldn't run in the top. Sometimes there were two cans to be lowered into the well.

I'll translate that for you young people out on a space station. A muley cow is one without horns. A cow is dry (doesn't make milk) before a calf is born. Cows have to be bred so they'll have calves and start over making a lot of milk. Milk has to be kept cool or it will sour or spoil, and we had to keep it down in the well, because we didn't have daily ice delivery and there was no electric refrigeration at the time. A well, in this instance, was a large hole dug into the ground to reach a good supply of uncontaminated water. The walls of our well were shored up with red brick and built on up several feet to form not only a safety barrier, but a working area for hauling up the water by a pulley and chain. Got it?

We owned at least one cow or another for the next twelve years. Mama sold the last one when Howard went off to the United States Naval Academy, saying, "I'm sure 'nuf not goin' to milk it and I'm not fixin' to let my girls milk a cow, either."

Howard: Mama sold that cow the very day I left for the Naval Academy. You don't own a cow, the cow owns you. She has to be milked twice every day; whether you want to or not, whether you're sick or well, whether you have a championship game or a date with your best girl, that dumb cow has to be milked.

With those two milk cows and plenty of chickens producing lots of eggs, we had homemade ice cream about three times a week. Mama loved ice cream all of her life, a taste passed on to most of her children, and we had a six-quart, hand-turned freezer to help her satisfy that taste. Ice was brought out from town and all of us took turns turning the handle, then licking or scraping with a spoon the last taste from the dasher when the ice cream was frozen. My children are still amazed how easily I dispose of a large dish of ice cream.

If Uncle Tad paid two hundred dollars for ol' Muley, Mama and Papa must have been renting the place from the Mobberly estate, of which Uncle Tad was executor. If they were renting on shares, the estate certainly didn't get rich off of that farm, because the first year Papa made only two bales of cotton, and cotton was probably selling for less than thirty-five cents a pound.

Berry: I remember seeing the cotton hauled to the gin between our place and town. It was hauled in a wagon with a team which must have been hired or borrowed, as we didn't have a big wagon with high sides, and we only had one horse, a pretty good sorrel which Uncle Tad had also bought. We used that horse both for plowing and pulling the buggy. We had bought a new buggy for $125.00 and I'm telling you it was the high point of our lives.

Howard: The buggy was used for hauling the whole family to Sunday School and church at the First Baptist Church of

Longview, a distance of maybe a mile and a half. When the family got too big for the buggy, some of us boys had to hoof it or ride our bicycles. One Sunday we had all gone to church together in the wagon and one of Mama's friends said to her, "Miss Ida, that is sure 'nuf a fine lookin' family you have there."

Mama replied, "Thanks, and you'll notice that they all have shoes on, too."

In my earliest recollection of the buggy, Papa and Mama had taken all of us down do the Mobberly Hotel, for some reason. This loading of the whole family in the buggy required a little planning. I don't know where everyone else was sitting, but I was sitting on a small box at Mama's feet. Some construction work was going on around the hotel and piles of gravel were dumped at what was going to be the curb. The wheels of the buggy rolled up on a pile of gravel, tilting the buggy which proceeded to run over my face. I'm sure I screamed bloody murder, but I wasn't seriously hurt, although for several years I had a fiery red line down one side of my face and under my chin.

Berry: Papa had about a half acre in garden. He built a six-foot, two-wire fence around it, and when he was plowing with that sorrel horse, the stubborn thing just wouldn't go where Papa wanted it to go, and that day, for the first time, I heard Papa say "Damnation!" I heard him say it a few times after that, but only under extreme provocation. Usually, the strongest expletive Papa used was "Tarnation!"

Fred and I had a green Studebaker wagon. We got it for Christmas and it cost ten dollars, which was a lot of money in those days. Papa bought us three goats, which we planned to train to pull the wagon, then we figured we'd get rich hauling vegetables and stuff like that to town to sell. Well, when the man who'd sold us the goats brought them out, we had him drop them out in the orchard where we kept the calf and the hogs. That weekend Fred and I started out to train those goats. They were wilder than a March hare and before we could get them even close to the wagon, they jumped the fence and got away. We chased them two or three miles and never did catch them. Never even saw them again. Somebody down the way probably had barbecued goat soon after that.

So we pulled the little wagon ourselves. The first money we made was from picking two bushels of sweet potatoes left in the potato patch right in back of the barn, and hauling them to town for sale at $1.75 a bushel.

We hauled vegetables and fruit and sometimes milk and butter in the Studebaker wagon down to the Mobberly Hotel, which was then being run by Mama's cousin, "Cuddin" Sam Mobberly and his wife, "Cuddin" Alma, and sometimes we sold them to the neighbors along Mobberly Avenue. We picked blackberries and sold them for fifty cents a gallon. We had a few rows of potatoes, Irish or white potatoes, in addition to the sweet potatoes, but it seemed like acres when we picked potato bugs off them, then dropped the bugs in a can where they were destroyed by kerosene. All of us, even the small kids, got involved with picking potato bugs. We also raised lettuce, leaf lettuce, not head lettuce, and cabbage, turnip greens, mustard greens, collards—what we didn't use at the house, Fred and I sold from the Studebaker wagon.

We had a red hog, a Duroc Jersey. The old sow came in heat and Fred and I had to drive her about one and a half miles down the road to get her bred. She was a stubborn, wild old cuss and we thought we'd never get her there and back again. She had a nice litter of eight pigs and we raised most of them.

My memories of the outdoors of the place are most pleasant. Mobberly Avenue continued to Young Street where stood the two-story red brick Pegues house. Mama's sister just older than Mama, Aunt Jessie, had married into the Pegues family. On Young Street we passed the old home of Grandpa and Grandma Young, full of potted plants and beautiful antique furniture. Grandma Young had a fascinating hard rubber, black trumpet-shaped device to hold to her ear as a remedy for her deafness. Grandpa Young had served in the Confederate Army with our grandfather Jim Mobberly, and the Young's daughter, Miss Lenore, was a dear friend of Mama's. Miss Lenore was married to Dr. F. M. McConnell, a former pastor of the First Baptist Church in Longview, who was prominent in Baptist work in Texas for many years. He had conducted Grandmother Mobberly's funeral. When the McConnells' young daughter Manon was married at her grandparent's home, there was much excitement for us small children when Mama made a large cake, beautifully decorated, and walked through the woods with it to the Youngs' home. It was the first wedding we'd been even that remotely connected with.

Next to the Youngs' old home was their pasture. One day out in our barnyard, Papa placed his fingers in his mouth and gave the loud, shrill whistle that could be heard all over that part of the county and meant we needed to come running immediately to see what he wanted. He pointed to the sky in the northwest and asked us what we saw there. At first we saw nothing, then we guessed a bird, and suddenly it dawned on us that the "bird" we saw growing bigger and bigger was an airplane! The first any of us had ever seen.

Here was a real, live flying machine from the new and still-mysterious world of airplanes, flying straight toward us. It passed low over us and circled south of the woods between our house and Young Street, and as it came in for a landing in Grandpa Young's pasture, we all took out running lickety-split, and we were in time to see the canvas-covered biplane with open cockpit taxi up close to the road.

Barnstorming was a popular pastime for some young men, a career for others, who had acquired a love of flying in World War I. The planes they flew, like the fliers themselves, were a surplus commodity of war. The usual practice was to buzz the town, locate a dry field free of trees and rocks, but not too far from town, and there land and offer rides for whatever price the traffic would bear. This young man stayed overnight and when he asked how far it was to Shreveport, Howard, feeling very grown-up, answered, "Sixty miles."

If we returned to the house by way of Young Street, we would have entered our place through the gap—or gate, to other people. It was not hinged, but a continuation of the barbed wire fence that had to be opened and closed on each entry. A black couple, Evalina and Hooper, lived in a house near the gap, with their sons, with whom my brothers played. I had occasion to be in Evalina's house only one time, but it still impresses me as the cleanest and neatest house I ever saw.

Evalina did our washing for us. This was done outside, with water heated in a big iron pot over an open fire. White clothes were boiled in the pot until they were white as snow, and all of the clothes were scrubbed with P&G soap or with lye soap on a rub-board or washboard until every grimy spot was gone. They were rinsed twice in washtubs, the white articles were run through bluing water, some things were starched, and everything was wrung out by hand and hung out to dry on the clotheslines in the chicken yard in back of the kitchen.

Through the years I have known women who thought that was the only way to get clothes clean enough to wear—not for them an electric washing machine, even the dasher type, and don't even suggest an automatic washer. When natural gas became available, a few highfalutin' women had a gas burner installed under the washpot.

Mama wasn't one of those die-hards, however, and did buy an electric machine about ten years later. She was never reluctant to use any labor-saving device she could afford, and was pleased as punch with the introduction of Rinso and other granulated washing powders.

The piney woods surrounding the house were accented in the spring with blossoming dogwood, redbud and plum trees, and in the fall with the bright red of oak. The lane from the gap passed through a sandbed, a wonderful play area sheltered by a mayhaw tree. The area around the front of the house, hard-packed and bare of grass or weed, made an even better playhouse. With a stick we scratched our house plans in the dirt and furnished the rooms with pieces of wood from the nearby woodpile. Our dishes were broken pieces of china that had suffered the fate of good dishes in the days before plastic. We also made dishes from red clay from the clay pit, budding pottery artists that we were.

Most of this playing house took place beneath two large hickory (pronounced "hickernut") trees, because the great oak near the back door of the house held two swings that were usually occupied by an ambitious Tarzan or gymnast or two. I once managed somehow to climb to the limb holding a swing (probably egged on by a brother or told to by Elsie) and slid down holding onto the rope, then went yelling into the house with badly rope-burned hands.

The boys made balls for their ball games and for "Annie Over" by wrapping the largest hickernut they could find with layers and layers of string, then covering it all with the toughest material available. Berry says the balls worked fairly well for a short while. The brothers camped out occasionally in the ravine at the back of the property, and all of us enjoyed the pond where there was a small beach and where all of us, even Mama and Mahaley, cooled off frequently during the summer.

Beryl: One of my early memories is of the time either Ida Rule or I fell in the pond and one of the boys pulled us out.

The orchard provided apples and peaches for jellies and jams. One Easter morning when the Easter rabbit had hidden the eggs in the orchard, we went out there and found that ol' Muley had dropped a calf in the orchard during the night, and we promptly named the calf "Easter." Easter was a favorite of the younger children for a long time.

Blackberries for cobblers and jams were picked from the large blackberry patch. My cousin Catherine Murphy Thomas writes, "I recall one blackberry picking Aunt Ida took us on. She got the horse and buggy ready and piled us in and took us way out in the field by the woods. She gave us each a bucket with the instructions, 'Don't eat—pick!' I'm sure Mahaley made us a blackberry cobbler that night."

Elsie and I picked blackberries to sell to the neighbors, and Mama told us that Mrs. Chatterbox wanted some. This was a neighbor who must have been quite a talker to have earned that nickname, but Elsie and I simply didn't know it was a nickname. We went up and down the road on the way to Campus Ward School asking, "Is this where Mrs. Chatterbox lives?" We never did find Mrs. Chatterbox, but we probably gave the neighbors something to ponder for a while.

The two-story red brick house must have been full to overflowing during our years there. There were two long porches, one upstairs, one downstairs, but no halls in the house. To get from room to room, we either went through another room or out on the porch. Papa put chicken wire around the upstairs porch to keep us from falling out on our heads, but it didn't keep the mosquitoes or flies away. If we slept on the upstairs porch during the summer, we slept under mosquito bars, which were just mosquito nets hung over each bed to discourage the pesky mosquitoes.

The first room at the front of the house was called "the front hall." The hall had a golden oak staircase, wonderful for sliding down, and was large enough to hold the davenport, the library table and that funny occasional table with the Victrola on it. I don't remember that room being used for anything except passage to and fro except for a couple of times: once when we girls played "cafe" on the steps, and another night when Mama and Fred had a party for Frederick's graduating class. That night the trees around and in the yard were hung with lighted Japanese lanterns, and the Victrola in the front hall had a burning candle on it to help us see to change the records. The Victrola ever after had a scorched place on the inside of the lid to remind us of what seemed a fairy tale night of magic to a gaggle of little sisters.

The front hall door opened into Mama's room that held Mama's oak bedroom set and another double bed as well, along with a big wicker rocker and Grandmother Mobberly's old heirloom "mother's rocker." The arms of that heirloom are long enough to support the mother's arms at a comfortable height, yet short enough to allow the baby to lie across the mother's knees when desired.

That rocking chair is another cherished heirloom in my home by virtue of the fact that when I was a young lady I made needlepoint pieces to replace the worn-out pieces of upholstery on the back and seat, which had replaced the original woven cane seat and back. I was leaving Mama's house with my newborn second child, Dick, and Mama said, "Is there a rocker in that apartment in Wyoming where you're takin' that child?"

"I don't know, Mama. Probably not."

"Then you take the rocker now. No grandchild of mine is goin' to go home where there's no rocker. It's best you have it now while you need it, than to wait until after I'm gone."

Grandmother Mobberly used it to rock her seven girls and

Mama used it with her ten children, but the thing finally collapsed under my husband and two children! Mama and Ida Rule took it back to Lubbock and had it restored professionally, and that was when the needlepoint was put on it. Mama had it in the living room of her home until her death, but most of the men of the family were scared to sit on the fragile thing.

The first Christmas in the old brick house, we gathered around the Christmas tree and Mama sat in the big wicker rocker, wrapped in quilts and holding the new baby, Beryl, who had been born on December 17th.

When we moved to Longview in August, Mama had sent a note by one of the boys to her old family doctor, Dr. Northcutt, telling him she was expecting a baby and asking him to come see her. When he didn't come, she sent for Dr. Louis Markham, a member of her high school graduation class, and he later delivered all of Mama's babies who were born in Longview.

"Some months later I was in the buggy holdin' the baby and spoke to Dr. Northcutt as we drove down the street. You could just see by his expression that he suddenly remembered the note. He sure 'nuf looked discombobulated," Mama said.

There wasn't a clothes closet in the whole house, so in their room Papa had hung a shelf on brackets in a corner, around which shelf they tacked a cretonne curtain. Such arrangements were to serve us as closets in houses for many years to come.

When a child was sick, he or she was usually moved into Mama's other bed. As the family grew, a trundle bed that slid under another bed was brought into use.

During the flu epidemic of 1918, Mama's room was a busy place. I thought Mama had told me that everybody, even Mahaley, had the flu, but Berry remembers it differently: "I know four of us had diphtheria because I remember getting antitoxin shots right in the stomach. They caused a terrible itching and we put baking soda on the itch so we could sleep. We'd been playing with two Negro boys the day I got sick. I became sick first, then Howard, then Fred. I remember the same old mockingbird singing outside our window every day. It was a rough time."

Mama and the baby, Beryl, were the only two who weren't sick. Papa and the boys were very sick and Mama actually hired a trained nurse to help her, but it was the last time she ever did that. Mama said, "I spent as much time fixin' her meals and waitin' on her as I did in waitin' on the sick."

My recollection of the time is: Elsie and I were on a cot or trundle bed at the foot of Mama's bed, and we kept teasing Berry Noel and Howard, who were in Mama's bed. We must have been getting better by that time. I did hear Mama tell a friend of mine many years later, "If you ever saw a child with diphtheria, you'd not put off even a day gettin' shots for your baby."

When the last patient was recovered, the old house had to be fumigated, a smelly process.

Through the years Mama had a lot of experience at both nursing and doctoring. It was in this house that Mahaley became ill and Mama diagnosed her illness as appendicitis. She sent word to the doctor to set a time for her to bring Mahaley to town for him to operate on the patient for appendicitis. He set the time; Mama took Mahaley to town, she was prepared for the operation and the doctor walked in prepared to operate. It was the first time he had seen Mahaley as a patient. As he started to make the incision he asked Mama, who was always in the operating room during all of our operations, "Are you sure it's appendicitis?"

"Well, maybe you'd best cut down the middle. I'm sure it's her appendix, but I reckon it's possible I jus' might be wrong," Mama answered. He cut down the middle of her abdomen, but it was truly a badly inflamed appendix.

Mama's room wasn't the only busy room in the house in the country. The door from Mama's room opened into the dining room (an early day family room. We ate three meals a day in there and then by the light of the two co'oil (coal oil or kerosene) lamps, we studied around the big table at night. The heating stove was in the dining room, and Mama told me, "The first winter we were back on the home place, the stove was the only thing that was dusted. I sat on one side reading books and Mahaley sat on the other side reading the *Saturday Evening Post* that she liked so much. Then right before time for the children to come in from school, we'd get busy and straighten up and start supper and look so busy that we'd be all worn out from our "hard day's work."

My memories of specific meals in the dining room are scarce. At one supper, Papa was scolding Frederick for not telling Mama and Papa that another boy had broken a leg in football practice. Frederick, who stuttered badly, said, "I was af-f-fraid you'd ma-ma-make me stop p-p-playing,"

I don't know how the crisis turned out, but I was so afraid of Papa's scoldings that I was scared to death. Mama, years later, said, "I feel sorry for first children. Parents have to learn on them. We made such hard and fast rules for Fred, it was prit'near impossible for him to keep them."

At the other memorable meal, one of the brothers had company. After the guest left, Mama said, "I want you children to learn a lesson from him. He didn't touch a thing on the table except the fried chicken, not the rice 'n gravy or the blackeyed peas or anything. He ate so much of that chicken that some of the rest of us just nearly didn't get any and I had cooked enough for Coxey's army.

"When you go somewhere for a meal, you be sure and eat something of everything that is offered to you, and you don't ask for seconds of any dish until the lady of the house offers it to you. That boy ate enough chicken to make himself sick."

All her life Mama said her recurring nightmare was to have a crowd coming to eat, and she didn't have enough food. She didn't want to have to say, "FHB! (family hold back!)."

The dining room opened both to the porch and to the kitchen with a big black iron Majestic cookstove heated by stove wood, which had been split by the boys and then stacked in ricks. When a child was too small to bring in an armload of stovewood, she would fill her skirt with wood chips or kindling to do her share of the chores.

The kitchen was the scene of meal preparations, as well as the place of Saturday night baths in tin washtubs. It was the room where Mama and Mahaley served tea cakes (big sugar cookies) to me and Elsie, seated on each side of a turned-over apple box, for my third birthday. A co'oil lamp with a fluted tin reflector in back of it hung on the kitchen wall.

The back porch had been enclosed at some earlier time the width of the kitchen, and we knew that room as the pantry. It was a big work room, or milk room, full of large crocks and milk buckets, washed and scalded and kept protected from the ubiquitous flies by clean dishtowels, because the churning process, which produced butter and buttermilk, took place in this room. Churning was a skill which each of us acquired at a very early age. Whipping cream, clabber (an early day form of yogurt) and cottage cheese were other by-products of the milking process.

When my own children came along, I had Mother Goose's Little Miss Muffet eating cottage cheese because they didn't know what "curds and whey" meant.

Right outside the back door was a cistern that once had been used to collect rain runoff from the roof, but it was no longer used for that, and some of the perishable food was lowered into the cool hole in the ground to keep a little better. Work tables in both the kitchen and pantry provided space for the food to be prepared and for the dishes to be washed and dried. It was here that we learned at a very early age to clean the soot from each lamp chimney each day, and then wash and shine each chimney until it sparkled. Mama or Mahaley scrubbed the wide pine boards of the floor of each room with Gold Dust washing powder every Saturday afternoon.

The front porch was as cool a place as they could find for the clothes-ironing operation on a hot summer day. Ironing clothes was no small deal at that time. Every article of clothing we wore was ironed, most of it starched. Every meal was served on a white damask tablecloth with cloth napkins that had to be ironed. Years later a friend asked Mama why she didn't have an oil cloth tablecloth, and Mama replied, "I've never used them, even when I had a whole passel of children at home, and I'm not goin' to start it now."

On ironing day, a legless padded ironing board was placed on the backs of two straight dining room chairs, and the heavy sad irons were heated, in the winter on the kitchen stove, in the summer on a small charcoal brazier. The clothes had been sprinkled and rolled up tight the night before to dampen evenly throughout, and the next morning Mahaley just started ironing. The ironed flat pieces were laid in the seat of another chair, and our dresses and the boys' and Papa's shirts were draped over the back of that same chair until they could be taken to their respective places at the same time. One hot summer day when Mahaley had been ironing all day and was just about through, some running kid bumped into the chair full of clean, ironed clothes and knocked it off the porch into the mud puddle where some of us had been making mudpies. It was another of those rare times when Mama cried. Mahaley cried, too.

Mama told me of another use for the porch, which I had

forgotten. "Mahaley could take a flying leap off that porch and chase your brothers all over the hill. It'd make her so mad when they called you 'Monkey,' but they delighted in teasing both of you with that. She usually caught them and gave them a good lick with whatever she happened to have in her hand."

When the church music directors of today forget and slip in an old, old song, I am reminded of Mama and Papa sitting on the porch while we children chased light'nin' bugs and Papa sang in his deep bass voice some of his favorite hymns. *In the Sweet By and By, Near the Cross, He Leadeth Me,* and *Leaning on the Everlasting Arms* are some that stir my memory of him.

A bench with a washpan and bucket of water was on the porch for us to wash our hands before each meal and to wash our feet before going to bed each night. We weren't about to get in bed on white sheets with those feet that had been running bare all over the hill.

Beryl: My earliest memory is the feeling of chicken mess squishing up through my bare toes. I headed for the house and my shoes, and I never would go barefoot if I could help it.

Some of the bedrooms had washstands with a bowl and pitcher of water, but most of the children's summertime cleaning took place either on the porch (where our baths were a lick and a promise: a lick with the rag and a promise to do better next time) or in the kitchen on Saturday night.

Most rooms also had a slop jar. Some people call it a commode or chamberpot, but we called it the slop jar and it took care of any emergency that couldn't wait until we could get out to the closet, which is what others know as an outhouse, privy, outdoor john or outdoor toilet. But we just called it the closet, out to one side of the area between the backdoor and the barn. It was a three-holer, the middle hole being quite small for little people. There was a screen to shelter it from view from the house, and when the big brothers escorted the little girls out there after dark, they delighted in scaring us with spooky shadows cast by the lantern, or by sticking the flashlight in their mouths and poking their glowing faces in the door, making us hurry and run all the way back to the house.

The upstairs of the house contained a large stair hall, the boys' room, the girls' room, Mahaley's room and the attic. When we weren't sleeping down in Mama's room, we girls slept in the room next to Mahaley. Mahaley's room was almost papered with the fronts of old *Saturday Evening Posts*. We didn't go in there much. Mama said Mahaley was entitled to her privacy and she needed to get away from us sometime. I walked in my sleep one night and woke up by Mahaley's bed, carrying a large, heavy Bible. In fact, it was so heavy I could not pick it up when I was awake, and it hit the floor with a thud, but Mahaley gently put me back to bed.

A door from Mahaley's room opened into the attic, a storeroom over the pantry downstairs. My cousin Catherine writes, "The greatest treat for me was when Aunt Ida let us go into the old storeroom, or attic, and look around. There were so many interesting things in there, remember?"

I remember, I remember. About ten years after we moved from the house in the country, I went with Mama and Aunt Noel for a tour of the old house at the invitation of the new owners. Mahaley's room and the attic were now a lovely nursery and bathroom; the wall between Mama's room and the dining room had been removed and a double fireplace installed in the center of the resulting large room; the pantry was converted into a modern kitchen and the old kitchen was made into a dining room. With its lovely landscaped lawn leading to a paved street in the Mobberly Addition, the old house was no longer *a* house in the country, and with all the changes made inside out, it was no longer *my* "house in the country."

CHAPTER 7

MORE COUNTRY LIFE

The old red brick house held our family well enough, but Mama didn't stop with our family. I don't know where Mama put everyone, but we seemed to have lots of company in that house. Aunt Elsie and her children stayed over at least one Saturday night, causing a traffic jam in the tin washtub baths in the kitchen.

Aunt Daisy and her two younger children, Margaret and Harold, came for a visit. Harold, about Howard's age, stayed with us for a year, and the brothers taught him to milk, too. When he came back for a visit a year or so later he said he'd forgotten how to milk.

"Milking is like riding a bicycle. Once you learn, you never forget how," Howard told him.

Grandma was there, too, much of the time. I believe she usually stayed with us girls in the girls' room upstairs. Bluford, Aunt Noel's son about Berry's age, came out from town often, but one visit he just kept staying. His mother had bobbed her hair and he said he'd go home when it grew out. Uncle Tad sent word to Bluford to cut out that foolishness and get himself home. Bluford is reported to have said, "Can't I just stay for dinner? They're having homemade ice cream." And he did.

Sunday afternoons the yard was full of visitors' vehicles, some horse-drawn, some motorized. We delighted in sitting in the open cars, pretending to drive, making "ah-ooga" sounds.

When Papa's sister, Aunt Willie, and her family were there one day, my cousin Catherine and I got in a hair-pulling, kicking fight, the only one I ever remember getting involved in. (Fights with sisters were usually verbal, not physical.) I don't have any idea what the fight was about, but we sure caught ol' Ned from our folks.

A few memorable Sunday afternoons, Aunt Noel would take as many as she could get in her big Chandler touring car with little jump seats that folded into the back of the front seat, and away we'd go for wonderful rides.

Those were the summer days. Christmases found us inside the house, of course.

Berry: The first Christmas we were there, Mama bought two dolls for Elsie and Rosemary from Duke & Ayres, the variety store. She paid a whole fifty cents for each of them, then made clothes for them, and the girls sho' did like those dolls.

Another Christmas, the big holly tree was upstairs in the girls' room. I remember that Christmas because we had lighted candles on the tree for a few minutes while Papa stood guard nearby with a bucket of water, just in case. It was also the year I received a play-like washboard from Santa Claus.

One Christmas we girls made Papa's Christmas present by stringing folded squares of tissue paper on a string. In those pre-Kleenex days, he tore off one square at a time to clean his straight-edged razor.

That first fall Frederick, Berry Noel, and Howard all started to school in Longview. Elsie started the next year and Mama sent me to kindergarten at the same time. Later I went through first grade, and when it was time for me to go to second grade, the rules had been changed. Since I wasn't seven years old by September 1, I was going to have to pay tuition. Mama would not hear to that and she took me out of second grade that year. Sometime during that year I went with Mama on a trip back to

Monroe, and during our visit there I rode the school bus for the only time in my life when I visited school one day with my cousins Dorothy and James Standley. I also ate the only hot lunch I ever had in school. Recently when I told Dorothy that because I was pokey and picayunish about eating breakfast, our mothers had put my bacon in a biscuit and sent me out the door so we wouldn't be late for the school bus and I didn't want the blasted biscuit and bacon and stuck it down between the seat and the wall of the bus, Dorothy said in that soft southern accent of a Louisiana native, "Why, Cuddin Rosemary, hon, it's mos' likely still there."

For a whole lifetime I considered myself smarter than Elsie because I thought she failed second grade. That was when I caught up with her and we went through all of our school classes together. Not many years before she died, she told me that she'd had erysipelas in her foot and had missed so much of second grade that she wanted to take that grade over. When I couldn't remember her being real sick a long time, she said, "It was when Mama took you and Beryl to Monroe. Grandma and Mahaley took care of me."

Elsie and I each had Miss Jodie McClure, a former classmate of Mama's, for our first grade teacher, a blessing for which I have been thankful ever since. No "Dick and Jane" for us; we had "This is Will. How do you do, Will?" and "This is May. How do you do, May?"

When I was in the third grade, several of us students were called from all grade levels to meet on the front steps of Campus Ward school. As we waited for some teacher to tell us what to do next, we tried mightily to figure out why and for what we had been chosen. I'm not sure we expressed it verbally, but we knew some of us were smarter than others, some were older, some were richer, others were poorer (This certainly wasn't true of me.), some were from "good families"

(This was certainly true of me.) and some were "poor white trash", although I know this last wasn't expressed out loud. We finally reached a consensus that we were to be in a play—that we could talk seemed to be the only thing we had in common. It turned out that we were all underweight; the Home Economics class in high school had us come to the nearby high school building every morning, for how long 1 don't remember, and they fed us milk and graham crackers and lectured us on the evils of drinking coffee. No one who has known me in the last thirty years has believed that story, at least the part that I was ever classified as underweight.

Frederick graduated from Longview High School in 1922. He was president of his junior class and had been a very popular, good-looking student with good grades and a good singing voice. As I have mentioned, he stuttered badly, but as is true of many stutterers, he could sing without difficulty. I heard him sing in a quartet at church, and I also heard him sing, "K-k-k-Katy, K-k-k Katy, you're the only girl that I adore!" I thought the song had been written especially for him.

Mama was determined that Fred should go to a school for stutterers in Tyler, Texas, a nearby community. Berry overheard Mama and Papa discussing it, and, as usual, Papa didn't see how they could afford it. Berry heard Mama say, "We must make any sacrifice for that."

Fred went to the school and it did help him a lot, although he stuttered to a lesser degree for the rest of his life.

The wonderful news of the end of World War I was brought to our place from over at Grandpa Young's house. It was an exciting time, and a time of relief also. Mama said, "If the war hadn't ended when it did, YaPapa would have been drafted very soon."

Mama later remarked, "There had been a shortage of potatoes during the war, but that didn't bother us a bit. We ate rice three times a day, almost, anyway."

Mama always tried to use as little sugar as possible, so the sugar shortage was not hard on us. She was a great one for offering us "biscuits, butter 'n' syrup" for dessert, anyway.

I have a hazy remembrance of a tall man in a uniform visiting our place. I believe it was one of Aunt Daisy's sons who had been in the service, and I was offered a sip from a glass of the stuff he had brought to the house.

"Phooey! It tastes like vinegar, and tickles my nose like the soda water Papa takes for his indigestion,' I said. And the grown folks laughed at my reaction to the champagne the soldier had brought home.

Howard: After World War I, haircuts at the barbershop went up from twenty-five cents to fifty cents. With a husband and three sons needing haircuts, this was too much for Mama, and she bought scissors and hand clippers and cut our hair for years. She cut the girls' hair, too, until they thought they were too grown up for that. Aunt Noel gave Bluford fifty cents to get a haircut at the barbershop, but Bluford, that early prodigy of high finance, persuaded Mama to cut his hair for twenty-five cents.

Papa was not a farmer at heart, and he soon went to work for one hundred dollars a month for Moore Grocery Company, wholesale grocers, calling on the retail grocers in the area surrounding Longivew, traveling by train some of the time, occasionally using a company car. One of the nights he had brought the company car to the house, it came in mighty handy.

Ida Rule, a toddler, stuck a dried pea or bean up her nose. The moisture in the nostril made the bean begin to swell, and it not only was impossible for Mama to remove it, but it also became painful. The folks piled all of us little ones in the car and took her to the doctor late at night—it seemed late to us.

The rest of us sisters stayed in the car under Dr. Markham's porte cochere while the doctor removed the culprit bean.

We enjoyed a couple of other gratuitous benefits from that job. Papa brought home to me and Elsie a sample portfolio of the fronts of school writing tablets he sold to merchants. There must have been a dozen front covers, and each one was a different paper doll and clothes representing that many movie stars, male and female. We had never seen a motion picture, but we certainly somehow knew who Mary Pickford and Baby Peggy were, and we were the envy of our contemporaries.

The other serendipity was a shipment of stale, no-good candy bars. They were brought to the house to be fed to the pigs, but you can bet those boys checked each bar before it was thrown to the pigs. If there were no bugs visible, the boys got them—not the pigs.

During these years, foodstuffs that we didn't raise on the farm were purchased from a local grocer. When Papa paid the grocer's bill each month, the merchant, in keeping with the custom of the time, gave Papa a large sack of candy to bring to the family. It was usually hard ribbon candy, probably left over from Christmas, not particularly good, but we ate it with gusto because it was the only sto'-bought candy we had.

Mama busied herself with church activities and with Parent Teachers Association work. She was treasurer of the church and taught a class of women; Papa was a deacon and Sunday School Superintendent, and both were faithful in attendance at nearly every service.

"When folks usta compliment me on how much work I did for the church, I told them they ought to honor Mahaley," Mama later told me. "I couldn't have done a lick of it if Mahaley hadn't been there to look after you children."

Parent Teachers Association met right after school and we always enjoyed being able to play on the school ground until the meeting was over, so we could ride home in the buggy with Mama, thus avoiding the long walk home.

Ida Rule was born September 16, 1919. Early that morning, Papa drove all of us to town to see the circus unload, and when we returned later in the day, we had a new baby in the house. About a year later, Mama bought Ida Rule a knitted wool suit of coat, leggings, and hat of orange with brown trim. It was a big occasion, the first sto'-bought thing that had been purchased for a girl in a long time.

"Poor child," Mama said. "Everything she's ever worn has been worn by three other sisters that has just prit'near worn them out."

Papa left Moore Grocery Company and bought a grocery store in Longview. He walked the mile and a half to work every morning, and that may have been why Mama wanted to move into town. "I was just not made to live in the country. YaPapa offered to put in a telephone and electric lights, but I just wanted to move into town."

Mahaley didn't want to move to town, however. She didn't think she'd like town life, so it was arranged for her to take the train to Arkansas for a visit with her folks. I thought our separation was temporary and was not too distressed, but Mahaley never did come back. The next Christmas, she sent to Elsie and me each a yoke she had made of tatting, another talent she had. Mama sewed a gathered piece of blue plisse on my yoke, pink on Elsie's, and we each had a nightgown we loved.

Mama had a letter from Mahaley after we moved to West Texas. She wrote that she thought we might have moved to Florida, which was having a big land boom at the time. She wanted to come back to live with us, but it was at a time when all nine children were at home, and we were living in a two-bedroom house, so Mama had to write her that we simply did not have the room or the money to pay even her small wages.

I wrote her, too, but if Mama ever heard from her again, I didn't know about it.

Even if Mahaley didn't think she would like town life, Mama surely thought she herself would. Maybe she thought there'd be more opportunities to help pay the grocery bill in town. So we moved to town, to a big house not too far from downtown Longview and only a couple of blocks from Papa's grocery store.

CHAPTER 8

IT WAS THE BEST OF TIMES

Suddenly, we were town kids, no longer country kids. (I can hear Mama now, "Don't use that word about my children. They're not billy goats, even if they do act like it sometime.")

We moved into the Perry House on Center Street, a short block from the church and right next door to the Kelly place.

The church, of course, was the First Baptist Church. I knew vaguely that Aunt Noel and her family went to the big red brick Methodist church near their home, but as far as I was concerned, the only church in Longview was the First Baptist Church. Because Aunt Noel's family was rich by my standards, and they were Methodists, for years I thought all Methodists were rich.

The Kelly house on the corner of Center and South streets was a lovely two-story white home with tall colonial pillars across the front. In recent years, I was surprised to find a section of an interesting museum in the historic old town of Jefferson, Texas, devoted to the Kelly family and their part in the development of the iron ore industry in northeast Texas. (You know you're getting old when you find the neighbors of your childhood honored in a museum.) At that time, however, we just knew that Mr. Kelly was the Kelly Plow Works, which, to us children, was a mysterious building near the staid old Magnolia Hotel. Mrs. Kelly was a distant personage who, as far as I know, never complained of the noise that must have emanated from the yard of the Perry House after that bunch of Duff children moved in.

But the personality that interested us girls the most was Daughter, the Kelly's girl who, as far as we were concerned, was a glamour girl fifteen or so years before the term *glamour girl* had been coined to describe such beautiful and exciting young women. We were agog at her comings and goings, at the cars that drove in and out of their curved driveway, and at her carelessness in lowering the shades at night when she undressed. After our move from the seclusion of our farmhouse in the woods, the importance of pulling down the window shades at night was our first lesson in city living.

We were impressed with her piano-playing talents, too, although she played *Carolina in the Morning* so much that even we wished she'd add another tune to her repertoire. But the incident that brought her down to our level occurred one summer evening when, through the open windows, we heard her mother call, "Daughter, I've told you and told you. The biscuits don't go in the ice box."

We giggled and giggled, because even we knew better than to put the biscuits in the ice box.

Howard: The land the Kelly and the Perry houses occupied was covered by a Sears automotive business for some years, but my friend Josephine Bodenheim tells me that it is today occupied by a branch of the Kilgore Community College.

When I think of our family during these years, each member seems to be going down a separate road, meeting at the hub of Mama in the Perry House.

The Perry House was a large, one-story, white Victorian structure with lots of gingerbread trim, a preponderance of porches and bay windows, and a big tower dominating the front. The big porch swing on the wrap-around front porch, nearly hidden behind wisteria and honeysuckle vines, was once too heavily laden with children, Duff children as well as neighbors, as I stood on the back of the swing, pumping us too high. The swing fell and Elsie went into the house calling for Mama, the bone in her injured arm exposed.

Soon after we moved in, Mama mailed to Aunt Mary in New York City bridal rosebuds picked from the arbor over the low front steps. Although the flowers were kept moist with damp cotton and were packed in an oatmeal carton with wax paper from bread wrappers, I wonder in what condition they arrived after a trip by regular mail, the only mail of the day.

A beveled glass front door opened into the big central hall of the house. This hall was a sort of living room for us, because it was large enough to hold the bookcase, davenport (when it wasn't in the bay window of the dining room), the Victrola, and a statue on a pedestal near the dining room door. Years later, I saw a large copy of that statue—a barefoot boy holding his head back, ready to drop a large grape in his mouth—in a city park in Idaho, and the sight brought back memories of the hall in the Perry House, because I don't remember our having that piece of home decoration after the Perry House.

The old-fashioned table-model phone in the hall with the receiver hanging in a hook on the side was the scene of what is called today "a learning experience" for me. (Again, I can hear Mama saying, "What do you mean *learnin' experience?* How can you have any experience and not learn anything from it?")

Over the telephone, I told one of Mama's friends that she was not at home, and she asked when Mama would return.

"Terreckly," I answered.

"When?" or "What?" she asked, understandably.

Now I knew what *terreckly* meant, and I also knew it was not a proper, grammatical word, but for the life of me, I didn't know what in the world it stood for. I hesitated so long, she said, "What did you say? When will she be back?"

"Innaminit," I answered.

That satisfied her, but later I asked Mama what *terreckly* meant and she told me, *directly,* one of Papa's words, which he pronounced either way. It had two different meanings the way he used it. "You come directly home," meant that you'd better come straight home, no goofing off, but "You come home terreckly" meant to come home pretty soon, after a while, or, as I said, in a minute.

Evidently the old house had not been built originally with a bathroom, because the back portion of the big hall had been walled off to make a bathroom, with one door opening to the hall, the other to one of the back porches. Berry tells me that the back porch was the site of one of the worst fights he remembers between Howard and himself.

We were excited to have indoor plumbing with toilet tissue(!) in place of the mail order catalogues in the closet on the farm. But modern conveniences came with their own problems.

We had a varied assortment of domestic help during these few years, looking for someone to take Mahaley's place. At least one of these women dipped snuff and used a toothbrush. Nearly every day, Mama told her not to throw the old twig in the toilet bowl; it might stop it up. Sure 'nuf, the sewer was stopped up one day and the plumber had to be called. Unable to find the obstruction from the bathroom end of the line, he had to dig up the sewer line, through the yard and down the alley to the street. One evening, a horse fell into the open ditch dug in the alley, and I remember lanterns shining in the dark as workmen labored into the night trying to get the horse free, which I suppose they eventually accomplished as all the excitement was over when we awakened the next morning. When the obstruction was finally found, it *was* caused by the woman's twig brush.

"Tarnation! This wouldn't have happened out on the farm," Papa was heard to mutter.

The first room on our left as we entered the hall was probably designed for the parlor, but it always served as a bedroom, sometimes Mama's room, sometimes a guest room, occasionally a room for one or more of the boys. Its outside door opened to the south porch shaded by huge magnolia trees.

The first Christmas we were in the Perry House, a big holly tree was brought in from the ravine on the farm and placed in the bay window that admitted the morning sun. In the days before electric Christmas tree lights, the beautiful tree was reflected from the big mirror over the walnut mantel of the fireplace on the opposite side of the room.

Christmas was one of the times when the roads of our separate lives came together. No one went into the Christmas tree room until everyone was ready; then Ida Rule, as the youngest, went in first, followed in stair steps by the rest of us, with Frederick, home from school, bringing up the rear.

Waking on Christmas morning is excruciatingly exciting at any time, but that year we had awakened to a white Christmas! It was the first snow I could ever remember. The familiar front lawn was so different; the dark green leaves of the magnolia trees held blobs of wet snow which, as we watched, slid off the leaves and mixed with the ground snow with a plop. We were anxious to get outside to play in it, but we wouldn't have delayed the Christmas tree for anything.

That best of all Christmases, Elsie and I each received a doll *and* roller skates! All other Christmases, there was only one big gift from Santa Claus, but there were two big gifts that year. Ida Rule and Beryl each received both a doll and a tricycle. We were firmly convinced our Santa Claus was the best in the world, although it never occurred to us to wonder whywe didn't receive a gift from Mama and Papa all the years we received gifts from Santa Claus.

The sidewalks were too slushy for us to use the new skates right away, but we tore ourselves away from the dolls to hurry outside to build, with the help of the boys, a gigantic snowman in the wet, sticky snow. The snow was melting fast, but all of that pleasant, sunshiny afternoon, the snowman watched our clumsy struggles to learn to skate.

After a big, midday dinner before the mahogany fireplace in the dining room, all four of us girls spent the afternoon with our skates and tricycles. Elsie and I pushed Beryl and Ida Rule on their trikes, theoretically helping them learn to ride their Christmas gifts, but actually trying to keep ourselves from falling down.

We fell down countless times, nevertheless, and tore out the knees of our long black stockings as well as the knees of the hated union suits we had to wear in winter. It was years before I heard them called "long handles." The stockings and union suits were so badly torn that Mama later patched them with pieces of completely worn out garments.This must have rankled her, because one of her more oft-repeated statements was, "A torn place looks like an accident, but a patch looks like premeditated poverty."

By the time the pleasant winter darkness settled, we felt we were the world's best skaters, and were ready to go inside and play with our reluctantly neglected dolls.

Elsie and I were playing happily with the dolls in front of the dying fire in that front room. The rest of the family was in Mama's room, across the dark hall and farther back in the house. We were occupied with changing the dolls' clothes, picking names for the new dolls and trying to make up to the dolls for our neglect of them in the afternoon. Suddenly we heard a slight noise on the side porch, and then, on the door to that porch, we heard, "Knock!" Pause. "Knock!" Pause. "Knock!" Loud and distinct, but each of the three knocks spaced several seconds from the others.

Without saying a word to each other, we rose from our cross-legged positions, taking the dolls and all the clothes we could pick up without wasted motion, and walked very rapidly through the dark dining room, across the dark hall and into Mama's room. The rest of the family was sitting around the golden oak fireplace enjoying the only five-pound box of chocolate-covered caramels I ever remember in our home. Two bug-eyed, white-faced little girls took their places in the circle, too scared to say a word.

We never did know who scared the livin' daylights out of us—the big boys insisted they didn't do it. It is the only time I remember being scared in that house.

The next day, Mama sent me back to the pantry, a storeroom in back of the kitchen, to bring something to her. There I saw boxes that had obviously contained dolls at some store. I chose to ignore them, or to believe that Santa Claus had just lightened his load of surplus material into our pantry.

Berry: Fred and I operated a fireworks stand at that Christmas season, and we netted a total of $105.55. Boy, was that a lotta money in those days! The popular southern tradition of using all sorts of fireworks at Christmas was sho' profitable for us.

That Christmas season had started off exceptionally well for me, too. My class at Campus Ward school had drawn names for the exchange of gifts. The whole class was commiserating with me—my name had been drawn by Beatrice, and no one was quite sure that I would receive a gift at all and, if so, they said it certainly wouldn't be much of a gift. You see, Beatrice was "Mexican," the only person of Spanish ancestry I knew at that time. What did she give me? A coloring book! It probably cost a dime, the price limit, but it was priceless to me as it was the only coloring book I ever owned, and I cherished it selfishly for years.

That front room was the setting for another occasion to remember. One Wednesday evening, we stood in the hall doorway waiting for Mama so we could all go to Prayer Meeting. Mama said, "Just a minute. Let me get my ring," and she reached up to the small, dark blue ring dish with the picture of Longview High School painted on it that she kept on the mantel. While she was busy with the innumerable chores around the house, Mama didn't wear the diamond ring Papa had given her at their wedding, but she always took it from its place on the mantel as she started out the door to go anywhere. The ring wasn't where it should have been. After searching around, Mama said, "Y'all go on to Prayer Meetin'. I'll be along terreckly."

When we got home, Mama had about turned the house inside out, but she still couldn't find the ring.

Thursday morning, when the current black helper arrived, Mama put her to work sifting the ashes in the front room fireplace to see if the ring had fallen there. (I truly do not remember the woman's name, but I will call her Rosy, because I know that was *not* her name.) When the ring still did not turn up, Mama eventually called the local law enforcement department. The first question they asked was, "Who do you have working for you?"

Mama told them about Rosy, but she added, "I know she's all right. She worked for the old Blank brothers for years." (*Blank* is another made-up name because I don't remember the real name of the brothers.) When the brothers were questioned, their reply was, "If anything is missing, Rosy has it. She stole us blind the twenty-three years she worked for us."

When the officers walked up on the porch of Rosy's house to question her, they saw her remove the lid from her cook stove and drop something in the fire. They quickly stepped in and with a fire shovel, reached into the fire and rescued Mama's ring!

Mama had her ring back, but she never could get over those brothers putting up with the woman's stealing for years.

Another day, Mama opened the big drawer of the dresser of the lovely cherry bedroom set in the front room and showed us girls a beautiful layette of baby clothes—the only time we knew in advance that another baby was coming. I believe the women of the church and Mama's old friends in town had given her a baby shower. It is easy to believe that the clothes left from the previous babies were pretty well worn.

Soon after that, Elsie and I were sleeping in Mama's big oak bed back in Mama's room, and I punched Elsie awake.

"Listen, I said, "I heard a baby cry. Do you reckon Mama has a new baby?"

We reached the astounding conclusion that Mama had a new baby, then went back to sleep. The next morning we were introduced to Lydia Ann as she lay by Mama's side in the big cherry bed in the front room.

Lydia Ann was a joy to her big sisters. We didn't need dolls, we had a real, live baby to play with. We loved to push her in her big wicker stroller. We were often on roller skates as we zoomed with her up and down the block. Sidewalks and neighbors were still a novelty to us and we spent hours pushing her carriage down the sidewalk and showing off our new baby to the neighbors on our side of the block: the Fullers, Meltons, and Skippers.

Mary Noel considerately forgot her bicycle and left it at the house for an extended time. Elsie and I taught ourselves to ride her bike, then we hitched the carriage-stroller on the bike and away we went! It's a wonder we didn't give that baby some kind of phobia or something worse, but she turned out fine in spite of us, not because of us.

My only other memory of that big front room: I am sitting propped up in the big wicker stroller with my feet on the handle, reading the tear-jerker novel, *The Wide, Wide World,* and shedding buckets of tears, while Mama was looking for me to come back to the kitchen and dry dishes.

Another time Mama found me sitting high up in the chinaberry tree in the back yard, reading again when I should have been drying dishes. It was usually Elsie's job to set the table, we both cleaned it off, and I had to dry the dishes. I was convinced I had the worst end of the bargain.

Two jealous little girls traveling down their own road was just another one of Mama's burdens to bear. Although we were in the same grade at school and had the same friends, I thought we were very different and resented it when people couldn't remember which was which. Elsie always dressed more neatly and acted more like a lady than I did. One teacher said admiringly, "That Elsie! You can always count on her to have a clean handkerchief." Conversely, you could always count on me to *need* a clean handkerchief.

When Mama made our dresses (they might be of identical material or they might be of the same print, yet different colors) we each resented her making the other a dress first. So she had to sew the left sleeve in one, then the left sleeve in the other; the same for the right sleeves and the fronts and backs so that she came out practically even. She should have scalped us.

"I had my children in pairs so they'd have someone to play with and so, if one of them gets in trouble, the other can come tell me about it," I heard Mama say many times. I also heard her make that statement years later, after Elsie's small son,

Jimmy, fell in the garbage can and his littler sister, Barbara Jean, came to tell Mama about it.

Now that we lived in town, we had a whole neighborhood of playmates. Mama often told of mothers who would call and say, "Miss Ida, can one of your girls come over and play with my child? She is so lonely here by herself."

"I can send two of them over, but not just one, or else *I'd* have a little girl with no one to play with," Mama said.

"But two can play well together, while three of them fight," the callers often said.

"You're so right," Mama might reply sweetly. "That's what happens when your child comes over here to play."

Elsie and I were one of those pairs of Mama's children, and Elsie, being the older of the two of us, was always getting me into trouble (I thought) by telling me I had to do what she said, because, she said, "I am the oldest and I'm the boss."

One day when Papa wasn't in his store, Elsie talked me into going to the store and telling Percy P. Painter, Papa's right-hand man, that he should give us the two dimes we needed to go to a Jackie Coogan movie.

"Are you sure it's all right with Mr. Duff?" Percy asked.

A kick in the ankle from Elsie prompted me to say, "Yes, he said we could."

I was lying through my teeth, because he had specifically said we couldn't afford it.

Percy reluctantly gave us the two dimes and we joyously went to see the Jackie Coogan movie, but it was I who had to take the scolding from Papa in spite of my vociferous protestations, "But Elsie told me to."

It was probably the worst scolding I ever had, and I surely never did that again.

Elsie and I might fight between ourselves, but we put up a united front against the rest of the world. The same could be said of the whole family. Through the years, we fought and squabbled, but let an outsider criticize one of us, and the whole clan quickly rallied together.

It was during these years that I first heard Mama say, "I declah I don't know how you children can carry on so here at home and behave so well away from home. People are always tellin' me, 'Ida, I reckon you have the best-behaved children in town. How do you get them to mind so well when they're out of your sight?'" Mama would continue with resignation, "I do declah I wish you'd behave as well at home as you do away from home."

All of us were taught from the time we were teachable to say, "Yes, ma'am," "Yes, sir," "Thank you," "No, thank you," "I'm sorry," "I had a nice time," "Please," and all of those little amenities. I tried teaching the same things to my children, but when they started to school up in this Yankee country, a teacher once reprimanded one of them for being impertinent when he said, "Yes, ma'am."

Mama taught us to stand when an older person entered the room, and to remain standing until the older person sat down or left the room. Life got complicated as Mama got older and her knees became painful when she bent them too much, and she often felt more comfortable standing for long periods of time. This left us and our friends standing there until she realized what was going on and either sat down or betook herself from the room.

We were taught not to talk with our mouths full, never to interrupt, particularly an older person and more particularly Papa, and certainly never to sass an older person.

She disapproved of chewing gum in general and taught us, "A lady never chews gum in public, only in the privacy of her own room."

Times do change. What would Mama think of the really

nice people who chew gum in public today? She's say, "Poor things. They haven't had a proper upbringing."

Giving us a proper upbringing was just another of Mama's burdens as she watched each of us travel our separate roads.

CHAPTER 9

IT WAS STILL THE BEST OF TIMES

It *was* still the best of times for Mama. She often quoted the line, "Life is so full of a number of things."

Frederick had finished Longview High School before we moved into town, where he had a job as custodian or janitor of the church. He worked there for a summer and at least part of one winter, because Howard remembers the four-foot logs required by the furnace of the church.

One weekday Fred lowered the great crystal chandelier from the domed ceiling of the church to the floor, and with the help of Mama and his little sisters, every beautiful prism was washed and polished to glisten spectacularly. I remember how important I felt in helping him (At last my dish-drying experience paid off!) and Beryl remembers that she and Ida Rule played "preaching" while this was going on, taking turns at the pulpit and preaching to the rest of us.

This was in those pre-Kleenex days and everyone always carried a clean handkerchief. Invariably a half-dozen or so were left somewhere around the church every Sunday and Fred collected them into a lost-and-found box. If they hadn't been called for in a reasonable number of weeks, Fred brought them to the house where they were washed and ironed, and we girls put some of them back into circulation, but when the officers went to Rosy's house to rescue Mama's ring, they found several dozen of those handkerchiefs which we'd never missed.

Berry: Fred and I went to the football game on Thanksgiving Day of 1922 at Marshall, Texas. Marshall and Longview were big rivals and the game was played in the morning so everyone could get home for Thanksgiving dinner. Fred and I got home, as I recall, about one-thirty and we all enjoyed a big Thanksgiving dinner in the dining room there at the Perry House.

Fred went to the stammering school in Tyler sometime during that winter, and then he went to Burleson College, a Baptist Junior College in Greenville, Texas. This was chosen because Dr. F.M. McConnell (the son-in-law of our neighbors out in the country, Grandpa and Grandma Young) was president of the school at that time. Fred probably had some kind of scholarship, and he had part-time jobs in Greenville while he worked and went to college.

Except for the chandelier washing, the only time I remember my road and Fred's road converging occurred after Lydia Ann was born. Fred returned from Greenville, jumped from a car full of young men and he was running into the house when we called to him to come and see our new baby. He stopped and admired her and asked what color her eyes were. When we told him, "Blue," he said, "Nice." Then he went on about his business.

Berry's separate road took him through his sophomore year at Longview High School after we moved into town.

Berry: When we first moved into town Mama bought a good-looking new suit for me, knickers and all. I wore it to a dance at Phillip Smith's home, maybe four miles west of town, and had to face Papa when I came in that night. That was the last short-pants suit I had and the last suit Mama bought me. After that I made enough money somehow to keep myself in clothes. I had a paper route for a few months delivering the Longview

Daily News to 110 subscribers in northeast Longview. The pay was three dollars per week.

Bill Francis, the son of Dr. Francis, the dentist, and I had a lawn mowing and lawn care service in the spring and summer of 1923. As I recall we kept pretty busy with some fourteen or fifteen lawns. We were making eight dollars to ten dollars a week, each, and as far as we were concerned it was a very successful business.

After working that summer of 1923, Berry started his junior year in high school. He and Barney Skipper, who lived down the block from us, enjoyed managing for a car, picking up a couple of girls and riding around for a time.

Berry remembers these good years as a time when he made many friends who would remain friends for the rest of his life. Although his social life was prospering, things didn't go so well in school. He actually persuaded Mama to let him drop out of school.

Berry: *I had just lost all interest in school and I was failing in nearly every subject. I didn't get too much static out of Mama. I convinced her that maybe leaving school and going to work for Uncle Jim and Aunt Elsie in Monroe would be just the thing to perhaps cause me to wake up and get interested in school and my studies. I did go over to Monroe in the spring of 1924 and worked in Uncle Jim's dairy that spring and all summer.*

The road Howard traveled was yet another road for Mama to watch. Berry had driven the cow into town when we moved, and she was stabled in the backyard, ready and waiting for Howard to take over the milking chores. The buggy we had been so proud of when we bought it had been sold (we could walk any place in town where we were likely to go), but the horse was also stabled in the old carriage house in the backyard, along with the light wagon used for making home deliveries for Papa's grocery store. Howard took care of the horse and wagon, and each afternoon after school he helped deliver groceries for Papa. During the school day, the full time delivery work was done by Fred Hudson, a black man.

Howard went through seventh grade that first year in town and graduated from grade school in the spring of 1923.

Howard: When I graduated from grade school and was preparing to enter high school, Mama was aware from her own experience that many youngsters had trouble shifting from arithmetic to algebra. Miss Jodie McClure was teaching a summer course in algebra. Mama scraped up the five dollars for me to take an hour's instruction each day for a couple of weeks from Miss Jodie. It did a lot of good for me, but it almost caused another problem. Another of Mama's classmates, Mrs. Irene Rosson, taught me algebra and after a few days of my super performance, she fixed me with a cold stare and said, "You must have taken Miss McClure's prep course in algebra."

"Yes, Ma'am, I did."

She was quite miffed that Ida Mobberly Duff had not trusted her to teach her son algebra adequately. But we lived over it, and I had a cordial visit with her when I was enroute to the Naval Academy, where two of her former Longview High students had recently graduated.

Later that winter Howard became seriously ill. He says he had pleural effusion, went to the hospital to have a tube placed in his pleural cavity, stayed there for a couple of days and then missed about two weeks of school. Berry remembers visiting him in the large private home converted to a hospital just west of the Gregg County courthouse in Longview.

All I remember is seeing him sitting in the sun in the big front porch as he recuperated, but eleven years later when I was ill, I overheard Mama say to the college doctor, "Doctor,

I've had one child with an abscessed lung and I know the symptoms. Don't try to tell me there's nothin' wrong with her."

Mama was always pretty good at diagnosing our various ailments.

Anyway, Howard recovered, but I'm sure that in those pre-antibiotic days such an illness must have been a burdensome worry for Mama.

Howard also had a daily paper route which he delivered on his bicycle, and because he was nearer our age and was at home more than the older boys, I have more memories of him during those good years: chasing Shep, the only dog we ever had, around the big front lawn; giving us rides on his bicycle; going to church with all of us and wanting to argue the finer theological points of the sermon.

BYPU (Baptist Young People's Union) was an organization for training in church membership. Elsie and I were in the Junior Department; Berry and Howard were in the Intermediate Department. We had officers, with a president to conduct the meetings, and if a newcomer wanted to join, he was "presented for membership" and voted on. One morning at a meal in the big dining room of the Perry House, Berry asked Howard, "What on earth did you mean voting against Joe Blow last night? Nobody ever votes against a new member, for cryin' out loud. What got in you to do that?"

Howard's reply was, "Well, I didn't think he'd ever come again. He wouldn't make a good member anyway, he just wanted to see if he could get in." And he and Berry got into as heated a discussion as Mama would allow at the table. I never heard of anyone else ever voting against a new member, but Howard was just doing what many others might have wanted to do through the years.

Just as we had had much company out on the farm, we had

lots of company in the Perry House also. Aunt Daisy and her daughter Margaret occupied the white room, the first big room on the right of the hall, with a white-painted French Provincial fireplace mantel and great mirror.

Howard: Aunt Daisy's two youngest boys, Francis and Harold, visited us for an extended time in the Perry House, too. Francis gave us an imitation of his father's oratory with big, fancy vocabulary and elaborate gestures, and the rising and falling of volume. He was pretty good, too—had W. T. Tardy's talent down to a T. While he was speaking, all of the lights in the house went out. Francis didn't bat an eye. In a deep, sonorous voice he intoned, "Let there be light," and the lights came back on.

It was during this stay with us at the Perry House that Harold informed us he had forgotten how to milk, which was a lot of hogwash.

I don't know where we put all the company. Four of the large rooms were used as bedrooms. The smallest of the four, in back of Mama's big central bedroom, I thought of as the "boys' room" although Elsie and I slept in there some of the time, too. I remember getting out of the warm bed in the cold room and running to a place by the fireplace in Mama's bedroom, then sitting there like a zombie.

"I declare, you girls are the best of the whole shebang at getting out of bed when you're called, but you just sit here starin' at the fire until I reckon you're not goin' to get any breakfast," Mama said.

The only specific night I remember sleeping in that bedroom back of Mama's room, I was in misery. I had spent the day at Aunt Willie's home on the Marshall Highway. Right in front of their house the road made a deep cut in the red clay hill, and my cousin Catherine and I had spent the day sliding down the slippery side of the cut, climbing back up to the top, then sliding down again. My white cotton undy-drawers were forever ruined with the bright red clay ground into them, and I thought my back and legs were forever ruined, they hurt so much. After I had soaked in the blessed old bathtub, I crawled into a cot in the boys' room and groaned with relief.

Mama had spent the spring day cleaning the house, airing the mattresses and pillows and changing the beds, and she said, "You're not so dumb. You go off and play all day, then come home and grab a clean bed in the cleanest room in the house. Wouldn't it be nice if we could all do that?"

Aunt Willie's family had also lived on the street right in back of us in one of three identical houses side by side. I have pleasant memories of us four older sisters playing with Catherine and her younger sister, Elizabeth, in that house, but between Christmas and New Years Day in 1923, one of the three houses caught fire and all three houses burned completely to the ground. It was a scary sight to see flames shooting high in the air from all three houses.

Catherine Murphy Thomas tells me in a letter, "Luckily we saved everything except the Christmas tree and some books that were behind a door. I remember Berry Noel was trying to get the tree loose because he hated for our tree to burn up, and Howard picked up the heavy cabinet sewing machine and carried it out. That morning I had made a small rag doll and when it was all over and we were sitting down to supper in the Perry House, Aunt Ida asked me what I had in my hand. I opened it and there was my little rag doll.

"After the fire, we stayed with you in the Perry House for a while until we could find another place to live. One day when Mrs. Kelly wasn't at home all of us girls went over and filled our dress skirts with pecans from the several pecan trees in the Kellys' yard and came home showing off our treasures. Aunt Ida marched us all back and we had to go back over to Mrs.

Kelly's and leave them."

We young children were introduced to other tragedies of life during these years. The father of one classmate was killed in a railroad crossing accident, and the father of another classmate died after an appendectomy. The little girl who lived across the street from us, an only child, was struck and killed by a truck as she ran across the street down at the very next corner. We children knew that her family put her Christmas toys on her grave, because we heard Mama say, "Oh, why didn't those poor parents give them to some little colored children who don't have anything?"

One afternoon Elsie's friend Julia Goodjoin asked us over to play after school. As we played on her front porch we asked what that unusual noise from the front room was, and Julia answered, "Oh, my baby brother is sick." The next day we heard that the baby died during the night. Mama was distressed. "I would nevah have let you two go over there if I'd known," she said as she prepared to call on the grieving family.

In those halcyon days most of the tragedies passed over us like water off a duck's back. We played with the Sparkman grandchildren in the big house across from the Kelly place (Berry had his first date when he took Mrs. Sparkman's granddaughter, Mildred, to a watch party on New Year's Eve) and we played with Thomas and Peyton Sweeney, who lived next to the Sparkmans. Our big front yard was full of children on July 4th when Papa brought home two full cases of soda pop.

We enjoyed going to church in the big, light brick building with stained glass windows and a great pipe organ with pipes making graceful arcs across the wall in back of the choir. There wasn't a nursery, a kitchen or a fellowship hall in the whole place. I don't even remember a restroom, but Mama wouldn't have let us leave services no matter how great the emergency. We sat strung out on the pew between Mama and Papa, and a glance from Papa was all that was needed to settle down a restless little one.

On Mothers' Day there were always two trays of roses on the table in the foyer of the church. If your mother was dead, the ladies in charge pinned a white rose on you. If your mother was still alive, they pinned a red rose on you. My cousin Catherine Murphy Thomas writes this recollection from her mother's stories:

"We were all in church on Mothers' Day in Longview. The boys were all sitting behind us. Mother said Aunt Ida punched her and said, 'Oh, my, Willie, look. Berry Noel thinks I'm dead.' There behind us sat Berry Noel as big as you please wearing a big *white* rose."

Class parties were held in the homes of our teachers, and one memorable spring Saturday, my Sunday School class went on a hike out in the woods near our old farmhouse in the country. The other girls were impressed by the wealth of spring blossoms, but I tried to be blase and let them know that I was used to that beauty. "It's nothin' special. It's just the ol' place where we usta live."

There were all-church picnics at Lake Lamond with tin wash tubs filled with blocks of ice and lemonade made from countless hand-squeezed lemons. O.L. Smith was pastor at this time, and we teased Elsie about having a crush on his son Brooks. During this time I put my trust in Jesus and was baptized in the cold water in the baptistry with a scene of the River Jordan painted on the backdrop.

My first memory of radio is hearing my brothers announce, "Mama, the President died." The boys had heard of the death of Warren G. Harding on the radio set they had built by wrapping wire around a cylindrical oatmeal box. There was only one set of earphones, but that earphone set could be separated so that two people could listen at the same time by holding one side to an ear and sitting as still as statues.

Berry: The newspaper put out an "Extra" when Harding died and I had to go sell the "Extras" when I wanted to be listening to that radio.

Another fellow, James Welch, had built his own radio set and he helped us put this one together. All parts were put in a Star Tobacco Box that was 8x12x2 inches. It had only one tube but that cost $5.50 and we had a hard time coming up with the money. Howard had received an honors award of a $2.50 gold piece when he graduated from seventh grade and he contributed that! This enabled us to get the necessary tube to make the radio work.

Howard: I remember that radio well, especially parting with the $2.50 gold piece. We listened to WCY in Schenectady, New York, KGO in Oakland, California, and KDKA in Pittsburgh, Pennsylvania. KDKA had received the nation's first call letters in 1920. We didn't care much for the programs, just hearing the call letters satisfied us. In one night we got twenty-three stations.

I also remember this about Harding's death: true to my Democratic upbringing, I strode up and down in front of the house, yelling at the top of my voice, "Hooray for the Democrats!"

Oh, it really was the best of times for some of us. Maybe not for everyone else in the family. When we moved into town in 1922 the cost of living index was higher than a cat's back, higher than it had been since the Civil War and Papa's business was good. The age of the jellybean and the flapper was upon us, and Howard heard Mama repeat a saying of the day, "If dresses get much shorter, there'll be some more hair to bob and two more cheeks to paint."

Motion pictures were popular and the Charleston dance was the rage. For several years Mama was not enthusiastic about our attending movies. I don't know whether it was the dime admission charge or the moral principle involved.

It was many years before Mama and Papa were reconciled to any of us dancing, and I believe they never approved of any of us going to a public, or paid admission, dance. Fred and Berry went to a dance one night in a hall over the Duke & Ayers Variety store, and when Papa found out where they were, he called to the place and told Berry, "You get yourself directly home," and Berry walked his date home early, then he did go directly home.

During these years Mama attempted her first money-making endeavor that I remember. Since I can't remember which of the years in the Perry House this took place, I don't know whether she really needed some extra money or just wanted to get out of the house.

In the days before electric heating pads were popular, Mama sold a hot pad that generated heat for hours by the simple addition of a teaspoon of water. She sold only to her friends and neighbors, but inasmuch as she knew practically everyone in town, she went from door to door with the sample heating pad wrapped warmly in baby blankets. One neighbor was heard to remark, "I didn't know Ida had a new baby." A perfectly logical assumption since Mama usually did have a new baby.

I recently asked Berry if he knew there was a Depression in 1924. He replied, "There was always a Depression in the Duff household."

An economics textbook makes a statement to the effect that the year of 1924 was a time of business recession. It began with the stock market fairly high, went into a time of economic depression and ended on a note of hope as the stock market began an upward spiral that ended only in October, 1929.

Having just turned nine years old, I had no interest in the stock market or economic theories, but I realize now that our family's financial condition paralleled the national financial condition very closely.

One Sunday afternoon I went charging from the white front room into Mama's room and almost collided with Papa on his knees, deep in prayer. I beat a hasty retreat. It was very soon thereafter that Papa closed his store.

Mama always told me that Papa's business failed because it was a credit business and people just didn't pay their bills. For whatever reason, suddenly Percy Painter was running the store (Papa had bought the store from Percy's older brother and in the closing of Papa's business the store was returned to the older brother), we had moved around the corner to a smaller, plain little house on South Street in back of the Kelly place, and Papa was planning to leave for West Texas.

Our best of times had ended.

CHAPTER 10

IT WAS THE WORST OF TIMES

Most of the details we, my siblings and I, remember about the house around the corner in back of the Kelly place are not very pleasant: a tiny front yard with no grass and no sidewalks, small front and back porches, a water hydrant on the back porch, and an outside toilet again. Elsie and I fussed because we had to rinse our hair in cold water after shampooing it. We just knew if we'd had warm running water, our straight, brown hair would be as pretty and curly as that of blonde Kathleen Melton, an older girl who lived a couple of doors on the other side of the Perry House.

However, we didn't live in the house around the corner very long. We moved in there in the dog days of summer, and Papa left for West Texas on September 6, 1924.

Shortly before he left, Papa had bought for far more money than Mama ever paid for a single book, a black leather-covered book, *The System Bible Study*, and he told each of us four older girls, "You just leave this book alone while I'm gone, you hear? If you tear this book, I'll spank you good, you understand?" And turning to little Lydia Ann he said, for our benefit, "And if you tear it up, I'll spank the one who let you get hold of it."

We always called the book "Papa's Bible," but when it came to me after Mama's death I discovered it is a book of Bible study helps which I have found useful in Bible study. In it, in Papa's handwriting are many of the dates I am using in writing this book.

On Saturday Berry arrived at home from Monroe to go with Papa ("I told YaPapa I couldn't manage two teenage boys by myself.") and Mama spent Sunday in washing Berry's clothes and getting everything ready for the early Monday morning departure. Mama hoped the neighbors wouldn't talk about her too much because she had Berry's clothes hanging on the clothesline on Sunday.

Berry: After working for Aunt Elsie all spring and summer, doing a little bit of everything around their dairy, including delivering milk to the families at the carbon-black plants near their place, I had enough money to pay my train fare back to Longview, and still had twenty or twenty-five dollars when we left for Sweetwater.

Earlier, when Mama had heard that the Texas Legislature had decided in 1923 to locate a four-year school called Texas Technological College in the city of Lubbock, way out in West Texas, she thought Lubbock would be a fine place to bring up all those children she wanted to see go to college. She always told me that when Papa's grocery store failed, they decided Lubbock would be the place to live, but Papa stopped in Sweetwater to visit with Mr. A. G. Winn who had formerly been in business in Longview, and Mr. Winn offered Papa a job. She said that's why we stopped in Sweetwater.

Berry's version of the original destination of the move differs from Mama's. He says the destination was always Sweetwater.

Berry: The vehicle we drove to West Texas, a Model T Ford pick-up, was owned by Mr. Gerald Nash, the other member of our party. The vehicle had a pick-up bed in which we carried our clothing, some cooking utensils, two bedsprings and two mattresses (full size), and all of this was covered by a white canvas tarp securely tied to the pick-up. I rode all the way to Sweetwater sitting on top of that bedding for two full days. The first night we stayed at a city park near the highway in Weatherford. I remember very well our passage through Dallas and Fort Worth with me sitting there on the top of the bedding and looking up at all those tall buildings.

We arrived in Sweetwater, our destination, around four in the afternoon and unloaded the bedding into the drive-in basement under the A.G. Winn Produce Company, and Papa and I slept down there until the rest of the family came to Sweetwater.

After we watched them drive away, Elsie and I went to school, slightly subdued by the knowledge that our family was much smaller now that Papa, Berry and Fred were all away. We still came home from school for dinner each day at noon as we had in the Perry House, and to save time for the couple of hundred extra feet we now had to travel, we found it expedient to cut across the Kellys' large lawn. One afternoon at the end of the school day, Elsie made a running jump up on the Kelly porch, ran across the porch and jumped down on the other side. I tried the same thing, only I missed and hit the concrete edge with my shin, then went home bawling. Mama scolded Elsie. "What'd you do to her? I've told you to quit pickin' on your sister."

Even I had to recognize the injustice of her attack and cried that I'd acquired my injury all by myself.

Her comfort? "You had no business jumpin' on the Kellys' porch." I still have the scar on my shin and it reminds me of the countless times children must have come to Mama with their injuries.

On Thursday, October 30, the very nice lady across the street from us, Mrs. O. L. Norton, invited all of us girls over to her house. She asked me to go in a front room and bring a diaper or something for her baby, which I did. She said, Didn't you see anything in there?"

"No'm," I answered.

"Go look again," she told me, and I came back reporting there was nothing in there that wasn't supposed to be, except a cake.

"But that's for you! It's *your* birthday cake." It was such an unexpected thrill to be the center of attention for once that I have remembered to this day that sweet and thoughtful woman.

The next night Elsie and I went to a Sunday School Hallowe'en party in the backyard of someone's home. The practice of trick or treating had not spread into our part of the country, and the weather was mild enough for us to bob for apples out in the backyard. We pinned the tail on the black paper humpbacked cat and played Flying Dutchman and other games until refreshments of cocoa and Oreo cookies were served, then Elsie and I were delivered to Aunt Noel's to spend the night.

It was always a delight to spend the night with Mary Noel in her family's big, lovely home. I sat on the piano bench by Mary Noel while she played their grand piano in the music room until Uncle Tad said to Aunt Noel, "Tell her to get away and let the child play in peace." I don't know why, in that society, grown men could speak to children only through a woman.

We bathed in the big white-tiled bathroom that always smelled of Ivory Soap. That bathroom always seemed cool to us in the winter because, since their home was heated by a furnace, they were not fortunate enough to have a cozy portable kerosene heater (or wood cookstove) as we had for warming our bath location.

The next morning at breakfast in the cheerful breakfast room Aunt Noel said, "Did you girls know you have a new baby at your house?"

"Yessum, we've had her for fifteen months."

"No, I'm talking about a new baby, a little boy baby. Your mama had a little boy baby last night!"

"Aw, I can't believe it. She didn't tell us."

Aunt Noel assured us that Mama had had a baby during the night, and she teased our cousin Bluford by telling him the baby was named for him and that he would have to buy the little fellow lots of presents all his life. Elsie and I were anxious to get home and see that the baby part was true, but that the part about the name Bluford was not true.

We stayed there all through Saturday, however, and on Sunday morning I went to the Methodist church with Mary Noel. The memory verse in Mary Noel's Sunday School class that morning was Deuteronomy 6:4-5. Now for the benefit of you young people, those verses are: *"Hear, O, Israel: The LORD our God is one LORD; and thou shalt love the LORD thy God with all thine heart, and with all thy soul, and with all thy might."* At least that's the way they are in the King James Version, the only version of the Bible in our family household at that time.

Now those are some of the best known and most often quoted words in the Bible, revered by Jew and Gentile alike, and, as far as I know, honored by all Christians. So, do you want to know what I said when it came my time to recite the memory verse? I'll tell you anyway.

I said, "I cain't say that. I'm a Baptist."

Every time I hear or read those verses I cringe with embarrassment for that little ten-year-old Baptist. If that good Methodist Sunday School teacher is still living, I'll venture to say (as Papa would express it) that she is still talking about that narrow-minded Baptist child and thinking, "What in the name of heaven are they teaching that child?"

We arrived at home on Sunday afternoon to find Beryl and

Ida Rule excited about showing off the new little ol' boy baby, and we began referring to Lydia Ann as the little girl baby. Mama was in her bed in the front room, with Mrs. Shackleford, a practical nurse, helping out.

How could Mama have a baby without two big girls of ten and twelve knowing about it? For one thing, Mama was never sick and nauseated in her pregnancies. About twenty years later, Mama was visiting me and my family in Ashland, Oregon, and we drove up on Mount Ashland to get a Christmas tree. Mama and Ann were sitting in the back seat of our car as we came down the mountain, when Mama became car sick. We had to stop the car so she could get out and throw up. She said, "I managed to have ten babies without throwin' up, and here a piddlin' little trip down a mountain is gettin' to me."

It was on that trip up to the Northwest that Mama was having to treat some stitches a physician had recently taken for what Mama called "a repair job from that last baby twenty years ago." She went on to say, "It's no wonder the doctor didn't take the stitches when the baby came—there was such poor light, a single globe hangin' from a cord in the ceiling."

The only indication I ever had from Mama of whether or not she had difficult deliveries came at a time we heard of a young woman who "went to sleep and woke up with a new baby." Mama said, "Oh, to think of what I went through to have mine. But think of my poor mother. She had a heart condition and couldn't even use chloroform the least little bit when her babies came."

From all I learned from Mama about having babies, I thought they came effortlessly and easily and that the term "labor" was a euphemism instead of an accurate description of the effort involved.

Mama had her babies when it was the considered opinion of the medical profession (or at least of the mothers of the world) that you had to have a big, big baby to have a healthy baby, and to have a big baby, the mother must gain a respectable amount of weight. Mama thought she had big babies, but there was never a scale around to weigh them, and later when she saw the next generation of babies weighing in at six or seven pounds, she said, "Those babies are every bit as big as my babies ever were. I reckon my doctor just held the baby in his hands and said, 'Oh, what a nice big baby—must be a nine-pounder, or ten-pounder' or however good the doctor was feelin' that day."

As I said, it was considered necessary to gain a lot of weight to have those big healthy babies, and Mama did gain a lot of weight. But she was never able to drink milk, and to gain that weight she drank beer. She said, "I'm the authority on beer in this family. I kept it around the house because I used to have to drink it when I was expectin' a baby."

I told that to my brother Fred at one time and his reaction was, "Why, I never saw any beer around the house. I just can't believe it." But why would Mama tell me that tale? Yet how could she have kept it out of sight?

But Mama said she did get big. "One time I was out in the barnyard and heard a rattlesnake and I couldn't see it for my big stomach. I was just too scared to move until it moved away, and I got away from there as fast as I could."

Mama said, "If the good Lord had meant for men and women to alternate in bearing babies, no family wold have more than three children, because there isn't a man under the sun who'd ever go through childbirth a second time."

Mama was ever amazed at young women of today who "kept goin'" until the very last minute, or whose babies came early. "I declare, I don't believe any of mine ever came until I thought I just couldn't live another single day—then they'd come a day or two later."

She told many young women, "That baby won't come until you think you can't live another minute, then he'll think about it, if he's of a mind to."

She thought the mother of a new baby should stay in bed for three weeks, and she was most distressed when doctors started the practice of getting mothers up in ten days, then five, three, and even the first day. She told one doctor, "I knew a woman who got up too soon, and she always had back trouble."

His reply was, "Mrs. Duff, how can you be sure it wasn't something else that caused her back problems?"

I'm not sure Mama ever was convinced.

Mama was also scandalized when the doctor's delivery fee for a daughter's baby was fifty dollars. She always added, "But my mama said the same thing about the fees I paid for my children. She just paid two, three, maybe five dollars for the delivery of her children."

I wonder what Mama and her mother would have to say about doctors' fees for her great-grandchildren.

Mama didn't breast feed either Lydia Ann or Little Boy. She said she always had a lap baby, a porch baby and a yard baby. If she put the smallest baby down for a nap with one of the larger ones, and found them both sleeping with an empty baby bottle between them, she always wondered if the big one or the little one had consumed the milk.

Mama was in good health most of her younger years and she had very few problems at menopause. One doctor told her, "That's Mother Nature's reward for having all those babies."

Mama told me she wanted a large family and never did anything to keep from having more babies, but since she was thirty-nine when Little Boy was born, she also said, "I worried for the next ten years that I'd have another one."

But she didn't, and all of us gave Little Boy our undivided attention for his too-short life. Lydia Ann was considered

Elsie's baby, and Little Boy was called "Manie's baby," Manie being the nickname used for me by the family at that time. We each took care of our babies in the time we had left from school, feeding them, watching over them, changing them, and whatever we could do to help Mama. She herself was able to cook a meal while holding a baby on her hip, but she wouldn't let me or Elsie carry either baby on our hips because she said it could cause stoop shoulders or curvature of the spine.

Mama's Sunday School class sent her a basket of fruit during her post partum recovery, and of course, she gave every piece of it to us children. I sat on the front steps enjoying the first Bartlett pear I'd ever had, with the delicious juice running down my chin. The locally grown pears were small, green and hard and not very much for eating fresh, although Mama certainly could make delicious pear preserves from them. But those Bartlett pears were something else! We had been introduced to fresh grapefruit the winter before and I thought I was becoming most cosmopolitan in my epicurean tastes.

On Saturday, December 6, 1924, Mama, with Little Boy in her arms, and her five daughters, ranging in age from sixteen months to almost twelve years, were on the platform of the downtown station in Longview, waiting to board the train for Sweetwater.

We had heard from Papa that he found a house in Sweetwater, and since the baby was old enough for Mama to travel, all of the furniture (except the cherry bedroom suite that was sold to the H.M. Lawrences) had been loaded into one end of a freight car. The cow was loaded in the other end, and Mama, expecting to freeze to death in treeless West Texas, had arranged for a couple of wagon loads of stove wood to be thrown in the door of the freight car in the empty space between the furniture and the cow. (Beryl remembers watching the men throw the wood into the freight car.) Howard went along in the caboose of the freight train to see that the cow was fed, watered and milked. In my hobby of studying pioneers' stories, I have read of many families who moved west using these "emigrant cars," both along the Union Pacific and the Texas and Pacific railroads. We didn't know we were part of history, we just thought we were leaving Longview.

Mama had planned to leave as soon as the furniture was loaded, but Aunt Noel insisted that we stay with her until we heard that the freight car had arrived in Sweetwater. Some of Aunt Noel's friends, the Sweeneys, had recently moved to Brownsville, and their furniture was several weeks getting there, and the Sweeneys had to spend those weeks in a hotel. So all of us had spent the waiting time at Aunt Noel's house.

The Junior BYPU at the church had given me and Elsie, as going away gifts, signet rings with our initials engraved on the outside and "BYPU" engraved on the inside.

We fingered our rings nervously as we listened to Aunt Noel try to persuade Mama to buy Pullman tickets instead of chair car tickets. With the chair car tickets we would have to change trains in Fort Worth, and Aunt Noel very sensibly argued that it would be more than Mama could manage to move all five girls, the little baby in her arms, and the luggage we had been living with at her house—not to mention our lunch—from one car to another.

Mama said she couldn't afford the difference in price and she was adamant in her refusal to let Aunt Noel pay the difference. Mama said, "Don't worry, Noel. I'll manage. The Lord'll look after us. My girls are good help."

Shortly before the train arrived, a man came hurriedly up to Mama on the station platform and said, "Miss Ida, I'm glad you're still here. I owe Mr. Duff a grocery bill and I wanted to pay it before you left town." And he pulled out his wallet and paid Mama a little over the exact amount she needed to change the chair tickets to Pullman tickets. It was an unusual amount, say thirteen dollars. Or $23.50, not a rounded-off figure like twenty or thirty dollars. I don't remember the exact amount needed, but when Mama told this story she knew the exact amount as well as the name of that nice man, the only person who ever paid an overdue bill.

She turned to Aunt Noel and said, "See? I told you. I told you. The Lord do provide." Then she had our tickets changed to Pullman tickets so we wouldn't have to change trains.

As I write this remembrance I wonder if the Lord used Aunt Noel to go find that man and give him the money and that story so she could get her stubborn and proud sister to take the money. However He worked it out, through Aunt Noel and/or the man, I agree with Mama, "The Lord do provide."

CHAPTER 11

IT WAS STILL THE WORST OF TIMES

By the clock, Sweetwater was only twelve hours from Longview, but by the change in Mama's lifestyle, it must have seemed decades away. I wonder about Mama's thoughts during those twelve hours. She was truly pulling up her roots: leaving the scenes of her childhood, and leaving her kin and old and dear friends.

The story is told that Chief Justice Charles Evans Hughes was sorely grieved when he heard that a childhood chum of his had died. His clerk asked him if they had been close all those years and the dignified, courtly Hughes is reported to have said, "No, it's just there's no one left to call me Charley." It would be years before Mama heard herself called "Ida" or "Miss Ida" again.

Mama knew that she would not be able to afford the domestic help that the women of the deep South depended upon. She knew that she was leaving the lush greenery and flowers, the soft water and the complexion-pampering moisture in the atmosphere of East Texas and Louisiana for the constant dry wind and hard water of West Texas. She was leaving a homeland where her family was one of the oldest and most respected in the community for an area where she was unknown. She must have thought there was little chance of even getting back for a visit for a long, long time.

Then again, she probably didn't have time for introspection. Mama could sit and read and be apparently unaware of what we

Mama Pays the Grocery Bill   111

children were doing, but let one of us get out of line and we discovered she had eyes in the back of her head, and that trip was no exception.

Mama said we children had emptied the container of conical paper cups near the water cooler in the Pullman car before we were well out of town. At one time the conductor asked Mama what were the numbers of our seats, and she replied, "This whole end of the car."

We disembarked into the windy night in Sweetwater to be greeted by Papa, driving a car borrowed from Mr. Winn. We were cold and sleepy, and one of us girls got a finger mashed in the car door, but we eventually arrived at our new home, where at least the beds and stoves had been set up.

We spent Sunday "getting the ox out of the ditch": unpacking, straightening the rooms, and in general, getting acquainted with the house that came to be known in our family as "the house across the tracks," because we had to go under a trestle of the Texas Pacific Railroad to get to school, church, and the main part of the business district.

Our horizons broadened, literally and figuratively. From our small front porch we had an unobstructed view of some low-lying hills south of town known as "Nine Mile Mountains." After living in the piney woods of East Texas, with limited horizons, all of us had a hard time believing it was nine miles through the open countryside to those hills. When Frederick came to Sweetwater for Christmas, he decided to walk over there to find out, and he announced it was every bit of nine miles.

The house was in town, but it had great empty lots on all four sides of us. Those lots had mesquite trees, cactus plants, big red ants, horned toads and ground squirrels living there, and all of these were new and strange to us.

On a hill some distance from us was a lovely, big white

house, remarkable to us for its white roof. The Mitchell family lived there. Mary Jane Mitchell was a popular, beautiful girl in our big brothers' graduating class, and Minnie Lee Mitchell, a little younger, we would eventually refer to as "Howard's girlfriend."

Mama had said we wouldn't have to start to school Monday because she needed our help in getting the rooms straightened, but we awakened Monday morning to snow—lots of snow and only the second snow I'd ever seen—and we begged to be allowed to go to school. We even said we'd put on the hated long union suits which Mama had promised we wouldn't have to wear any more, and away Elsie and I went to enroll in the fifth grade of East Ward School. The school was eight or nine blocks from the house, but both Elsie and I had "rubbers," rubber overshoes left over from wet and muddy East Texas and they kept our feet warm. After they were outgrown I don't remember that we ever had any more "rubbers" because excessive dampness was a rarity in West Texas.

When we returned home we were introduced to "snow ice cream": clean snow mixed with milk, sugar and vanilla to make a frosty and delicious treat.

This house had a living room which, for a change, was actually used as a living room instead of a bedroom. The four of us older girls slept in two double beds crowded into the front bedroom, which was as cold as all git out. When Little Boy outgrew the big laundry basket on the foot of Mama's bed and moved into the baby bed, Lydia Ann was transferred into the double bed with Beryl and Ida Rule, an arrangement which continued for several years. The dark, cold back bedroom was the boys' bedroom, while Mama and Papa's room in the middle received a little heat from the wood stoves in the living room and kitchen.

The second Sunday we were in town we all went to church

together and moved our memberships to the First Baptist Church. The pastor made quite a fuss over Papa because he was a deacon and because he had been Sunday School Superintendent in Longview, as well as in Monroe. But poor Papa had to work on Sunday mornings and couldn't go to morning services, and I don't remember his ever being in a place of leadership in a church after this move. He was faithful in attendance and stewardship, but he was unable to fill a place of responsibility in the churches after we left East Texas.

The preacher called on Mama the next week and he made a big impression on Beryl who remembers him saying, "The mother sets the tone for the Christian faith in her household." Mama remembered him saying, "Mrs. Duff, it's a pleasure visiting with you. You're not mad at anybody and you haven't been here long enough to take sides in any disputes!"

I once moved from one town to another over Thanksgiving weekend and I learned how difficult it was to settle into a new place and prepare for Christmas at the same time. It made me wonder how Mama ever managed that Christmas of 1924. When I was grown, she told me she never had liked Christmas because she never had enough money to do for her family all things she would have done, and this Christmas was probably the roughest one she ever had.

In the first place, she told us we wouldn't have a Christmas tree. There were just not any to be had for the going out and getting them as we had done in Longview. Then Berry came to the rescue. One Sunday he and a friend of his, both of whom worked at the Piggly-Wiggly grocery store, borrowed the Chevrolet delivery truck belonging to Mr. Terry, the owner of Piggly-Wiggly, and drove out to the hills south of Sweetwater to bring back some bushy cedar trees, thus saving the holiday for us children.

We went to a Christmas tree program at church—the

first time we had seen a Christmas tree in a church building. The Sweetwater church was quite new and had a new-fangled fellowship hall where the Christmas tree was erected. I don't remember a program or refreshments, although we probably had both. I just remember that every child was given an appropriate gift with his or her name on it. Mama later said, "Somebody sure 'nuf went to a lot of trouble to pick out just the right thing for each child, wrap it and put the name on it. What a lot of work!" If the church had a Christmas tree and gifts for the children the other three Christmases we lived in Sweetwater, it certainly didn't make the impression on me that the first one did.

It was a memorable Christmas also because as we walked the not inconsiderable distance to church, we passed a house with a string of electric multi-colored lights on the tree in the window, the first electric Christmas lights we had seen.

Mama had written her sisters an SOS saying, "If you're ever going to send my children Christmas gifts, this is the year to do it," and they had come through admirably.

In recent years I was asked in a writing class to finish this sentence: "The worst Christmas I remember—," and I finished it with "happened when Santa Claus left for me the very same doll he had brought to my rich cousin the year before." That was this Christmas. Here, supposedly from Santa Claus, was a special doll that Mary Noel had received the year before, and one that I had enjoyed playing with at her house. Elsie also received one of Mary Noel's old dolls, but she already knew about Santa Claus, so it didn't bother her any. I lived over it.

For the rest of the years that I lived at home, Aunt Noel always sent each of us children a Christmas gift. As we got older the gift was always silk stockings for the girls and a pair of socks for each brother, but there was never anything more needed and appreciated than those silk stockings. We always eagerly opened her Christmas box to see how she had wrapped the gifts each year. Her gifts were the first we ever saw wrapped in all dark blue paper with silver ribbon, which we thought most elegant. She was also the first I knew to use transparent sticky tape—one of the great technological developments of my lifetime. If you don't believe me, try gift wrapping without it.

The other gift I remember that year came from Mama's sister Lydia in Louisville, Kentucky, the only time I recall receiving a gift from her. She sent me a small volume of Robert Louis Stevenson's *Treasure Island*, and she sent Elsie a copy of Sir James Barrie's *The Little Minister*. I liked my book, but Elsie never did get interested in her book, and I often wondered if that determined my love of reading and Elsie's disinterest in books.

That winter, all of our senses received new impressions. The smell of coal smoke on a frosty morning can take me back to Sweetwater in memory, because while practically all heating was done with wood in Longview, wood for heating was a rarity in West Texas. When the stovewood had been offloaded from the freight car, Papa reported that a crowd of onlookers watched the process and wanted to know if it were for sale.

We learned to recognize the dark blue line on the northern horizon for a Texas blue norther and we soon learned to get the clothes off the line quickly and to shut the doors and windows before the wind hit the side of the house with a thump and lowered the temperature thirty or forty degrees in a matter of minutes.

The smell of the first drops of rain on dry, dusty ground also brings back recollections of Sweetwater.

We were even introduced to a new food, pinto beans. We called them "red beans," but after I left home I learned that red beans are different. The beans we had been eating all those years were really pinto beans. In East Texas and Louisiana, there had been fresh vegetables all year 'round, and this was our introduction to dried beans. They became the standard midday dinner on wash day.

In East Texas, rice had been one of the staples of our diet. I grew up thinking that "rice'n'gravy" was one word, but we ate it other ways, too: rice and butter, rice pudding, rice in soup, left-over cold rice with sugar and milk for Sunday night supper, and Spanish rice, to name some of them.

We still ate rice, but this was the winter of our butter'n'grits. We had eaten grits in Longview, too, but the way I remember it best was with what we called "ham gravy." Some persons call it "striped gravy," and others call is "red eye gravy"—those browned skillet-drippings left from frying ham, mixed with hot water. By whatever name, it made good eating when poured over boiled grits. But that first winter in Sweetwater we seemed to have grits and butter every night for supper, together with biscuits, butter and ribbon cane syrup.

One evening Mama sent a couple of us girls to the neighbors' house about a block nearer the railroad tracks to buy some milk because our cow was dry. It was supper time and that family was fixin' to eat a supper of great bowls of hot oatmeal with butter, cream and sugar saturating the cereal. I felt so sorry for those poor people having to eat oatmeal instead of grits—anybody in their right mind knew that oatmeal was for breakfast!

Years later, when I had exhausted the canned soups from asparagus to zucchini, I tried to think of something to serve my own children for supper on cold winter nights, and I remembered those grits and butter suppers, but there just wasn't a package of grits in the state of Wyoming. I wrote Papa to send me some grits, which he did, and the mailman delivered the package in a blinding snowstorm.

"You'd better not let that Yankee mailman know what's in that package," my husband said. "He'd leave it on the sidewalk and make you come get it."

Usually, all of us came home for midday dinner, but on the two or three very cold and stormy days, Mama gave me and Elsie ten cents each to eat in a little lunchroom across the street from East Ward. We were supposed to get a bowl of red beans and a half pint of milk with that dime, but Elsie and I both usually bought a candy bar and a soda pop. For some reason we thought that was much better than the biscuit and steak sandwiches we used to take for our lunches when we lived in the country.

We always had plenty of fruit, however, and the brothers and sisters today talk about being raised on overripe bananas and rotten tomatoes. That is gross exaggeration. The produce company where Papa worked sold to retail grocers in the days when electric refrigeration was almost non-existent. For the fruits and vegetables to keep well, they must be delivered to the merchants in an almost green condition. The crates of fruits and vegetables had to be "worked" daily so that any piece with a spot of over ripeness on it could be removed. Those fruits and vegetables that were just getting deliciously edible were set aside to be taken home by the employees, and Mama was already an expert at making applesauce, jams, relishes, chili sauce, banana puddings, and any number of other goodies for our delighted palates.

We thrived on the diet, although we suffered the annual bout of the flu when Elsie, Beryl, Ida Rule, and I were all sick at the same time in that crowded front bedroom. Mama's treatment of the annual colds and flu included mustard plasters (which we hated), Vicks Vapo-Rub, soft boiled eggs, hot tea with lots of cream and sugar, milk toast, and Mama's own brand of tomato soup—canned tomatoes and milk heated together. Somehow it never curdled for her.

In those pre-antibiotic days, we had to stay in bed for a week after the fever left because of the fear of having a relapse, which was considered more dangerous than the original illness. Usually we strung out the various illnesses one patient at a time until I'm sure Mama must have been ready to climb the wall.

During my recuperation I became a literary critic of sorts and went through a volume of stories, marking each in large letters, "No good," "Very good," "Don't read," "O.K." or some such nonsense. Mama gave me a lecture I never forgot about books being my best friend and said she presumed I knew better than to pull a stunt like that.

That spring and summer an epidemic of the dreaded disease infantile paralysis (poliomyelitis) hit the community. That was usually an annual scourge that struck fear in the heart of every parent, although it could affect adults as well as children. Beryl remembers that in some years Sunday Schools and movie houses were closed at the height of the polio season, but I saw that happen only once and that was in Wyoming when I had children of my own. That summer of 1925, however, when we passed a home known to be stricken by the disease, we were instructed to cross to the other side of the street. It would be about thirty years before Dr. Jonas Salk perfected the polio vaccine that halted the spread of the disease.

About forty-five years after that hot summer in the house across the tracks, my granddaughter Joan and I were watching a television movie about a child stricken with polio. Joan asked, "Grandma, what's polio?" and I thought that was one of the most beautiful sounds I ever heard—just knowing she had never heard of it.

Elsie and I entered into the activities of the fifth grade at East Ward School. We were invited to a tacky party at Vernice Henthorne's home across the street from East Ward, and Mama dressed us in our pre-school sisters' coveralls which struck us about the middle of the legs and arms. She painted our faces with crayons, and we made a pretty good pair of tacky clowns. Howard came over to walk us home after the party.

In that fifth grade I developed my first interest in American History. I told Mama I was the smartest person in my class because I could spell the word "Baptist" when no one else could. She replied, "Well, I think not. You'd be the dumbest dumb bunny in the class if you couldn't spell it after all these years."

The study of the Civil War fascinated me, but it would be ten years later, when I took a summer course in American History at the University of Wyoming, that I found out there were two sides to the Civil War question and that my Yankee classmates, for some reason, thought that the North had won.

In those earlier times, however, when I asked Mama questions about her father's experiences in the War, she told me what she knew, but she was prouder of the record of her maternal grandfather, Charles Todd Noel. In talking, she said casually, "I presume you know his cousin was Mary Todd who married Lincoln." This excited me and I asked why she'd never mentioned it before. "Oh, I reckon my mother's people were ashamed of her. I presume they thought she'd disgraced the family by marryin' that Yankee, and they just nevah talked about her."

Since that time I've never been able to read about Mary Todd Lincoln without a sympathetic frame of mind.

Our horizons broadened in other ways. The Christian Church was catty-cornered across from the Baptist Church, and one of my good friends, Beth Patterson, was a Presbyterian. Before we left Sweetwater my best friend was Hazel Hodges, and the whole Hodges family were faithful Methodists. In school one of the most popular families was half Catholic (the females) and half Baptist (the father and sons). At an Interscholastic League meet I saw one of the sisters of that family blissfully eating a hamburger until she realized it was Friday. Suddenly she clasped her hands to her face and said, "Oh, my goodness, it's Friday!" She paused a second or two, then resumed eating, remarking, "Oh, well, I'll just have to pay the priest tomorrow."

I didn't even know what she was talking about and had to have it explained by Mama later.

Another day I went home after school with a classmate, Esther Levy, to work on some sort of school poster. Making posters to illustrate some subject in school was a form of visual aid for that day and time. Esther and her sister, Helen, were well-liked girls in the school, and their mother received me cordially into their lovely home. They were the first Jewish friends I had known, but I could not see that they were any different from us except they seemed to be richer, but then everybody was richer than we were.

Life went on. I have no memories of Papa in that house. He went to work before we children got up, traveled much of the week, and when he did come in it was after we were through with supper.

Frederick had come home for Christmas, and in January 1925, he went to work out at Sweetwater Cotton Oil Company.

Berry continued working until the middle of January of 1925, when he entered Sweetwater High School.

Berry: My first job in Sweetwater in the fall of 1924 was at Bradford Wholesale Grocery Company. They had just completed a new building on the north side of the tracks, just west of the passenger depot. There were four of us employees, plus the foreman, and we unloaded cases of canned goods from the box cars to hand trucks, then wheeled the hand trucks to the warehouse where we stacked the cases in the building.

Mama Pays the Grocery Bill

The job was from 7:00 A. M. to 6:00 P. M., ten hours of really hard labor, six days a week, at twenty-five cents an hour. We had an hour for lunch and ate at a little cafe nearby—a big plate lunch, plus drink and dessert for fifty cents.

In October I also stared to work at Ferris Drug Store "skeeting soda" as it was called in those days. I worked on Saturday nights and Sundays from one P. M. to ten P. M.

In November I went to work for Mr. L. D. Terry in his Piggly Wiggly Store, six days a week from seven A. M. to seven P. M. for fifteen dollars a week. I stocked shelves and made home deliveries in those days when all grocery stores delivered.

Mr. Terry was a fine Christian man, a Baptist of course, but he was a bit close with his money. I recall that to heat the back of the store we had to burn the cardboard and wooden boxes that canned groceries came in. There was a place down on the railroad tracks where coal was unloaded from coal cars and where a considerable amount of good coal had been spilled on the ground in the unloading process. We—the other fellow who worked with me, and I—would go by this place on the tracks when we were making deliveries and pick up enough coal to keep the stove going in the rear of the store. I don't know how Mr. Terry heated the front part of the store.

I worked full time for Mr. Terry until I started to school in January, then I worked part time for him until spring. When the weather warmed up I quit working at Piggly Wiggly and worked every night and Saturdays and Sundays at Ferris Drug.

I was really glad to get back in school. I appreciated it more after I'd laid out of it for nearly a year.

Berry had his tonsils removed by Dr. Dudgeon in the spring of 1925, if his memory serves him right, as Papa would say.

We were living in the Roaring Twenties, the time of the flapper and her male counterpart, the jellybean. Wide, very wide-bottomed trousers were the style, and a gooey cream called "StaComb" held a fellow's hair slicked down in a Rudolph Valentino style.

Howard continued in his sophomore year at Sweetwater High, delivered newspapers, milked the cow, became active in Boy Scouts, and eventually became an Eagle Scout.

Our nearest neighbors were the Reavis family, who lived down the street a short distance. Their children were all grown or nearly so, and we youngsters really had no neighborhood playmates.

Howard: The Reavis' son and his partner bought an old ranch northwest of Midland, Texas, near Shafter Lake, and plowed it up to plant cotton. In the summer of 1925 I cooked for them for two weeks and got a pair of shoes and five dollars for my trouble.

Howard had a reputation for having quite a temper. He once got mad at me for some unremembered reason and chased me all over one of those mesquite-covered blocks. Fear gave wings to my feet and I outran him until Mama "put a stop to that foolishness."

We spent a lot of time playing in the living room that winter and spring. One of us tried to reach Lydia Ann to say some word, and we were using baby talk. For instance, it may have been she was asked to say "cool" for "school." She just glared at her young teacher and said clearly and distinctly, "School!"

Using a big rubber ball Mahaley had sent to Beryl and Ida Rule, we played jacks with small pieces of coal for jack stones. When we did get to use a proper ball and regular jacks, we turned out to be pretty good jacks players.

The boys took apart the earphone of the radio and then screwed it into the dismantled arm on the Victrola in the living room and the sound was magnified enough for the whole family to hear it if we sat quiet and close enough. It was a time when we would rather hear a squawk or squeak, a crackle or a pop, from Honolulu or Pittsburgh, than a good clear program form WFAA Dallas or WBAP Fort Worth. I first heard of Schenectady, New York, over that radio and nearly learned to pronounce it before the batteries died. That was the end of radio for our family for about eight years.

Mama said I learned to iron at the same time she did. She had always had black helpers to do the washing and ironing in her former homes, but in West Texas there were fewer black people, and Mama could not afford to pay the higher wages they could get. As Little Boy outgrew his pretty, long, batiste baby dresses, Mama made for him a whole collection of blue-checked gingham aprons, plain and tailored, and short enough to allow him to crawl around easily. In those pre-knit days, this was the accepted dress for little boy babies, easy to change and easy to wash and iron. It was with these aprons that I learned to iron.

We did have electricity in that house, but the iron was a big, old heavy number with no thermostatic control. It had to be connected and disconnected at the plug to control the heat. The big boys and Papa wore starched shirts every day, and Elsie and I usually wore starched cotton dresses that had to be ironed. There is little wonder that Mama put the others—the pre-schoolers—in coveralls that kept them warm and clean, yet didn't show dirt easily. Those coveralls also didn't have to be starched and could be ironed with a lick and a promise.

We again had a back porch hydrant for running water, baths in the washtub in the kitchen, and the clothes washing process taking place in the same, old iron wash pot in the backyard. Of course, the outside toilet was also out there in the backyard. Those were some of the many reasons for moving.

Mama must have wanted not only an indoor bathroom, but

she probably wanted to be nearer the action so she could make some money to help pay the grocery bill. About the first of July we moved to a house across the street from East Ward—a house with an indoor bathroom and nearby neighbors, but only two bedrooms for those nine children and two adults.

CHAPTER 12

ACROSS FROM EAST WARD

"Across from East Ward" is the way we brothers and sisters refer to the year in our lives when we lived in the house on North Third Street, across from East Ward School.

The only thing I remember about the move is that Mama did the biggest washing she had ever done up to that time. She had changed all the sheets as usual the week before we moved, but the details of packing and moving had precluded her washing at the house across the tracks, and when we moved into the new place, she, of course, put clean sheets on all the beds just as soon as the beds were set up. Our first day in the new house was spent washing about two dozen sheets, plus all the other clothing, in the same old iron washpot in the new backyard.

The cow was duly stabled in a small shed in the back alley, but Howard couldn't stake her out in mesquite-covered lots, as he had done previously, for the simple reason that there were no empty lots in that part of town.

The East Ward neighborhood was well settled. We had a paved street, sidewalks for our skates, a scraggly lawn of Bermuda grass, and neighborhood playmates galore. The Risingers lived on one side, the Tolers on the other. There were other children in the neighborhood who came over so much that Mama had to make a rule that we quoted for years after. When dish washing and dish drying time came around, one youngster or another would claim, "I can't dry dishes (or wash or whatever needed doing) because I have comp'ny." The company might have been there morning, noon and night, day in and day out, so Mama early on resolved the problem by saying, "They're not comp'ny if they've been here a dozen times. They can wait for you, they can help you, or they can go home and come back, but you get yourself in here and do your chores p.d.q., you hear?"

We children used and heard used the letters "p.d.q." frequently and discussed what they stood for. We decided they meant "pretty darn quick," although the word "darn" should really be translated with a stronger word that we wouldn't say. Whatever they stood for, "pretty darn quick" is what they meant.

The house was the one where Elsie and I had gone to a tacky party the winter before, but somehow the former tenants' one child didn't fill it as we did. The front bedroom had two double beds crowded into it—Elsie and I occupied one, two of the brothers the other. When Fred was at home, he and Berry slept in the bed and Howard set up a folding cot in the living room each night. About Christmas time, Howard's cot was placed in the bedroom because of the Christmas tree in the living room and then our room was so crowded we had to move antigogglin' to get around in there. Elsie or I turned over in the dark one night and a baby doll left on the bed cried, "Maa-Maa," and whichever big brother was in the process of going to bed at the time jumped sky high. We—Elsie and I—got the giggles and that made him even madder.

The back bedroom—Mama's room—had Mama's big golden oak bedroom suite, a fold-up bed for Beryl, Ida Rule, and Lydia Ann, and the baby bed for Little Boy. It, too, was so crowded at night when the little girls' bed was open that we had to walk sideways to get around in there, too.

But we had a bathroom with an indoor toilet and running

water! Ah, luxury.

I have no memories of Papa in that house, either. He worked early and late and still traveled to neighboring towns for Mr. Winn. Berry had access to a camera by this time and I do remember seeing a snapshot of Papa in front of that house, kneeling with his arms around Little Boy and Lydia Ann, so he must have been around some of the time.

Fred still worked as an accountant for Sweetwater Cotton Oil Company. He was a handsome young man with black hair and dark brown eyes, who was known as "that young man who never wears a hat" in a time when practically all men wore hats. Although he never went to school in Sweetwater, he made friends with other young persons and had an active social and church life, but I can remember long summer twilights when he would be "it" and let all the children in the neighborhood hide from him. His method of seeking in our game of Hide and Seek was just to sit tight and eventually we'd try to sneak in and touch base before he saw us—but we never did. Ordinarily, Mama wouldn't let us play over on the school grounds when there wasn't a responsible person in charge. She said if something happened or a window was broken we might be blamed for it. But when Fred played with us, we could play on the school ground. I recently watched a young single man playing in just such a manner with neighborhood children, miles and years away from my childhood, and those young space age children loved it just as much as we did.

Fred worked at the Cotton Oil Company through the cotton ginning season of 1925, and after Christmas he returned to Greenville to continue his education at Burleson College.

Berry continued his work at the soda fountain at Ferris Drug Store and would work there, off and on, at least part time, for much of our stay in Sweetwater. His title was "soda skeet" or "soda jerk," either of which meant he worked behind the soda fountain, a counter in the drugstore equipped for preparing and serving soft drinks, ice cream, combinations of soft drinks and ice cream, and even, in a few drugstores, sandwiches. Depending on the size of the store and the length of the counter, there were one or more apparatuses with faucets for dispensing soda (carbonated) water and plain water.

In the counter were multitudes of heavy crockery containers holding flavorings, syrups, cherries, chopped nuts and other toppings, all dispensed either through pumps or ladles. From the creative combinations of these goodies could be prepared and served a limitless variety of tempting drinks or ice cream dishes. In the early days, the ice cream cabinets and counters were kept cold with huge blocks of ice, although within a few years practically all of them would boast electric refrigeration, even though the bin for holding twenty-five or thirty pounds of shaved ice for the drinks was always a necessity.

There were tall stools for customers at the counter, and tables and chairs under overhead fans for more leisurely visits. The wrought iron ice cream parlor tables and chairs were soon relegated to the second-hand stores to become, eventually, much prized collectibles. They were replaced by bentwood tables and chairs to accommodate walk-in customers.

Ice cream parlors themselves were old hat. The first one had been established in Baltimore in 1851, and ice cream cones had been introduced at the St. Louis Exposition of 1904. What made the soda fountain counter different was its integration as part of the drugstore, and the thing that made the drugstore fountain itself the social center of that time and culture was curb service. The proprietor designated all the parking places in front of his establishment as "reserved for curb service," and if he was fortunate enough to have a corner location he had that many more spaces. The people of the town would drive up to the curb, honk, and be waited on by one of the soda jerks or soda skeets, whichever he was called. If there were two persons in the car, the order might be as simple as "two Cokes" and the customers would get the royal treatment for that ten-cent order just as if it were a big-dollar order. Six people in the car might order six different nickel drinks and be accorded cheerful and gracious service, always without a tip for the soda skeet.

Although the drugstore was the original destination for many young dating couples, it was also the place to stop after a movie or football game. Carloads of girls driving around might stop, ostensibly for a Dr. Pepper or Eskimo pie (a vanilla ice cream bar covered in chocolate and wrapped in tin foil and introduced in the 1920s), but their primary objective was to flirt with the soda skeet or the "drugstore cowboys" who gathered around the street light. Families going for a drive in the evening to "get a breath of cool night air" or to put the children to sleep, usually stopped by the drugstore for a cool drink or ice cream cones.

This congenial and delightful social practice lasted probably no more than twenty-five years, from the advent of the widespread use of motor vehicles to World War II, with its shortages of gasoline and of available young men for soda skeets.

Curb service began to disappear with the advent of air conditioning (drugstores were some of the first businesses to be air conditioned) and with the establishment of food and drink drive-ins further away from downtown. Gradually, the drugstore fountains were replaced, one by one, by counters full of hardware, sporting equipment or even groceries, although a few have been preserved in private recreation rooms or public museums. I didn't realize drugstore fountains with curb service were a sociological and business phenomenon peculiar to our culture and locale until I talked to persons too young to have known of them, and to others who grew up in communities either too large or with weather too severe to have utilized this curb service convenience.

The friendly soda skeet or soda jerk, with his expertise at concocting any number of delicious treats, was usually a good-looking, personable, and popular young man. Berry fit into this category and, in spite of working most evenings, he began to develop quite a social life.

As long as he worked at the drugstore, Berry usually brought a pint of ice cream home to Mama each evening because he knew her weakness for ice cream. Often she had gone to bed, but would get up and eat the whole pint while she visited with him.

Berry: About the first of August, as Mama was eating the usual pint of ice cream in the dining room about ten that night, I told her about the pain I had in my stomach and that before leaving the drugstore I had taken a purgative because I thought I had eaten something that disagreed with me. Before daylight the pain was so severe that I was miserable.

Mama called Dr. Dudgeon and he took Mama and me to the hospital early in the morning. My appendix had burst and gangrene had already set in.

I was in a coma for exactly seven days. The only thing I remember about those lost seven days was that when Dr. Dudgeon came (at least three times a day) he would be humming "Nearer My God to Thee." Finally, Mama told him to hum a more cheerful song, and he did just that. I can't remember what song he started humming, but "Nearer My God to Thee" was laid to rest.

Mama stayed at my bedside at least twelve to fourteen hours a day. I came out of my coma almost seven days to the hour after the operation. It was rather early in the morning and Mama had not arrived at the hospital. The nurses tried to call

Mama to tell her that I was out of the coma, but Mama was already enroute to the hospital. When she arrived in my room she was so happy and thankful that she was crying, and she went down on her knees to thank God in prayer for my improvement. She told me later that the doctors and nurses had just about "given me up," but **Mama never did!** Dr. Dudgeon told me later that there was no way I could have survived my condition had the operation been performed a day later.

My own memories of that time of Berry's illness have to do with how worried Mama was and how she was gone most of the time. Louise Toler, our friend who lived next door, had several older brothers who gave Mama rides across town to the hospital. Mrs. Risinger, our neighbor on the other side and the mother of Billie, a girl our age, and Maurine and Dorsett, about Berry's age, supervised Elsie and me as we did whatever we could to look after things around the house.

Berry's hair, which had not been particularly curly up to the time of his illness, came out to a great extent and came back in quite curly. He'd always been good lookin' enough, but now he was known as a real lady killer.

I think of this as the summer of lettuce and tomato sandwiches for supper, although some of the brothers brought home some lunch meat, probably bologna or minced ham, and introduced us to lunch meat sandwiches, a summer supper stand-by in Mama's house for many a summer.

Fifteen years or so later, when Mama and I were talking about wedding rings, I asked her what happened to her ring; I just realized I'd not seen her wear it in years, evidently about fifteen years, because she said casually, "Oh, I paid Dr. Dudgeon's bill with it when Berry Noel was so sick in Sweetwater. I just gave it to Dr. Dudgeon and we called it even."

Berry: In those days it was unheard of to play football

within six months of an appendectomy, and I was really disappointed that I was unable to come out for football that fall. But that disappointment was partially offset because I was elected president of the junior class that fall of 1925. That school year was really something and I won't attempt to review things that happened in the rivalry between the junior and senior classes. Those events would make a book by themselves.

Howard stayed busy that summer with his paper route, milking the cow (she just wouldn't stay milked) and working in Boy Scouts. He, too, was a junior in that fall of 1925 and a very good student.

Elsie and I enjoyed being nearer to town. We went to town and church more easily than we had when we lived across the tracks. Not long before her death Elsie told this tale, which I do not remember at all, when she and I were reminiscing about our childhood. She said, "'Member there were a lot more Mexicans in Sweetwater than we'd seen down in Longview? One day you and I were walking home from town to the house across from East Ward, and there was a Mexican man walking along a little distance in back of us and a black man walking in front of us. We let our imaginations get the best of us and worked up a p.o.d. scare about that Mexican. We hurried and caught up with the black man and asked him if we could walk along with him, we were used to people like him, but we were scared of that man in back of us. Of course, he said it didn't make him no nevah mind, and we walked along with him to our house. He went on about his business and the Mexican man went on about his business as he had been doing all along. Weren't we silly?"

When we first moved to town, the public library was in the basement of the Nolan County courthouse, and we became some of its most faithful patrons. It later moved to the brand new and beautiful combination City Hall and Auditorium, and

I remember reading all the Tom Swift books (early day science fiction), *Billy and Miss Minerva* and its sequels, *Pollyanna, Tom Sawyer, Five Little Peppers* series and the Horatio Alger books, among many others in the Sweetwater years.

Elsie was already demonstrating her aptitude for things domestic in that she learned to cook more easily than I did. One wash day in that house, Mama told me to put some flour and milk in the new potatoes that were cooking on the stove. Now, years later, I realize she wanted me to mix the flour and milk to make a cream sauce for the little new potatoes, a dish we all relished when served over cornbread, but I just poured milk in and dumped some flour on top of it. When Mama came in from the washtubs, expecting to find what we called "potato gravy," there was dry flour floating around on top of the milk and potatoes and sticking to the sides of the pan. She sighed deeply and said, "I do declare. You'll nevah make a cook and that's the pure-d truth."

On Saturday evening after we'd been to the movie (admission ten cents), I was holding forth with a dramatic declamation of why I was mistreated because I always had to dry the dishes, and Mama said, "Well, Sarah Bernhardt, you're just takin' those picture shows too seriously. You just get yourself too involved with them and can't come down to earth. Watch out or you'll have to cut 'em out altogether, you hear?"

Elsie and I started in the sixth grade that fall and survived it in due course. My most vivid memory is of the spelling class. The teacher, who shall be nameless for the purpose of this tale, threatened to "thresh" us if we missed a single word in spelling. Although the dictionary tells me that a rare meaning of "thresh" is "to discipline severely," when that teacher dramatically rolled the "r" in that word and threatened us if we missed a word, I purely knew what she meant. I studied and studied and prayed and prayed and somehow I never missed a word that year.

I don't know what happened to Elsie in that class. She never did get a "threshing," but she never was much of a speller, either. For years, when she was writing, she'd ask me how to spell nearly every other word, and Mama would say to her, "It'll do you no good for her to spell it for you. She's not always goin' to be there. Look it up in the dictionary yourself."

Beryl started in the first grade in East Ward in the fall of 1925. She tells me that Mama sent her to school when we first moved into the house across the tracks, but because her birthday is in December, the authorities wouldn't let her go to school and sent her home. Since she was almost eight years old when she did get to school, she did very well and eventually skipped a grade.

While we were going to East Ward, a couple of programs were put on in the auditorium, one at Christmas with angels with lots of tissue paper wings and the other in the spring with lots of dancing nymphs with long, colorful crepe paper fringes hanging down from each arm. Sounds fine, doesn't it? Except that some lighted candles were to be carried by some of the participants. Mama tried to get the principal (that spelling teacher) to eliminate the candles for safety's sake, but she refused to do that. Mama called the fire department and demanded they send a fireman to stand backstage as a precautionary measure. When he saw the set-up in both programs he forbade the use of the candles. A tragedy may have been averted, but Mama certainly did not endear herself to the staff at the school.

When school started in that fall of 1925, Mama and Papa built shelves in the little closet in the living room. Papa was always a great one for building shelves, and then Mama stocked the shelves with candy bars, penny candy, gum and a few school supplies to be sold to the school children—they hoped. I can't remember that business was overwhelming, but I also don't remember getting to eat any generous amount of that candy. So maybe Mama made enough off of that enterprise to pay, if not the grocery bill, at least for our school supplies.

Fred received his Associate of Arts degree from Burleson College in the spring of 1926, and Berry hitchhiked to Greenville to see him graduate.

Fred returned to Sweetwater and to his job with the Sweetwater Cotton Oil Company. One of the benefits of his job was a larger house over on Elm Street which he could rent from the company for a very reasonable rent.

So without much ado, we moved again. This time Mama just went off and left the big iron cookstove sitting in the kitchen on East Third Street, and we began life with a kerosene, or co'oil, cookstove.

CHAPTER 13

MISSIONARY BOXES FROM HEAVEN

We had hardly unpacked the wooden apple boxes full of books to arrange them in the living room of the nice, three bedroom house on Elm Street, when we packed them up again to move to a little bit less nice, two bedroom house next door. The W.G. Davis family moved into the first house. Mr. Davis was superintendent at the Sweetwater Cotton Oil Company and he either bought the house from the company, or exercised the prerogative of an older, long-time employee in a more responsible position than Fred held.

Whichever, the Davises made good neighbors and we got along well during the couple of years we lived on Elm Street.

The cow, of course, moved with us, and there were some large mesquite-covered lots between our house and the high school, where Howard could stake her out during the day.

The washing was still done in the backyard, but during our years here Mama bought a washing machine and a new electric sewing machine the same week. It was a traumatic time for Papa because Mama had her long, thick hair bobbed the same week, and this distressed him mightily. He thought she ought to have a washing machine, but he saw no need for an electric sewing machine; the old pedal model was serving its purpose very well. Mama said, "With these five girls comin' along and needin' to learn to sew, they need an electric machine."

I don't know if Papa ever was reconciled. A couple of

Mama's daughters did learn to sew, but I think they learned on sewing machines at school. Two out of five isn't too bad, I suppose. Years later, Mama insisted that Fred take the sewing machine to his wife because, she told me, "Fred came to our rescue and finished paying the installments when we couldn't meet them."

With the Maytag dasher machine housed on the small screened back porch, washing was a little easier than it had been, but most of the water was heated in the iron washpot in the backyard over the fire built by Howard.

We did have the first hot water tank we'd ever had: a kerosene side-arm heater located in the tiny hall between the two bedrooms and bath. Fred often called from work or downtown and asked us to light that hot water heater so he'd have hot water for a bath when he got home. He'd pay us a nickel or a dime for lighting it, but sometimes he'd ask us to iron a shirt for him and then maybe he'd give us a whole quarter.

For one of the Christmases that we lived in that house, Fred gave to Elsie and me each a bathrobe, the first we'd ever had. The other Christmas he gave us autograph books. I still have mine filled with a few pictures (We are all wearing dressy hats even on picnics.) and many souvenirs of those years in the Elm Street house. They remind me of how Elsie enjoyed entertaining, because there are souvenirs of Valentine, Hallowe'en and summertime parties. I liked to go to parties, but I didn't care a fig for the work involved in putting on a party.

Beryl overheard Mama and Fred talking of things to buy from the Sears Roebuck or Montgomery Ward catalogues for all the family. Mama said, "Oh, Beryl would like this, and Ida Rule wants that," and Beryl nearly died of curiosity as she listened from the little hallway.

The first Christmas we lived on Elm Street, Helen Davis, the college-age daughter of the family next door, invited Fred to a party to which he was supposed to bring a gift. He purchased a full-length long union suit and some red dye and asked Mama to dye the long underwear a bright red. Mama was a little bit scandalized, but she did the dye job, and Fred took the red underwear to the party. He knew few of the young people there, but his risque (for the time) gift to the hostess made a big hit, although it kept Mama and Mrs. Davis wondering what the world was coming to when these modern young people started exchanging underwear as gifts.

The next year Helen wrapped the red long johns elaborately and returned them to Fred. For many years, even after they were married to their respective spouses, they continued to send those red long-handles back and forth to each other at Christmastime.

Aunt Noel and Mary Noel came by train (Uncle Tad was lawyer for the T&P Railroad) during one Christmas vacation. Mary Noel had a deck of playing cards with her, the first Mama had allowed in the house, and Mary Noel taught some of us to play auction bridge. Mama let us play a card game called "Rook," but bridge was taboo in our house for quite a while.

The next summer Aunt Noel sent her son, Bluford, out to Sweetwater for an extended visit to "keep him out of mischief." Berry had been voted the most popular boy in the school, and one of his rewards was a pass to the local movie house. Bluford had the money to go to the picture show every day, and Berry had his pass, so they went to the movies every day until they became so familiar with the dialogue (words flashed on the screen in that day of silent movies) that they would recite the lines with the silent actors before the lines were flashed on the screen. They did this in rather loud voices, changing to falsetto for the female lines, to the amusement of some of the audience, to the annoyance of others, until, according to Mama, the manager of the picture show gave them an ultimatum, "Shut up or get out."

Elm Street was paved (black-topped) soon after we moved into the house, closing the street until the top was cured, and that opened the street wide for our enjoyment with roller skates. Elm Street sloped slightly to City Park and City Lake, and we'd coast to the park and then skate laboriously back up the street.

There are other pleasant memories of this house. Beryl and I both recall the long twilights when all the neighborhood youngsters played "Kick the Can" or "Hide and Seek," using all the neighborhood for hiding places. Mama paid the small membership fee so we could swim in Santa Fe Lake. The trouble was, it was too far to walk out there and we had to bum rides with Dorothy Davis, our next door neighbor, and other playmates' families so that we could splash in the cool waters and refresh our dog paddlin'-technique, neglected since we'd left the pond in the country.

During the time in this house Mama endeavored to sell red and white (Sweetwater High School's colors) felt hats and beanies or skull caps to the pep squad. Although the idea didn't catch on, Elsie and I had red and white felt hats (the demonstration samples) to wear to the football games when we did get in high school.

During those summers Mama undertook what we called the Corset Caper and the Drapery Dodge. Mama walked to homes by appointment and measured the ladies for custom-fitted foundation garments. She also sold a special drapery-cleaning service recently installed by a local laundry. The owner of the laundry furnished a car, and Berry drove Mama around the town, as well as to rural homes and smaller towns in the area, as she peddled the service. Berry tell us Mama made quick judgments: "That house doesn't even have curtains, much less drapes. We won't stop here." Or, "They look like they can afford this service. Stop here." She hoped she'd make more than one hundred dollars with the drapery cleaning enterprise, but after much hard work by Mama and Berry, she made ninety-nine dollars.

Sometime during these years Mama also took orders for Olson Rugs. This was a deal where a homeowner could collect a bundle of worn out wool rugs and carpets and send them in for credit by weight on a new rug ordered from a colorful catalogue. We didn't get rich off of that project, either, but we did get one new rug.

That first fall on Elm Street, Elsie and I started in seventh grade, which met in the basement of the high school building. All seventh graders were required to take a course in Agriculture, which was pretty much wasted on us city kids. We also had Art Appreciation, in which we viewed traveling exhibits of copies of works of the Old Masters and were supposed to learn something about the artists, but I don't remember ever being challenged to try to develop our own artistic talents, if any.

For several years we had a Music Memory class, the likes of which I have not seen offered to grade school students since that time. On a wind-up phonograph, the teacher played records of the works of well-known composers, and we were supposed to learn to identify the tune, the opera and the composer. Years later when I heard some of that old music played, I sang, "Ahb-a-nera" or "Tor-e-adore from Car-men by Biz-zay" or "Bark-a-ro-ole from Ta-yels of Hoff-man Ah-a-ahah-fin-bock," and my own children looked at me as if I'd finally lost all my marbles. Other than that, I'm not sure that Music Memory did us any good.

In this area also, the schools did not give instrument instructions, nor was there much emphasis on developing vocal talents. In the sixth grade, the students were seated at their desks mumbling along at some song the teacher valiantly tried to teach us. She finally called me to the front of the room and told me to stand facing the class while we sang. I just knew she finally appreciated my wonderful voice and I nearly busted a gusset with pride. Imagine my chagrin when she told the class to watch me as I sang—I opened my big mouth wider than any of the rest of the class!

I did learn about "every good boy does fine," and "FACE," and thirty-five years later when we bought a piano for my own children I was able with no further help, but with hours of practice, to teach myself a repertoire of about fifteen or twenty hymns that I could play with four fingers. So my grade school music was finally put to some use.

Our English teacher labored diligently trying to correct our class's grammar and our pronunciation of certain words. She labored mightily to change our "git" to "get" and to eliminate the ubiquitous "ain't." We didn't use "ain't" very much in our family. There were too many others to jump on the one who let it slip out: "Mama, she said 'ain't!'"

But everyone in the community used "chunk" for "throw." I forgot about that until I recently saw a copy of *Campfire Stories*, autographed by its author, Tanner Laine, to Beryl's husband, Gene Barnett, in this manner: "Gene, I have always admired you since the days we were in Texas Tech and you were chunking for the Raiders. All best wishes, Tanner Laine."

My dictionary tells me "chunk" is a nasal variant of "chuck," one of whose meanings is "throw." That good teacher tried to eliminate our usage of "chunk" and was doing a pretty good job of it, too, until one day in her exasperation with certain individuals in the class, she exclaimed forcefully, "You boys quit chunking that chalk back there, you hear?" The class burst out laughing. She must have had some effect, however, because that year is the last time I remember using "chunk."

Ida Rule started to first grade that fall of 1926 and walked with second-grader Beryl the six or eight blocks to East Ward; Berry and Howard were both seniors in high school, and as I said, Elsie and I were in the seventh grade in the basement of the high school building. All of us came home for dinner in the middle of the day.

This was the first house where we ate in the kitchen and it wasn't a particularly large kitchen. The long, oak dining table must have been stored in the garage during this time because we ate on a square kitchen table in the corner of the kitchen. Most of our seats were apple boxes so they could slide under the table when the table was shoved into the corner between meals. Mama cooked the meals on a kerosene stove, and the old safe (antique dealers today call them "pie safes") was in the corner near the back door.

The main reason I can remember those noontime dinners is because I heard Mama complain, "I do declah, it's so aggravatin'. Howard reads the assigned books and sits there at the dinner table and tells Berry Noel the plot. Then Berry Noel goes to school and makes a book report that afternoon just like he'd read the book and prit'near makes a bettah grade than Howard does. It's just not fair."

We ate in the kitchen instead of the dining room because the potbellied stove, as well as the double bed for Elsie and me, were in the room designed for dining. The three brothers occupied the front bedroom, and Mama's room at the back of the house was essentially as it had been across from East Ward: big oak bed, foldaway bed, baby bed, wardrobe and dresser.

Nearly twenty-five years later Ida Rule lived with me and my family for nearly a year at our home in Casper, Wyoming. It was during that time that I realized what entirely different memories we each had of our earlier lives. You'da thought, as we expressed it, that we had been raised in different homes. She told me this story:

"Elsie, Beryl, Lydia Ann, and I all had our tonsils taken out on the same morning by Dr. Dudgeon at his second-story office in downtown Sweetwater. Beryl and Ann and I got along okay, but you remember Elsie was a bleeder, and Mama and Dr. Dudgeon worked with her for a long time trying to get the bleeding stopped. Finally, Mama said to us, 'No use in you children just sittin' around up here. You'd best go on home.' And Beryl and Ann and I—what age were we then?—no more than seven and nine, and Ann just four—proceeded to hot foot it the eight or nine blocks to our house, just a little while after our tonsils were removed."

I remember that occasion because that night when Elsie and I were sleeping in that middle room, she started bleeding again, and the blood came gushing out all over me in the bed. Mama called Dr. Dudgeon to come and they worked over Elsie again for a long time and eventually stopped the bleeding. After that, Mama was ever mindful of Elsie's condition of having blood slow to coagulate.

When Ida Rule told me that story, I later repeated it to Mama and she said, "Oh, I think I wouldn't have sent those little girls walkin' home so soon after a tonsillectomy."

I replied, "Well, how in the world would they have got home? We didn't have a car."

Mama said, "Well, I reckon Rulie might be right. I must've done it." Neither Mama nor Ida Rule had any memory of how they got to the doctor's office, or how Mama and pretty sick Elsie got home.

Berry reports that Mama had a contract with Dr. Dudgeon to remove six sets of tonsils, cheaper by the half-dozen. Since Howard's tonsils had been removed in Longview, Mama must have had in mind Little Boy and the five girls, but I waited to have mine removed later.

Elsie and I graduated from the seventh grade in the spring of 1927. The graduation exercises were held in the old high school. A new high school building was under construction that year and Elsie and I would be freshmen in a new building the next year. Mama let me have my hair marcelled for the graduation ceremonies, and she even hired a young lady to come to the house with her electric curling iron, which was different from Aunt Willie's curling iron that was heated in the chimney of a kerosene lamp. With the curling iron, she pinched my normally straight Buster Brown haircut into what must have been unbecoming, tight, frizzled waves. I had begged for this beauty transformation, and after Mama had to pay the young woman seventy-five cents, I didn't dare express my disappointment.

While the young woman was there, she mentioned that she'd met Fred around town, that he was a very good dancer. Mama was a mite discombobulated. She didn't even know until then that Fred knew how to dance.

At the graduation exercises, the whole class sang what our teachers called "Spring Song," the words of which I can still remember. Mama said that the seventh grade classes of all three of her sons had sung the same song, although they had been in different towns. The tune is well-known, and every time I hear "Melody in F" by A. Rubinstein, it takes me back to those words of "Welcome, sweet springtime, we greet thee in song," which Mama had to listen to so many times.

I suppose the dresses Elsie and I wore for our graduation came from our cousin, Mary Noel. All of our "nice" dresses came from her in what we called "missionary boxes," a phrase we appropriated from the *Pollyanna* books. We have a snapshot of Elsie and me taken in front of the house across from

East Ward, and I'm wearing a neat-looking coat dress of pastel striped wool (the picture, of course, is in black and white, but I remember those lovely colors) and Elsie is wearing a brown velveteen with fancy trim. That's indicative of the difference in our tastes in clothes. I favored tailored things and Elsie liked them fancier. Mama said Elsie got her tastes in clothes from Aunt Willie, but we received enough pretty clothes from Mary Noel to take care of both of our likes and dislikes. Another snapshot of me in front of the Elm Street house shows a neat, knitted wool two-piece dress of tan and brown, short enough to meet the bobtailed styles of the Roaring Twenties.

Mary Noel's clothes were always right in style, usually ahead of those worn by our peers. Mama assured us that we were doing Mary Noel a favor by taking the clothes off of her hands because that enabled Mary Noel to clean out her closet with a clear conscience and then make shopping trips to Dallas to restock. Most of her clothes had famous store labels in them, and we always knew we were pretty classy dressers. Later, when I was in college, I applied for a job and removed my hat and coat before taking dictation from the prospective employer. He saw the label in my hat and said, "I see you shop at Neiman-Marcus; that's where my wife gets some of her clothes when I can afford it."

I mumbled something about my aunt giving the hat to me, but he evidently didn't believe me because I didn't get the job. He told someone if I could wear Neiman-Marcus clothes I did not need his puny little job.

Mama wouldn't alter the clothes, saying surely with all those girls, there was someone around they'd fit without her having to take the trouble to alter them. Mary Noel was a few months older than Elsie, but Elsie soon outgrew the clothes and I was the lucky recipient of most of them. Mary Noel favored blue, my favorite color, and Elsie didn't care for it so much.

Beryl and Ida Rule could hardly wait to grow into Mary Noel's clothes, then lo and behold, the younger girls sprang up in height so quickly that from the arrival of one missionary box when the girls were too short, to the next, they were too tall. It was a bad day for them. Beryl had thirty-five cents and kept threatening to buy thirty-five cents worth of white material to insert a white belt in the waistline of each dress.

Elsie was an inch or so taller than I was, and the three younger sisters, taking after Mama, grew to be several inches taller than I am in spite of their threats to take up smoking to stunt their growth. The one big advantage I could see in my lesser height was that most of Mary Noel's clothes fit me.

Beryl: I did get to wear a good looking long dress from Mary Noel to my seventh grade graduation, then promptly tore it in the spokes of a bicycle I rode while I was still all gussied up.

In Lubbock High School, Ida Rule was working on some letter writing project in English class. Her partner Betty was a girl who flaunted the fact that much of her shopping was done at Neiman-Marcus. In the course of the letter writing, Ida Rule was insistent that Neiman-Marcus should be hyphenated and Betty was just as insistent that Ida Rule was wrong. It gave Ida Rule great pleasure to say, "Look at the label in my sweater," and Betty was properly impressed and convinced. Of course, Ida Rule didn't bother to mention that her sweater was from a missionary box.

I was blessed by those good-looking clothes all through high school and college and I remember many of the dresses, hats and coats with pride. It was a bad day for me when Mary Noel married and moved from Aunt Noel's home, but I was through college and working by that time and could afford to buy myself a few clothes, although never as fine as Mary Noel's.

Mama often said, "It was a bad day for this family, too,

when your Uncle Tad lost lots of weight and his suits no longer fit YaPapa."

Mama could never bring herself to cut up outgrown or worn-out clothes to make patchwork quilts as some women did, saying, "As long as anybody else can get some use out of them, as long as they'll keep someone warm, I'm not goin' to cut them up."

Consequently, when we got a new missionary box from Aunt Noel, Mama would make up another missionary box of last year's clothes to send to Aunt Willie's family. This went on for years. After we were married and after Aunt Willie's death, Mama might appear for a visit and announce she wanted to "clean out your closets to send a missionary box to Catherine Murphy."

I recently heard from my cousin Catherine Murphy Thomas who wrote: "Through all these years Aunt Ida continued to send me 'missionary boxes' as she and Mother used to call them. My girls delighted in dressing up in the clothes when they came. My son Buddy was still quite young when Aunt Ida died, but he remembered her. When I told them of her death, Buddy asked, 'Mommie, will Aunt Ida still send us missionary boxes from heaven?' Aunt Ida would have appreciated that."

Mama made dresses for us, also. During those years of Elm Street, her specialty for me and Elsie was "sleeveless, Basque waist and full skirt." She made so many of them that the big brothers asked Mama if we couldn't have something else. We had graduated from black, cotton stockings to a tacky shade of tan cotton lisle, and the brothers asked if we couldn't wear some other kind of stockings. Silk stockings were out of the question (other than those we received from Aunt Noel at Christmas), but the boys bought us rayon stockings that were at least stocking-colored. They cost a dollar a pair and we had to take mighty good care of them, but it would be several years before we bought silk stockings, and almost World War II before we had our first nylons.

I have more memories of Papa in this house than in the two before this. It was in this house that he scolded me so severely for getting home late one Sunday afternoon, and it was from this house that he took us on the July Fourth picnic out in the mesquite pasture. We returned from a Christmas program at the church one Friday evening to find that he had brought us a string of electric Christmas tree lights. He and Mama had already put them on our tree, and we just knew it was the most beautiful tree we'd ever had, even though they were the series type of lights so that when one colored light burnt out or was loose, they all went off and we might have to try every single bulb before we found the culprit. This went on for years and after we acquired three or four strings, it seemed that someone had to be constantly working the whole Christmas season to get the lights turned back on.

The thing we remember most about Papa in those years was his early Monday morning departures. He had to leave about four o'clock in the morning to cover his territory for the A.G. Winn Produce Company. He'd go out to his Model T Ford coupe and start it up, and then sit there racing the engine louder and louder to warm it up until he had the Davises and Crenshaws and the whole neighborhood awake. Everybody knew full well when it was Monday morning and Mr. Duff was leaving. I heard the brothers griping to Mama about the noise, but certainly never to Papa.

In an emergency he might come home on Tuesday night, but usually he was gone until Friday night, and then he worked on Saturdays in Sweetwater. Mama said she told Mr. Winn, "This would be a fine job for a couple who don't care anything about each other. He's out from under foot all week and I get his paycheck, and that's a good enough arrangement for some folks, but it happens that I love my husband and I want some other arrangement so my children can get to know their father."

I don't know whether Mama's plea influenced Mr. Winn (she thought it did), or whether in the due course of transacting his business, there came a time for another arrangement for Papa. Mr. Winn built another wholesale produce house in Big Spring, eighty miles west of Sweetwater, to take care of the western part of the territory served by his company, and he said Papa would be manager of the new place and we could move to Big Spring so that Papa could be home every night.

But things came up that kept us from moving for another year.

CHAPTER 14

THE HAMBURGER STORE

As Elsie and I had graduated from seventh grade in the spring of 1927, so Howard and Berry had graduated from Sweetwater High School that spring. Howard and Berry had each been an outstanding student, though in totally different areas. Howard was an exceptional scholar, having the second highest grade average in his class. Berry had played football and was very active in other areas of school life.

Berry: A local service club gave five hundred dollars each year to four graduating seniors from Sweetwater High School: a one-hundred fifty dollar scholarship or award went to the boy with the highest grade average, and one-hundred fifty dollars to the girl with the highest grade average. Then they gave one hundred dollars each to the senior boy and girl who they felt were needy, deserving, and outstanding in school activities. This latter award was the one hundred dollars I received.

I still wonder why I chose Texas College of Mines at El Paso (now known as University of Texas at El Paso) over Texas Technological College (now known as Texas Tech University). At that time Tech had been in existence only about three years and it was considered a "country school," but El Paso had an appeal for me, and at the time I thought I'd like to become a civil engineer.

I had continued to work at all sorts of jobs in Sweetwater—Ferris Drug, Piggly Wiggly, and for the latter part of the summer I worked out at the U.S. Gypsum plant, moving four-by-eight sheets of wall board around for thirty-five cents an hour. After paying my railroad fare to El Paso ($13.45), I arrived in El Paso with about fifty dollars. The award money came out after I had enrolled.

Howard also had a decision to make about college.

Howard: For second highest grade average, I was offered a scholarship by the University of Texas for thirty-five dollars, which wasn't much help for starting a college career. As Mama and I began looking around for a college for me, Mama suggested that I try for the United States Naval Academy, since Aunt Daisy Tardy's brother-in-law, Walter Tardy, had graduated from there in 1898, and he liked it. I had seen Ramon Navarro in the movie "The Midshipman," and it looked good to me. That is how it started for me.

In the days before she picked up the long distance phone easily, Mama called Congressman Thomas L. Blanton in Abilene and asked him how to go about getting an appointment through him. Fortunately, he gave appointments through competitive exams and we found out the requirements for admission to the Academy. Most of the candidates had some college education before trying for the Academy, and I found I had one intolerable hole in my education. I had not taken physics in high school, and physics was an absolute requirement for admission. I also had an orthodontic condition that needed correction.

Our dentist, Dr. Russell Wimberly, said there was only one man between Fort Worth and El Paso who could do the job—Dr. Guy Marvin Gillespie in Abilene. I was reluctant to see him because I knew the family could not afford the costs, but Russell Wimberly said, "I told him about you and he said, 'Heck, we can't all have money. Tell him to come on over.' So you get over there to see him."

Dr. Gillespie believed he could correct the condition in a year and he also said, "If that boy is ambitious enough to try for the Naval Academy, I reckon I can wait for my fee until he graduates."

So when Mr. Winn said Papa could move the family to Big Spring, it was decided that Mama and the family would stay in Sweetwater another year while I took physics at the high school and started the orthodontia with Dr. Gillespie in Abilene. I took physics from Ina Wood, I took public speaking from Bob Payne, and I hitchhiked the forty miles over to Abilene every week to get the orthodontia started.

In 1938 I finally got Dr. Gillespie paid off.

At the newspaper office, Howard had heard about Charles A. Lindbergh's successful solo flight non-stop from New York to Paris where he landed on May 21, 1927.

Howard came in from delivering papers one afternoon about the time of their graduation and called out to Mama, "Hey, Mama. That young man made it."

Mama's reply was, "Oh, I'm so thankful. I've been prayin' for him."

It is difficult to convey to persons who didn't experience it the great outpouring of hero worship that was the result of that historic flight. That young man seemed to strike the right chord in everyone all around the world, male and female, young and old. Upon landing in Paris he was mobbed by madly cheering Frenchmen. President Coolidge sent a cruiser to France to bring back Lindbergh and his plane, *The Spirit of St. Louis*. When he arrived in the United States he was given 55,000 telegrams of congratulations, and most Americans agreed that they had found in Lindbergh a hero they could really admire and respect.

How did he become such a well-known personage, beloved near and far, in the days before television, before total radio coverage? Our family did not have a radio and the families of most of my friends did not have radios at the time. (While we lived on Elm Street, one of the New Year's Days found me in the Davis home next door, watching Helen Davis and her boyfriend playing some two-handed card game while they listened to the Rose Bowl game on the radio, the first time I'd heard a radio since the batteries had given out on the one my brothers had made several years earlier.)

We took the daily Sweetwater paper and the Fort Worth *Star-Telegram*, and through the years we subscribed to several magazines, perhaps not all at the same time: *American, Saturday Evening Post, Literary Digest, Woman's Home Companion, Liberty, Collier's, Ladies Home Journal,* and *Good Housekeeping* to name some that I remember, and all of those publications had multitudes of stories about Lindbergh. We went to the Saturday matinee at the picture show and saw the newsreels, *Pathe News* and *Fox Movietone News*, filled with what Lindbergh was doing. Various merchants posted bulletins in their windows to keep interested citizens abreast of news of Lindbergh.

Colonel Lindbergh took his plane on a tour of the nation, promoting interest in aviation, and in each town or city where he appeared, he was greeted by thousands of admirers. Most authorities said he probably moved aviation ahead fifty years in that first year. The fall afternoon when his plane was expected to arrive in Abilene, I spent my English class looking out the east window of the new high school building in Sweetwater, hoping against hope to catch a glimpse of his plane, but I was not that lucky. That day our English teacher told us we must keep a scrapbook all the school year on any subject we chose. I, of course, chose Lindbergh, and I must say that with Mama's help, I had no trouble finding a wealth of material to fill probably two hundred pages of scrapbook. A classmate also chose Lindbergh, and her book, small and orderly, was voted the neatest in the class, but my big, messy, cluttered book, with no semblance of order, was voted the most interesting at the end of the school year.

That same teacher required us to bring to class some joke about English or grammar, and Mama came to my rescue with, "A preposition is something you should never end a sentence with."

Mama helped Elsie out with the story of the lady who said to a passing child, "Little boy, your mother's calling you," and he replied, "Her not call we, us don't belong to she."

That same teacher asked us to bring some unwritten folk song passed down from generation to generation. Again, Mama told us of a song that the colored women sang to their babies back in Kentucky: *"Way back in Kintucky, where Kinbuck was born/He swore by his master he'uz fresh from a storm/And Kinbuck he fluttered, and Kinbuck he flew/And Kinbuck skeered Molly clean out of her shoe."*

I felt sorry for the other students who didn't have Mama to help them out.

Mama told us the teachers had her permission to discipline us if we misbehaved or were bad, but they couldn't punish us for being dumb. If we misbehaved, that was our fault, but if we were stupid, that was not our fault, that was hers (Mama's).

The church in Sweetwater had a balcony in the auditorium, but Mama wouldn't let us sit up there, she said there was too much carryin' on up there.

Mama didn't like Mother's Day. She thought it didn't make any difference to those whose mothers were still here, and just made those folks whose mothers had died feel bad. On one of the Mother's Days in Sweetwater, however, the preacher asked for families to sit together, for all children to come together to sit with their mothers. Mama later said, "Oh, my, I was so proud of my family. I was scared to death that you wouldn't want to come down and sit together—some of you can be so cranky at times. But one by one you slipped into the pew until we ran over and had to use the pew in back of us. I'll tell you, I was as proud as all git out—sinfully proud."

It is the only time I definitely recollect (as Papa always expressed the word "remember") that all of us were together—from Papa to Little Boy. At mealtimes at least one or another of us, usually the big brothers or Papa, was away. It's too bad there wasn't a camera around for that Mother's Day.

At the end of summer Berry left for El Paso to enroll in the College of Mines, and Mama rented a small store building across the street from the high school, and in the days before hot lunch programs, she opened a hamburger stand. Howard opened the store—a simple frame structure—every morning. The store had school supplies, pop, candy and a few basic groceries for sale, and Howard tells me there was a gasoline pump, the old kind with a glass ten gallon container, hand pump and gravity flow, but very little gas was sold. He compares the place to a 7-11 store, forty years too soon. The hours certainly weren't the same because he closed early enough so that he could take care of his paper route in the northeast section of Sweetwater and then still have time to milk the cow.

Mama walked to the store each morning in time for Howard to go to his classes. Immediately after she arrived she began frying hamburgers by the dozens, wrapping them in wax paper and putting them in tall, crockery churns to stay warm until lunchtime. Each hamburger had lettuce, tomatoes, dill pickle slices and mustard, and all except one churnful had onion slices. "With or without?" referred to onions only. And they sold for a nickel. The standard lunch of hamburger, large doughnut and soda pop cost a grand total of fifteen cents. We did have half-pints of milk for sale, but nearly everyone chose soda pop, and some of the boys had more than one hamburger.

When I return to the scenes of my adolescence, old friends often remark, "Your mother made the best hamburgers I ever ate." Some of these days I may tell them that she mixed a little moistened bread in the meat to hold it together, but what they didn't know didn't hurt them.

Elsie and I helped in back of the candy counter, Mama passed out the hamburgers, and Howard presided at the soda pop case. Ida Rule and Beryl walked up there from East Ward for their lunches except on cold or extremely bad days, when they were given a dime each to get a bowl of red beans and a glass of milk at the East Ward store. Our store had a couple of long tables with benches, but unless the weather was very bad, most of the customers preferred to stand around outside to eat their lunch. The south wall of the store made a good bulletin board where the scores of the Sweetwater High School football team—undefeated in 1927—were tallied. It was a good noontime hangout.

As I write of that year, I wonder what Mama did for a babysitter. Lydia Ann and Little Boy were preschoolers. Ann now insists that they stayed by themselves—that she babysat Little Boy and was supposed to call on Mrs. Davis if she needed any help. I have a hard time believing that Mama would have done that; the house was heated with a potbellied stove that burned coal and they couldn't have kept the fire going, for crying out loud.

Papa's stepmother, our Grandma, came for an extended visit, her last visit to us. While at Aunt Willie's in Hanna, Louisiana, she died a couple of years later at the age of eighty-one. Papa's recently divorced cousin, Gertrude, and her little boy, Billy, also lived with us until things worked out for her.

I suppose Gertrude or Grandma babysat during their visits, and Mrs. Townsend, a childless widow in the neighborhood, filled in when needed. Mrs. Townsend was an interesting character who told stories of her youthful days in the Midwest when large bicycle clubs took long touring trips on their bicycles. At the time I thought she was so old I wondered how she could ever have ridden a bicycle. Mrs. Townsend would help Mama out a year or two later when Ida Rule needed a quieter place than our big household in which to live.

Mama went with me and Elsie to hear some woman lecture to the girls of the high school. I realize it was supposed to be a form of sex education. Afterwards I heard Mama say to another mother who had stopped in the store, "I don't know how a girl could hear that talk and not remain a good girl." And I didn't even know what the lecturer had been talking about.

Berry came home from El Paso shortly before the Christmas holidays. He had been boxing with another young man, Malcolm Madera, and had been knocked out so thoroughly that he was unconscious for fifteen minutes. Madera was one of the few students on campus who had a car, and he took Berry to the doctor who told him he had had a severe brain concussion and should go home and stay in bed in a darkened room for an extended time. Madera took Berry to the station and even paid for his ticket to Sweetwater, and they later became quite good friends.

I remember Berry's being in bed in that darkened front bedroom and I marvel that he was able to find any peace and quiet in the hojang, as Mama called our family life.

The school year finally ended and we said goodby to our friends as we prepared to move to Big Spring, where Papa had found a house which he and Mama decided to buy.

Mama made arrangements for Fred to rent a room from

Mrs. Crane, and couldn't get over the fact that Mrs. Crane said she would wash Fred's sheets every two weeks, he could just sleep on one side of the double bed one week and move to the other side the second week.

I overheard Mama tell Mrs. Davis she didn't mind leaving Sweetwater. We had lived there four years and she had never been invited into a home for a social occasion. Beryl recalls that in one of the houses on Elm Street, Mama let Beryl invite several of her friends for an Easter party when Mama fixed an Easter egg nest for each guest, and not a single guest showed up. Nevertheless, Mama had encouraged us to have parties in our home for our Sunday School classes and for B.Y.P.U.

Mama had been active in PTA and church and she got along well with her neighbors, but it was a time when no grown woman was called by her given name, and Mama of course, called all her friends by their married names: Mrs. Davis, Mrs. Risinger, Mrs. Crenshaw, to mention a few. After living the first half of her life in the scenes of her youth, she missed hearing herself called "Ida" or "Miss Ida."

Some of us were more reluctant to move to Big Spring because the Big Spring and Sweetwater high schools were arch rivals in all sports, but once again we packed the books and everything else and moved farther west.

CHAPTER 15

BIG SPRING BOARDING HOUSE

Papa wrote in his old Bible that we moved from Sweetwater to Big Spring on June 6, 1928.

Early June is not the best time for youngsters to move from one town to another. The neighborhood of the house on Runnells Street in Big Spring had plenty of playmates for the younger members of the family, but the children in the Bow, Riggs, and Jones families, and the McKenzie's grandchildren ranged in age from Little Boy to Beryl, and Elsie and I would not deign to play with them.

Because there was nothing much to do, Mama actually let us get some regular playing cards (there were no Rook cards for sale in the town), but we had to play some simple game with them, Fish, or some such, certainly not bridge. Fred came over from Sweetwater one weekend and as he left he said to me, "How'd you ever get those cards in the house? She (meaning Mama) would never let me bring anything like that in the house."

To keep the summer from being unbearably long, Mama let Elsie and me visit in Sweetwater three different times that summer, and she also planned another trip that hurried us on to the end of summer. Mama's itchy foot and love of travel began to manifest itself soon after we arrived in Big Spring.

We still had no car of our own, but Mr. Winn lent his Studebaker sedan for this occasion, and Fred came over from

Sweetwater to be the chauffeur. I don't know how all eight of us, six kids ranging in age from three-year-old Little Boy to Elsie at fourteen, plus Mama and Fred, were packed in that Studebaker with the food and bedding for the three or four days we were to be away. We left Big Spring and drove over the old "Broadway of America" to Pecos where we turned south on a long, straight road stretching ahead over dry, flat land, the monotony broken only by dips made in the graveled road to drain the desert from the infrequent rains. We children squealed every time we hit one of the dips until even Fred's monumental patience began to wear thin.

In the late afternoon, almost dusk, we came to an exceptionally deep dip that was running high with water, our first experience with a flash flood. Heavy rains in the distant highlands had run down the arid countryside through this particular dip, making the highway impassable at this point. The occupants of another car stranded there were making the most of their enforced layover by playing a wind-up portable record-player, which we, of course, called a Victrola. We spread our covers on the ground under the clear, starry sky, and with the strains of "My Blue Heaven" sounding from our neighbors' instrument and the melodious gurgling of the stream nearby to lull us, we soon dropped off to sleep.

How did Mama ever feed us on that trip? We had no car ice box, no air conditioning to keep food or kids from spoiling, and no camp stove, although we were traveling through an arid, treeless country with little prospect of finding firewood. I don't know what we ate, but we didn't go hungry, although we certainly didn't eat in a cafe or restaurant.

The second afternoon, as we journeyed down the winding road leading into the town of Alpine, a tire went flat. With remarkable good humor, Fred set out to change it, but though he struggled and struggled, he simply couldn't loosen the nut that held the tire on. He knew he was twisting it the right way because on the other side of the car he could easily remove the nut. After struggling with it for an hour or more, Fred finally flagged down a passing car and asked the driver to send a service man out from Alpine. The service truck eventually arrived and that man had the tire off and changed in a very short time. The problem: on Studebaker cars the nuts turned one way on one side and the opposite way on the other side.

Mama took fifteen one dollar bills from her purse and paid the man, leaving mighty little money for us to finish our trip. The repair man left, and Mama rounded up kids and loaded the car, preparing to leave after the long delay. As Fred started to pull out, Mama said, "Where's my purse? I presume you children have it back there." Fred stopped the car; we searched the car and all around the car, high and low, but we never did find the purse. Mama always believed the tire-changing man had taken her purse. Distressed, she wired Papa collect to send $25—almost a week's salary to Papa—and we spread our covers on the ground and slept under the starry sky. Waking up, we found we were right in the middle of a goat pasture, with goats all around us, nuzzling us awake!

We spent our last night on the road in Christoval, a small resort community on the Concho River, where we thought we were in the lap of luxury in a primitive tourist cabin. We arrived home the next day ready for a bath, good food and a clean soft bed.

Mama never did let any difficulties incurred while traveling discourage her from making more trips, either that summer or later. The day after we arrived home, Mama, Papa, Howard and Fred left in Mr. Winn's Studebaker for a trip back to Longview and Monroe, and these two trips were just the beginning of many such trips Mama was to take for the rest of her life. We teased her that she couldn't stand to see a car with an empty seat in it going anywhere. If she couldn't go, she'd put one or more of her children in that space.

John, one of the men who worked for Papa, and Doris, John's wife, and their small boy stayed with us while the grown-ups of the family went to Longview and Monroe. John and Doris, the first adults we children called by their first names, stayed in the big room that had been built on the very back of the house as soon as we moved in. Opening off the kitchen, that room was Mama's room, and as usual, held all of Mama's big furniture, as well as the four younger children and their belongings.

The five-foot crawl space under Mama's room was not enclosed, making it a good playhouse for the little kids until, according to Beryl, Mama took a hoe and killed a coiled rattlesnake under that room.

A large closet had been built into that room, and before the year was over I heard Howard call out, "Hey, Mama. I've found the holy of holies." Over the door frame, inside the closet, was the only place that poor Papa could find to call his own where he could keep his personal belongings, such as his razor and aftershave lotion.

There certainly wasn't much privacy for anyone in the Big Spring house. Located on a corner lot across the street from the backside of the high school and junior high school campuses, it was an older house whose yard was planted with more shrubs, trees and flowers than we had had in Sweetwater. Pretty carnations bloomed in the side yard; the lilac hedge bloomed our first spring there, but never again, although that lilac hedge was a help in keeping the caliche dust blowing from the street corner from smothering the house. That first summer, Howard emptied the ice bucket of the ice cream freezer on one of the trees, and the salt water killed that tree. Small apricot trees and peach trees bore beautiful blossoms, but never any fruit. The side yard was quite large, and Mama and Papa had a small three-room house built there to rent out in the booming times.

As soon as we moved in, half of the front porch was enclosed with canvas, with a window opening on the yard, and a door opening to the front porch. This was Howard's room that first year.

When we moved to Big Spring, ditches were being dug for the installation of natural gas for the town, but gas was not turned into the gas mains until after cold weather arrived. Mama cooked on the kerosene stove until that time and then she purchased a new gas cookstove as well as four room heaters, which were doubly appreciated after we had endured the chilly mornings.

The bookcase was in the front hall, as usual. On the right of the hall was a bedroom that Mama kept rented out much of the time. On the left was the living room which we used as a parlor all of the time we were in Big Spring, although the davenport served as an uncomfortable bed many times.

Wide, sliding double doors led to what was probably built for a dining room, but was used as a bedroom for me and Elsie. Two other doors led from our bedroom, one to the kitchen in back of our room, and one to the big dining room at the end of the front hall. To get to the bathroom, which evidently had been built as an afterthought between the back porch and the big room, we either had to go through the kitchen and the cold back porch, or we went through the dining room, which was often full of boarders. The bathroom didn't have a lavatory, only a stool and tub. For use as a lavatory was an ever-present apple box with a white enamel wash pan on it.

That big dining room (every time she swept it, Doris said it was as big as an airplane field) was the scene of Mama's first experience with a large boarding house. The community was experiencing an oil boom, and eating and sleeping places were much in demand. Mama served meals to about sixty boarders three times a day in two shifts from two big tables, and she apologized for having to charge fifty cents a meal, but she *was* able to pay the family's grocery bill with that business.

One of the boarders, Raymond McDaniel, manager of the Coca Cola Company, was always kidding Mama by making up tales about a landlady of a boarding house in Abilene who served wonderful meals for a quarter. The next summer when Mama had occasion to be in Abilene, she called him and said, "Well, Raymond, I've come over to get one of those two-bit meals."

Raymond replied, "Oh, Mrs. Duff, that lady got rich and retired!"

As I recall many of those boarders, I remember Mama's interest in them and their problems. There were several school teachers, including Johnny Coffey (to me and Elsie he was Mr. Coffey, our math teacher), before he married and brought his young wife to Big Spring. More than thirty years later I ran into Mrs. Coffey at Glorieta Assembly grounds in New Mexico and she remembered all of us and asked about each of my sisters by name.

Tiny Reed, the principal at Junior High, and his wife, also a teacher, were another two I recall because they each went to his or her parents' home for Christmas and didn't spend Christmas together. Mr. Reed, who could see our back gate from his office, teased the young woman who helped Mama in the kitchen about how long the bakery deliveryman stayed when he came each morning.

When Mama was worrying out loud about trying to get enough money together for Howard to take to the Naval Academy (Howard needed to arrive with one hundred dollars on hand either to pay on uniforms or to buy a return ticket home in case he failed the entrance physical), Mr. Reed, having been raised on a farm, said, "Oh, Mrs. Duff, don't worry about it. You can always sell one of the old sows for a hundred dollars."

Mama's reply was, "Oh, sure. We just don't have any old sows."

Another boarder, a beautiful young grade school teacher, introduced us to Dr. J. R. Dillard, to whom she was later married. Dr. Dillard ate many meals with us and later brought his mother, who often spent the day visiting with Mama. Dr. Dillard brought a big-city heart specialist consultant out to sample Mama's meals, and Mama, never reluctant to get any free medical advice, told him why she thought she had heart trouble. The big city doctor looked at Mama's roomful of boarders and at her houseful of children of all ages running in and out, and replied, "Mrs. Duff, if you can handle this, for all these years, there's nothing in the world wrong with *your* heart. It must be as strong as an ox."

Miss Clara Cox, who taught Senior English in high school, and who, according to Berry, had the only Master's degree in the school system, helped Howard prepare for his second competitive entrance exam for the appointment to the Naval Academy by furnishing the books he needed to read and study to fill in some of his weak spots in English literature.

Two of the young men, Mac and Jack, were "bug hunters," employees of the Department of Agriculture who were part of the project to eradicate the cotton boll weevil. One of those young men, C. D. McGehee, was later Superintendent of City Parks in Lubbock when we lived there.

Another of the boarders, a carpenter, came in for supper one night and announced he had been robbed that day. He was working alone in a new house, separated from other nearby houses by slight hills, when a man came in and demanded his wallet. Mama asked the boarder if the robber had a gun and he said, "Not a gun—a cannon. At least it looked like a cannon to me looking down into it."

Red Lyons, another working man, had been an airplane mechanic in World War I and he had interesting stories to tell about his wartime experiences. Mama urged him to have his sister, Lois, come to Big Spring to work in the telephone office, and Mama put a single bed in the room with Elsie and me for Lois to become a live-in boarder. When Lois' shift ended after dark, Red waited for her outside the telephone building and walked her home. Mama often asked him to bring some ice cream from Shine Phillips' drugstore across the street from the telephone building, and he always brought it, grumbling, "There I stood outside the telephone building, freezing to death, and holding a package of ice cream, for gosh sakes. You're crazy for wanting ice cream in this weather."

Lois was a PBX operator. When Mama was in Sweetwater one evening, she asked the PBX operator in Sweetwater to tell the PBX operator in Big Spring that her mama would not be home that night. Lois got the message and for a little while was puzzled by it because her own mama was in Louisiana, but she quickly figured out that it was Mama's way of letting all of us know she wouldn't be home that night, and saving the cost of the long distance call.

Mrs. Higgins and her young son, Tommy, had a room in a house on the other side of the high school, but took their meals with us. Mr. Higgins worked for the railroad and was with them occasionally. Elsie and Mrs. Higgins became very good friends and enjoyed Mrs. Higgins' favorite pastime of draggin' Main in her green Hupmobile coupe, while Mrs. Higgins sang a parody of a popular song, "We drug the Main together, sang love's refrain together . . ."

A roly-poly Englishman was polite enough not to question

all the Texas accents around him, so we never commented on his English accent. One evening, however, he said, "Please pass the coslu." When we passed nearly everything on the table to him without meeting his request, he just kept repeating, "coslu." He finally stood up and pointed to the cabbage salad which, until that time, we called "slaw," never having heard it called "coleslaw" before.

Oh, it was in interesting conglomeration of characters. The front room was rented by Mrs. Redford, a beautiful young woman, and her small child. Mr. Redford had some position in the oil field and was seldom around. (Twenty years later my husband worked in the oil industry and I knew countless couples who lived in circumstances similar to the Redmonds.) A touring company was coming to the big auditorium in Sweetwater to put on a road show of the musical "Rio Rita." In spite of the fact that Mr. Redmond couldn't attend, Mrs. Redmond wanted to go so much that Mama suggested that Howard drive her over there in her car. He did, and I almost drooled when I heard them talking about the different scenes and musical numbers.

Mrs. Jenkins and her young daughter Frances were the next tenants of the front bedroom. Mr. Jenkins was another oil field person, but we saw a little more of him than we had Mr. Redford. The Jenkins' son, Manon, came home on furlough from Army service in the Panama Canal Zone, and I didn't know he asked Elsie for a date. Elsie had matured socially much faster than I and our paths were diverging rapidly. After supper Manon and Elsie kept sitting at the table while I loudly and ostentatiously cleaned the dishes in front of them. Then I began to bang pots and pans around in the ktichen, griping loudly that it was time for Elsie to start washing dishes. There in the ktichen, Mama finally grabbed me and gave me a shaking as she said through her teeth, "Now, you just hush your mouth, young lady. Elsie has a date with Manon and they're goin' to stay here. I told her she didn't have to clean up tonight."

How'd I know? Nobody ever told me anything.

Miss Lytle, the public health nurse for Howard County, was the last tenant in the front room that winter, and I would get to know her better than any of the others.

Mama was friendly with all of the boarders. She said she ate with every shift, from those working men who came at six in the morning for breakfast, to Papa who usually came in for supper after the last boarder finished at night, and she blamed her habit of eating with each group for the fact that her weight began to go up. It was about this time that I first heard her say another one of her screwball poems: "Tell me not in mournful numbers/Life is but an empty dream/When the girl who weighs two hundred/Drinks a quart of whipping cream."

Mama served what she called "basic everyday food, nothin' fancy, but plenty of it." She had only one main dish for dinner and supper, not two or three as some boarding houses did. She must have made pretty good mashed potatoes (and without an electric mixer, too, for the benefit of you space age descendants), because one of the boarders said it was a pleasure eating Mama's mashed potatoes after eating in cafes for so long. He said, "Cafes get their mashed potatoes from a tank car that the railroad delivers right to their back door."

I think the boarders got to order their breakfast pretty much individually, within limits, but for the family I only remember the usual oatmeal, toast and cocoa.

Elsie and I set the table every night, always damask cloths and napkins that had to be ironed. The boarders' napkin rings were spring clothes pins with their names written on them. We ran home from basketball practice in our high-top tennis shoes and sweaty school dresses—no basketball uniforms for the girls—just in time to get everything on the table and in order before the boarders arrived.

Mama didn't serve an evening meal on Sunday. On a beautiful Sunday afternoon in April, all of us went out to Signal Mountain for a rare family outing: Papa, Mama, Howard, five girls and Little Boy. We must have gone in a produce company truck because we were all in the same vehicle. The big kids promptly set out to climb Signal Mountain, and even the youngsters gave it a try. Lydia Ann and Little Boy returned to Mama, and Little Boy handed her a rock they'd picked up on the steep side of the mountain. "I went half up it, Mama, half up it," he said proudly. When Mama's old dresser was sent to me after she died, in one drawer was that small stone glued to a small copper plate, and in Mama's handwriting are the words, "half up it."

Mama enjoyed visiting with the boarders and this presented a problem for Little Boy. We had all been taught never to interrupt when someone was talking, and since someone was always talking, Little Boy couldn't get a word in edgewise. After standing by Mama's knee for a time too long to suit him, he learned to reach up and put his hand on her mouth to get her attention. She, of course, had to stop talking, and then he could say what was on his mind.

As usual, Mama's attention was divided between many different concerns that winter of the Big Spring Boarding House.

CHAPTER 16

MAMA NEVER SANG IN CHURCH AGAIN

Howard kept busy that year he spent in Big Spring. He had a multitude of jobs: driving a wholesale candy truck; screening gravel for the construction of the Settles Hotel; working on the construction of a pipeline in the oil fields; dragging a chain for the surveyor of the Cosden Refinery, and night watchman of the cotton gin where he kept up steam, cleaned up, graded cotton, and phoned in reports to Fred at the cotton oil company in Sweetwater on the cotton purchased.

He also hitchhiked back and forth between Big Spring and Abilene every week or two to see the orthodontist. He said, "I not only know every sunflower along the road, I know every petal of every sunflower."

We were in the backyard one day when Lydia Ann and Little Boy came running around from the front yard, scared spitless. They were followed by a woman who said she had been driving by when Little Boy threw a rock and broke her car window. The neighborhood children had been having a fight, throwing rocks at each other across the street, and Little Boy just had not stopped throwing when the car passed. Mama told her to have the car repaired at a certain place, saying, "We'll pay for it, of course." After the woman left, all I remember Mama saying is, "Now you see why I've told you and told you, never throw rocks." The new window cost them seven dollars and fifty cents.

We thought Little Boy was pretty special. Someone had read somewhere that most United States presidents had been born to fathers who were over fifty years old when the future president was born. Since Papa had been over fifty years old when Little Boy was born, we were thoroughly convinced he was a future United States president.

Sometime during that winter, Ida Rule, who was nine years old, was diagnosed as having St. Vitus' dance, a nervous disorder technically know as chorea. The brothers and sisters still living remember few details. Beryl says it was diagnosed because Ida Rule's hand shook so badly.

Ann: Mama tried to blame herself for Ida Rule's illness. She said when Ida Rule was small she got real, real dirty one time and Mama bathed her so stringently and washed her hair for such a long time that Ida Rule caught a bad cold and was pretty sick, and Mama thought that was the cause of this illness.

Mama took Ida Rule to a specialist in Dallas, who advised that Ida Rule be placed in some environment where there wasn't such a hullabaloo going on as in our household. Mama brought her back to West Texas and made arrangements for her to stay with Mrs. Townsend, the widow in Sweetwater who had done some babysitting for Mama. Mrs. Townsend had a small apartment, and Ida Rule spent a quiet time with her. We can't remember how long, but she was at home by early summer. Mrs. Townsend taught Ida Rule to embroider so well that Ida Rule could always do prettier handiwork than the rest of us. Mama berated herself many times because she had scolded Ida Rule for being clumsy, saying, "I told her to swat flies in the kitchen, and she jerked the fly swatter over and hit my leg and snagged my stockings. I smacked her arm a good one. Oh, I feel so guilty about that."

I once told Beryl I'd read that chorea was caused by a

Vitamin B deficiency and Beryl said, "That makes sense, because Ida Rule had to eat lots of yeast. Mama came home pushing yeast down the rest of us. Oh, it was yucky, but we ate it. Mama made us."

When Mama had gone to Longview the summer before, she had bought an antique Morris chair, an early day lounge chair with wooden arms, an adjustable back and removable cushions. The chair had been crated and shipped by freight out to Big Spring. When the crating was removed, Little Boy and Lydia Ann had fun playing with a hammer and pieces of lumber and nails from the crating, until one day Little Boy swallowed one of the nails.

He and Lydia Ann came running to Mama to tell her. Mama promptly called the doctor who told her to feed him lots of soft bread and the nail would most likely pass through his system with no trouble, to watch his stools and note when the nail passed. Little Boy started using a slop jar instead of the bathroom toilet, and he was as interested as Mama in watching for the nail. After a week or so, Mama told the doctor it hadn't passed and he said, "It must have. You just missed it."

About three weeks after he swallowed the nail, Little Boy said as he prepared for bed, "Mama, my tummy hurts." Mama promptly wrapped the four-and-a-half year old in a quilt, and Papa drove them to the doctor's office in the hospital a few blocks from the house. When the child was placed in front of a fluoroscope, the nail was there as plain as anything, lodged in his appendix. He was operated on that night.

Mama stayed with him almost constantly, yet with the aid of the woman who helped in the kitchen, she didn't miss serving a meal until Thursday when she called and told Elsie and me what to fix and serve for supper. Papa came from the hospital and when Miss Lytle, the nurse boarder, asked about Little Boy, Papa told her he was running a high fever. I heard

Miss Lytle murmur the word "peritonitis" and saw her shake her head, but I didn't appreciate the significance of her reaction. When he left to go back to the hospital, Papa told Elsie and me to clean up the living room and to close up the davenport, which had been open since Berry and Fred had come over the previous weekend, which had been Mother's Day.

We washed up the dishes and forgot all about the living room. I was sitting on the floor of our room digging through some magazines for a school project when I looked up and saw Papa standing in our door with tears running down his face. I burst into tears because I knew without being told that Little Boy was dead.

Papa tried to call Fred and Berry in Sweetwater but couldn't reach them; then he called our former neighbor, Mrs. W.G. Davis, to ask her to get in touch with the brothers, but he reached the wrong Davis household. Fortunately, that Davis family knew Berry and Fred and did get word to them.

Papa went back to the hospital, and Mama picked up Little Boy and held him in her arms as they drove to the house. Mrs. Jones, our neighbor from across the street, whose children were his playmates, came over and bathed the little fellow and put his little Sunday-go-to-meetin' sailor suit on him, and when Elsie and I awakened on Friday morning he was lying in a little white coffin on the library table in the living room.

Friday morning, some of the boarders arrived for breakfast, not having heard the sad news. They wanted to leave, but Mama insisted on serving them breakfast, saying, "No, stay. I need to be doin' something."

Mama had been so pleased when we moved to Big Spring to find that the First Baptist Church building was all paid for. "We moved from Monroe just as that church building was completely paid off; we moved from Longview just as their building was paid for, and we got to Sweetwater where they'd just built a new building and we helped pay on that. It was such a relief to get to Big Spring and not have a church debt to worry about." Then, what happened? The First Baptist Church building burned to the ground soon after we moved to town, and the congregation met some of the time in a new movie house (built for the new-fangled sound pictures) and some of the time in the combination gym-auditorium of the high school.

I tell of this at this point because Mama always believed "Funeral parlors are for people who don't have a church home." Little Boy's funeral was held from our living room Friday afternoon. Mrs. Higgins, who had taken Elsie and me to breakfast at the Douglas Hotel Friday morning, had put a tiny nosegay of flowers near Little Boy's face and he was beautiful with his curly blond hair and long black eyelashes.

Elsie was so distraught she wouldn't leave our bed so we opened the sliding doors between our room and the living room. Beryl, Ida Rule and Lydia Ann joined us there. They were sick with the measles back in Mama's room and couldn't go in the front part of the house, which was full of people standing in the hall, in the dining room, and in our bedroom. Mama said, "I didn't think we'd lived here long enough to know that many people."

Little Boy was buried in the Big Spring cemetery and Mama broke down only when she had to leave the gravesite.

Ann: I was not quite six years old when Little Boy died. Somehow the phrase "six weeks" had just come into my vocabulary and I thought for the longest time that Little Boy would come back in six weeks. I didn't know just how long six weeks was, but I was sure he would be back then. For some months Papa took Mama and me out to the cemetery every Sunday afternoon. I remember Mama sitting there by the grave, crying, while I wandered around trying to find some straggly wild flowers to put on his grave. That was pretty heavy for a six-year old.

We moved from Big Spring in about three years, but Howard later had a permanent marker put on Little Boy's grave and a curb made around the lot, and since that time, Papa, Mama, Ida Rule, and Fred have been buried there.

Ann: Mama used to tell us we were lucky that Papa went first, because if she had gone first Papa would have given us no peace until somebody took him from Lubbock to Big Spring so he could have visited her grave every week. She was right about Papa that time, too.

The old table-model Victrola had gone kaflooey and we had a portable, wind-up record player purchased by one of the big brothers. Mama told us that we would never again like the records we were playing during this sad time: *"Sonny Boy," "Carolina Moon,"* and *"The Parade of the Wooden Soldiers"* to name some of them. She was right. Ann tells me of a time three or four years later when Mama came into the room where *"The Parade of the Wooden Soldiers"* was heard on the radio and, crying, said, "Why don't you turn off that piece of music that you know upsets me so much?"

On Sunday, two days after Little Boy's funeral, most of us went to church services in the gym-auditorium of the high school across the street. We were a fraction of our former group, with the three younger girls still sick with the measles and Little Boy no longer with us. Mama didn't join in the congregational singing. In fact, Mama never sang in church again after Little Boy died.

CHAPTER 17

MISS IDA AGAIN

The day after Little Boy's funeral Mama began serving meals to the boarders again, but the fun had gone out of it for her. Mama soon let her boarders go; many of the school teachers were leaving for the summer anyway, and the oil boom had leveled off.

Miss Lytle's plans for the summer were to go to Arizona to visit her brother's family in Phoenix and to go to college in Flagstaff in the latter part of summer. She said to Mama, "Mrs. Duff, I surely wish you could go with me."

"Much as I'd like to, I just can't go, but how about one of my girls goin' with you?" Mama answered.

Miss Lytle allowed as how that would be fine with her. I don't remember whether I volunteered or Mama volunteered me, but I was the one chosen to go.

Papa didn't think I should go—we couldn't afford it. Mama said, "It won't cost much," and Papa replied, "It'll cost what it would take to paper their room you want papered."

Mama answered, "Seein' some of the world will be better for her than paperin' their room."

Mama's plan was for me to get a job as a "mother's helper" when I got to Arizona. Her advice was, "Don't you be any expense to Miss Lytle, you hear? When you get a job, don't stand around waitin' to be told everything to do, look for things that need doin'. And if any man tries anything funny with you,

you walk out and go to the YWCA."

Miss Lytle and I visited her brother and his wife who lived in a lovely home on a desert acreage across a big irrigation canal from the more settled part of Phoenix. In 1929 Phoenix wasn't the city it is today. Mr. Lytle was in the real estate business, determined to keep his few acres in its natural desert state because he thought in years to come a desert environment would be a rare phenomenon. At any rate, I was out in the boonies without any idea about how to get to town to look for a job, and never did need to find out if Phoenix had a YWCA.

After a week or so, Miss Lytle drove me to a spot near Prescott for a meeting with my cousin Noel Pegues (about Fred's age). Noel took me back with her to the company town of Clarksdale where she worked in the company office and supported her mother, Mama's sister, my Aunt Jessie. The whole visit was arranged by mail by Mama. After a delightful visit with Aunt Jessie and Noel, with plenty of time for swimming and reading, I met Miss Lytle at the same spot near Prescott and went with her to Flagstaff where she went to college for the second term of summer school.

Miss Lytle and I stayed in a rustic housing complex provided for summer students, and ate at least one meal a day in the cafeteria. I kept the cabin clean and did our washing on a rubboard in the community wash and bath house, and read Zane Grey novels checked out of the college library. One weekend we went to Grand Canyon, another up on San Francisco Peak where we returned after dark in order that we could visit Lowell Observatory. Another Sunday we went on an outing in Oak Creek Canyon (I had just read Zane Grey's *Call of the Canyon*, which is set there.) and by chance ran into Noel Pegues and some of her friends who had driven up from Clarksdale. It was the last time I ever saw Noel, who died about ten years later.

A letter from Mama told me that Mr. and Mrs. Bob Bow and their sons, Robert and Jimmy (our neighbors in Big Spring), were on a vacation in California where they had been to visit Mr. Bow's relatives, one of whom was Clara Bow, the "It Girl" of movie fame. Mama wrote that they would be returning via Phoenix and she instructed me to take the train to Phoenix where they would give me a ride home, but "Don't be any more expense to Miss Lytle."

I said to Miss Lytle, "I don't know how she expects me to get a ticket. I don't have a solitary nickel."

Miss Lytle was quick to say, "I'll buy your ticket."

So at age fourteen I rode the train all night (I think it went from Flagstaff to Kingman or Needles and then back to Phoenix) and stepped off the train about seven-thirty in the morning to find the Bow family had just driven up and were waiting for me. We left immediately for the two or three day trip back to Big Spring.

When I think of Mama's arranging all of that via mail, I marvel that it all worked out. I asked her years later what would have happened to me if the Bows had been delayed, and she said, "Well, they weren't. The Lord do provide, and that's the p.o.d. truth."

Mama did send Miss Lytle the cost of my train ticket.

It isn't as if Mama had nothing else on her mind. Howard had left on June 1st to go to Annapolis for his final physical examination. He milked the cow that morning (the last time he has ever milked a cow), and the man who had bought her from the folks came and picked her up before nightfall. We never again had a cow.

Howard: I still have the telegram of congratulations that Mama sent me when she learned that I had passed my physical exam and had been admitted to the Naval Academy. That had been touch-and-go because of a heart problem. I had so little confidence in passing (the exams were given at the Academy in those days) that I had left my hundred dollars in travelers' checks for uniform deposit in my hotel room and had to hustle to get them.

I had borrowed the hundred dollars from John Millsap in Sweetwater. In a time when the usual rate of interest was four percent, I had to pay him ten percent, compounded annually. Fred paid the interest for me the first year, but when I graduated from the Academy I owed Mr. Millsap a hundred and forty dollars, which I soon paid off. Another thing that worried me: I was doubtful also that the incomplete orthodontia in my mouth would be acceptable. When I got out of the dentist's chair and saw his "Dentally Qualified" written down, I knew I was IN.

To add to Mama's worries, Papa was very ill during that summer. Mama took him to the doctor who had looked after Little Boy, and he said Papa needed gallbladder surgery, but he wouldn't operate on him because Papa was too old and too fat.

Ann: Papa didn't want to have the operation because that doctor said he couldn't expect to live more than six years even after the operation. I heard Mama cry, "Give me that much time. You've got to help me raise these children."

Papa was taken to Abilene and the operation was performed there. Papa was dangerously ill. Mama stayed in a room near the hospital and spent long hours by his bedside. One night the surgeon made a special trip to the hospital to see Papa in the middle of the night, and Mama always figured Papa came close to death that night, but they didn't let her know of it. He recovered enough to come back to Big Spring and spend his recuperation period in the front bedroom at home.

While Mama and Papa were in Abilene, a young couple, Isham and his wife, stayed in Mama's big room. They had a new baby that summer and the baby cried *all* the time, greatly disturbing Papa in the front bedroom. Mama, with her wealth of expertise in looking after small babies, diagnosed the problem as hunger. The young mother was breast feeding the baby and refused to give it a supplemental feeding. Mama finally talked Isham into taking his exhausted wife to the picture show on Saturday night while Mama looked after the baby. As soon as the parents were out the door, Mama gave the baby a bottle, which he took with gusto, and then he went sound asleep and slept all night. The young mother was so hurt she wept saying, "Now anybody can look after my baby. I liked it when I was the only one who could satisfy him."

It took her some time to acknowledge that the good night's sleep she had that night enabled her to make milk enough so that she could breast-feed the baby for some time.

By the time I returned from Arizona near the end of summer, Papa was almost fully recovered and the young family were in their own home. Mama had thought she never wanted to see the Morris chair again because it reminded her so painfully of Little Boy's death, but she told me, "That was just foolishness on my part. YaPapa needed a comfortable chair while he was recoverin' and I just had the Morris chair fixed up for him so he could get some use out of it." And the old chair was a comfortable part of Mama's household for the rest of her life, and is now in the home of her grandson, Berry Noel, Jr.

For the little time I was there in that summer I remember the required nap or rest time after dinner dishes were washed, mid-afternoon baths, and then playing tennis on the two concrete courts on the high school campus across the way. Berry had left a racquet and balls for Elsie and me, and although I never did become an experienced player or give Helen Wills any cause to worry, tennis was a source of enjoyment for me all the years we lived in Big Spring.

After working hours, young professional and business men came to play, and if the courts were full, they said to a couple of inept, clumsy girls, "I'll take the winner of this game." They learned not to say of this "set" because we might drag the set out indefinitely. The winner of our game wasn't about to play those young men, or challenge the winner of their set, so we learned to get to the courts and do our playing in the middle of the hot afternoons. One of those young men whose tennis playing scared the bejabbers out of us was Curtis Bishop, who, if I remember correctly, was a state champion both in high school and the University of Texas. He worked on the local newspaper in the summertime and would later become the author of many published books.

In the summertime, when I was at home, I was supposed to listen for the whistle of a train that passed through town about 11:40, and that was my signal to go in and make the daily bread, cornbread, that is. We might "make" cornbread or battercakes (our name for hotcakes or pancakes), but we "fixed" breakfast, dinner and supper. "Fix" in various forms was a well-used work in our vernacular: "I'm fixin' to study," "Are you fixin' to go to work?" or even, "I'm fixin' to fix dinner." When I moved away from the scenes of my youth, I missed the utility of "fix" and I never have become accustomed to "making" breakfast, lunch or dinner.

We washed and dried dishes by the carload while we argued long and seriously about the possibility of inventing a mechanical dishwasher or dishdryer. The discussion continued over the years between any two sisters washing and drying dishes, and we finally reached a considered and erudite consensus that an automatic dishwasher was not feasible—shortly before the electric dishwashers appeared on the market.

Our dishwashing sessions often degenerated into loud arguments between the two or three sisters doing the job until, on many Sunday afternoons, both in Big Spring and later in Lubbock, Mama said, "You girls just hush your mouths. If you can't do those dishes quietly, leave 'em alone and I'll do them, but Sunday afternoon is the only time YaPapa and I have to rest, and how can we rest with that hojang goin' on?" That would shut us down for the afternoon, at least.

While we swatted flies, we peeled peaches and tomatoes on the screened back porch that was hotter'n blue blazes. Mama canned some of the peaches, but many of the ripe ones became her delicious jam. She sold many quarts of chili sauce and chow chow to our neighbors. Years later I tried making chili sauce from her recipe which included the direction: "Boil until thick." By the time I had boiled away most of the juice from those ripe tomatoes, three hours had passed, and I wondered how many, many hours Mama had spent "boiling off the juice," whereas I found out I could pour it off and save hours of time.

Mama didn't can tomatoes by themselves. "They're just too hard to keep." I don't know what experience had produced that attitude, but she told me about it when I mentioned my efforts at canning tomatoes when I was first married. I'm glad she didn't tell me sooner, because, not knowing any better, I found tomatoes the simplest and easiest fruit to can.

Years later, when Ida Rule lived with me, we gathered a few green tomatoes ahead of an early Wyoming winter. Now, Ida Rule purely loved chow chow, and we tried every recipe for green relish that we could find, but none of them produced the taste of Mama's chow chow, so we wrote Mama for her recipe. She sent a page torn from her old, old cookbook, and in her handwriting she begins, "Silver and gold have I none to leave to my children, so I leave them my recipe for chow chow." It begins with "1 bu. Green tomatoes" and among other ingredients includes a "10¢ box of pickling spice." I never did gather a bushel of green tomatoes, and I never saw a box of pickling spice for ten cents, so I never did try to make Mama's chow chow. Elsie, as well as Ann's daughter, Judy, had a recipe that duplicated the taste of Mama's chow chow as we remembered it.

In 1929 Berry worked in Monroe for several months, but in September he came to Big Spring and worked as night clerk at the Douglas Hotel until the next June. He worked from 7:00 P. M. To 7:00 A.M. for one hundred dollars a month. He tells me he got in a lot of tennis playing during his off hours. As they had been in Sweetwater, the girls in the family were back in the position of hearing the high school girls say to us *"That* good-lookin' fella is *your* bro-ther?" and wondering if they wanted to be our friends because of our brothers.

Nevertheless Elsie and I did have lots of friends, good-lookin' brothers notwithstanding or because of. We were in the H.I.K.E. Club whose members went hiking nearly every Saturday morning on the rocky hillsides all around Big Spring. Mama let me and Elsie go only if we promised to go to Sunday School and church without any argument. "If you can get up that early on Saturday, I presume you will get up early enough to go to Sunday School with no argument." When Mama presumed something, you'd better believe it would come to pass.

We were always accompanied by Miss Kitty Wingo or Miss Georgia Kirk Davis, or both. Those high school teachers deserved a special reward for the extra hours they spent with us, but they probably didn't even receive as much salary as the male teachers did.

In a time when females seldom wore pants, Elsie and I had hand-me-down (from Berry) corduroy boot pants to wear on the hikes, and Berry bought each of us high top lace boots at five dollars a pair, which certainly made hiking easier for us.

By the time we graduated, beach pajamas had become stylish, but they were very wide-bottomed, dressy pants, impractical for hiking.

Mama let Elsie and me give parties at the house. Mama made one of her large, especially delicious banana cakes, and the younger kids of the family were highly indignant that the slumber party consumed every crumb of it, along with all the milk in the house.

We didn't have enough milk left for that many breakfasts, so two or three of the girls volunteered to take the one car parked in front of the house to the store and pick up some milk. They did, only they didn't go to the store. They picked the milk up from someone's front porch and just forgot to mention that little detail until years later. I thought Mama was going to spank us grown women when she heard us laughing about that milk and where they got it.

I remember all of those girls with affection, but three of them, Pauline Melton, Dorothy Vandagriff and Jennie Dorinne Rogers, discovered that the first names of their mothers were respectively, Cora, Dora and Flora. The sound-alikes were just too good to resist and they, and their friends, began to call those mothers "Miss Cora," "Miss Dora," and "Miss Flora." Since I felt left out, they began to call Mama "Miss Ida" and the once-familiar name became familiar again. I haven't been in touch with Jennie Dorinne since my college days, but Pauline and Dorothy have been near and dear to the family all these years, and Mama always seemed to relish hearing "Miss Ida" from our friends.

She was Miss Ida again.

CHAPTER 18

MRS. DUFF TOOK CARE OF HER OWN

During the winter of our last year in Big Spring, Papa's sister, our Aunt Willie, and her family moved to our community from Louisiana. I recently asked my cousin Catherine Murphy to tell me of their move to Big Spring.

Catherine Murphy Thomas: Coming to Big Spring was like coming into paradise. Aunt Ida had the place they'd found for us clean and furnished. Uncle Berry brought all kinds of things from Winn Produce—goodies that we hadn't had in ages, and that's where we started our climb up from the hard times we'd been having.

After being in school for awhile there, I had a study hall the last period. Someone told me if your schedule was like that, you could go home, and so I did. After about a week of this I was called to Mr. Gentry's office and was going to be expelled for a week. My mother was fit to be tied and was going to the school to tell Mr. Gentry off. Aunt Ida said, "No, Willie, you are too angry, and since I know Mr. Gentry better, I'll go."

So she took me with her and went. I don't think my own mother could have been angrier. Aunt Ida gave him a piece of her mind. She told him I was her niece, I was new there and did not do it intentionally. It ended up that I got an apology from Mr. Gentry and was not counted absent for any days and the slate was wiped clean.

Years later, when I was making George Gentry's picture for

Mrs. Duff Took Care of Her Own

the annual, we talked of that incident and laughed over it.
He said, "Yes, Mrs. Duff sure took care of her own."

I have many memories of incidents when Mama took care of her own.

Elsie and I were both sophomores in high school our first year in Big Spring. W.C. Blankenship, the Superintendent of Schools, and George Gentry, the principal of high school, were both graduates of Baylor University and quite active members of the First Baptist Church. They had such a proclivity for hiring other Baylor graduates as teachers—Mr. Coffey and Mr. Matthews, to name a couple of them—that, according to Mama, the school board told them to quit hiring so many Baptists.

They didn't seem to push the Baptist beliefs that I noticed. We didn't have daily prayer in schools, and we didn't have scripture readings. When Miss Clara Cox, our teacher of senior English, quoted a halfway familiar phrase and said, "Where do we find that in literature?" by pre-arrangement half the class would say, "The Bible," and the other half would say, "Shakespeare," and one or the other was usually right.

Elsie and I both took second-year Latin our first year in Big Spring, and Elsie didn't like it at all. She wanted to drop the course, but Mr. Gentry, wouldn't let her. Mama realized that to make Elsie stay in the course she disliked so thoroughly might sour her on the school year completely, so she went to see Mr. Gentry, the first of many visits Mama had with him. As Mr. Gentry extolled the advantages of having a knowledge of Latin, he asked Mama (condescendingly, Mama thought), "Mrs. Duff, how many years of Latin did you have?"

Mama was pleased to reply, "Four years. How many did you have?"

He confessed ruefully that he'd only had two years of Latin and eventually he consented to let Elsie drop the course.

I asked Mama what she'd learned in her four years of Latin

that I didn't learn in my two years of Latin. "Well," she told me, "I read Cicero's *Orations* and Virgil's *Aeneid*, among other things, and I learned a great poem."

She proceeded to recite the poem: "Boyibus kissibus girla galorum/Girla she likeibus, wanta somorum/Papibus seeibus breach of decorum/Kickibus boyibus out of the doorum."

So that's what they learned in the good old days.

During Christmas vacation of our first year in Big Spring I wanted to go to Sweetwater so much in spite of a pain in the roof of my mouth that Mama let me go against her better judgment. Mama told me to call Fred if the pain worsened. It did, and Fred told me to go to his friend Russell Wimberly and tell him to send Fred the bill. Well, sure 'nuf, the dentist pulled a front tooth and made a bridge to replace it, and it was the bill for that major job that Fred had to pay, probably half a month's salary.

Mama said, "And you were about the *only* one of the children who had good teeth!" If Mama had been there, she'd probably have found some less expensive treatment for me.

Howard returned from one of his many trips to the orthodontist in Abilene, mad as all git out. He had a very good friend in Sweetwater—they'd been close friends and classmates for several years—and that fellow told Howard his father, a successful businessman in Sweetwater, had forbidden him to be friends with Howard, saying, "He's nothing but a tramp, spends all his time hitchhiking on the road." I can imagine Mama as mad as a wet hen. I don't know whether she made a special trip to Sweetwater for this specific purpose, but the next time she was in Sweetwater she made it a point to call at the father's place of business. She didn't tell me how the first part of their conversation went, but the father said, "Well, you know, Mrs. Duff, that's why we all work so hard—to have some money to leave to our children."

Mama replied, "Mr. So and So, I'd rather (and Mama always used a very broad "A" in her "rathers") leave my children a good education and a good character than all the money in the world."

Howard tells me today that this incident had no effect on the friendship between the two young men and they remained good friends for life.

Mama wanted Lydia Ann to start to first grade (there was no kindergarten in Big Spring) in the fall after her sixth birthday, but she didn't want to pay the four dollars a month tuition for the whole year. "I presume any child of mine—and particularly Lydia Ann—should be able to accomplish in half a year what it takes ordinary children a year to accomplish." So Lydia Ann started to first grade after Christmas and did make the whole year's curriculum in half a year, with no difficulty. Mama always knew Lydia Ann was pretty bright. She told Ann, "You don't need to learn to cook. You're too smart to have to cook."

Ida Rule was operated on that year for appendicitis. Dr. Dillard diagnosed the appendicitis, but a surgeon performed the operation, and for once, Mama wasn't in the operating room. Later Dr. Dillard told Mama, "Her appendix wasn't in the place where it should have been. If you think I wasn't sweating it out! The surgeon had to make a second, or central incision, and follow her intestines to find her appendix up high and in back of the center part of her abdomen. But her symptoms all came from the normal place for the appendix to be. Why, I'd even begun to wonder if she had an appendix."

Mama's family never did have simple illnesses.

In June of 1930 Berry quit his job at the Douglas Hotel, bought a 1926 Model T Ford for seventy-five dollars, and went to Sweetwater to pick up his friend Ray Booth before they left for Boulder, Colorado, where they attended the University of

Colorado for the summer session.

That same summer I went to the resort community of Laporte on Galveston Bay via another complicated trip arranged by Mama. Mama had spent some time in Dallas when she had taken Ida Rule to the specialist there. She had stayed in an efficiency unit of a lovely apartment house owned and operated by Aunt Daisy's sons, Williams and James Tardy. In Dallas Mama had renewed her old friendship with her girlhood friend "Miss Lenore" Young McConnell, whose husband, Dr. F. M. McConnell, was editor of the *Baptist Standard*. The McConnell's daughter, Manon, using the pseudonym Gloria Young, was editor of the children's page of the *Standard*, as well as a good right-hand to Dr. McConnell. Manon wanted to vacation down on the Gulf Coast, and of course, Mama suggested that she needed a Duff girl along to help her with her two young children.

Mama arranged for me to get from Big Spring to Colorado City, where Fred (who had recently purchased a Plymouth sedan) drove over from Sweetwater during his lunch hour to get me.

Fred and I drove the thirty or so miles from Colorado City to Sweetwater without saying a word to each other. The next morning he picked me up at my friend's house and took me over to the apartment he shared with some other young men and left me there to clean the place. After work, he, two other young men and I drove to Dallas. In the middle of the night he let me out at the big apartment house run by William Tardy, and I found the apartment where Mama was staying and spent the rest of the night. Early the next morning Fred appeared with still another young man added to his group, and we drove to Houston. There he let me out at the home of Manon's cousin, Mr. Young, and his wife, saying, "If they don't offer you supper, drink lots of water to fill up."

I drank lots of water.

After I spent a week with these nice strangers, Manon, who was also really a stranger to me, known only through Mama, arrived with her children, Gloria and Buddy, and all of us—the Young cousin and his wife, Manon and her children, and I—drove to Laporte where we spent a pleasant couple of weeks on Galveston Bay. Manon let me write a fiction story for children for the *Standard* but she said it would have to be published under the name of Gloria Young. The only resemblance between what I wrote in longhand and what was published was that the heroine's name was Rosemary.

We awakened one morning to find Fred dozing on the front seat of his car parked in front of the cottage, just champin' at the bit to get back to Sweetwater. He had been on a tour through the South. He and I were in Sweetwater by late afternoon, a hard day's drive in any conditions, but especially so with the roads as they were in 1930.

While I lingered in Sweetwater, I saw Berry, who had brought his friend Ray Booth back to Sweetwater from Colorado, and I arranged to ride in the Model T back to Big Spring to finish out the summer there. That fall Berry went to work as night clerk at the Settles Hotel, Big Spring's seven-story skyscraper.

The great stock market crash had occurred in October of 1929, but it had little immediate effect on our lives. By the end of 1930 we blamed our lack of money on "the Depression," and we blithely explained why we had no plans for college with, "Haven't you heard about the depression?" as if we'd have all the money in the world if it weren't for the depression.

My memories of our last three years in Big Spring have little to do with the financial condition of the country, however. Instead, they are a collage of household chores, and church, school, and social activities.

The First Baptist Church had built a beautiful new building after the old one burned, and I have happy memories of my Sunday School and BYPU activities, including weekday picnics and Friday night volleyball games in the city park. Mama cautioned Elsie and me with lectures about staying close with the group, saying, "don't you be disappearin' into the dark, like some young people do. Those BYPU leaders have enough to worry about without worrying' where a couple of nincompoops have strayed off to, you hear?"

R. E. Day was pastor of the church the last few years we were in Big Spring, and Berry often brought the Days' beautiful college-age daughter to church "after the collection plate was passed" as Brother Day was quick to tease them. The most memorable revival held while we were there had as song leader B. B. McKinney, writer of so many well-used hymns in our hymnals today, and B. H. Carroll as evangelist, both of them guests for a meal in our home.

Beryl, Ida Rule, and Lydia Ann were growing up along their own paths during these years. Sometimes it seems that Beryl and I were a generation apart instead of three years. For instance, Beryl never did wear long black stockings or long union suits, and I never did wear ankle socks. There was a rule against high school girls wearing those new-fangled ankle socks. Melva Gene Handley was only fifteen years old when she graduated with our class, so when she entered Big Spring High School at the age of eleven or twelve, she was still wearing her childhood ankle socks. Mama said, "Poor Mr. Gentry. He had to explain to that child that she couldn't wear them in high school."

My path didn't cross the paths of the younger girls very often. They got to go to cartoon shows on Saturday mornings (Beryl and Lydia Ann were even elected Queen Minnie Mouse on separate occasions.), and I never even went to a Saturday morning cartoon show.

As the three girls continued in school, Mama continued her interest in PTA, and Beryl remembers Mama was a district officer at this time. Mama was often at the school on some sort of PTA business, and with her eyeglasses that pinched onto her nose when she pulled the small chain that held them to a pin on her lapel, she was a memorable sight. Beryl thinks it was while Mama was an officer of the PTA at this time that the organization was instrumental in getting the law passed that required diphtheria vaccinations before a child could enter school.

Mr. Blankenship was supposed to teach Beryl's fifth grade Texas History from a cartoon book of Texas history (she seemed surprised that I wasn't familiar with such a book as she told me it was used for years), but his administrative duties kept him from showing up in the classroom most of the time.

Mama had said we couldn't have a radio in the house until the last child had graduated from school, but soon after Elsie and I graduated, Fred brought a nice, small-sized walnut cabinet model Brunswick radio to the house, and like the fictional Kitty Foyle, Beryl and Ida Rule were members of our first generation that learned to study and listen to the radio at the same time. We had listened to the radios at our friends' homes, hurrying to someone's radio every night at ten o'clock to hear Herman Waldman's band play "Lazy River" from station WOAI in San Antonio. Now that we had a radio in the house, we hoped to be able to listen to Bing Crosby, but his time conflicted with Mama's favorite show, "Amos 'n' Andy." Of course there was no argument, and we usually just got to hear Bing sing only the opening and closing lines of *"When the Blue of the Night Meets the Gold of the Day."*

Beryl went to the seventh grade in the basement of the high school building and graduated from seventh grade in 1932 as valedictorian of her class. Her valedictory speech ended:

"Climb ever onward, upward. And climb and climb and climb."

That must have inspired Billy Jo Riggs, who made that graduation night so memorable.

The Riggs family were our good neighbors across Runnells Street. Dorothy Belle Riggs was in Beryl's class, and Mama and Mrs. Riggs sat together on the main floor of the gym-auditorium, and the Riggs boys, Durwood and Jack, were up in the side balcony supposedly keeping an eye on Billy Jo, the little three-year-old daughter of the Riggs clan. During the program Mama noticed that little Billy Jo was climbing around on the iron safety railings of the balcony, standing on the lower pipe and leaning over the upper railing. Billy Jo decided to take Beryl's advice literally and climb and climb and climb.

Mama began waving at Billy Jo to get down, but she just waved back at Mama and started lying down in the lower pipe. Both Mama's arms were waving in the air by this time, trying to attract the boys' attention, and Mrs. Riggs started to the back of the auditorium to go upstairs and get the child.

By this time Billy Sunday could have been preaching and an angel choir could have been singing "The Hallelujah Chorus" and no one would have paid attention to anything but Mama and that child. Finally, at a moment of quiet in the program, Mama called out, "Durwood, get that child back away from the edge before she falls." He did, Mrs. Riggs arrived to bring the child downstairs, and the program went on, I understand, but all I remember is Mama in her dignified blue serge suit and hat, waving her arms, and Billy Jo waving back.

My most vivid memory of never-ending chores in Big Spring is standing by the ironing board, running that heavy electric iron over countless starched garments, tablecloths and napkins that dried out too fast in the summer heat. Elsie and I were supposed to do equal amounts of ironing, timewise (to use today's word), but although I was pokey slow because I thought I had to keep the music going by winding the phonograph and by keeping the records turned and changed all the time I was ironing, I could do a lot more family ironing during my hour or two than Elsie did. Mama was the first to comment, "I"ll declah, Elsie spends her whole time doin' just her own clothes. They do look mighty nice, but she sure 'nuf isn't doin' her share."

Elsie was a very meticulous dresser and always looked nice. She had taken home economics in school and besides being a good cook she was an excellent seamstress, making lovely dresses for herself. Beryl remembers watching Elsie spend hours ironing her own clothes, particularly when Elsie was getting ready for a date.

It was the painstaking care that Elsie gave her clothes one Saturday in November of 1930 that gave Mama the idea that Elsie had run away to get married. I don't know how they managed it, but Mama and Papa found her in a hotel in Midland with the young man she had been dating for some time. Since Elsie wasn't of legal age to marry, Mama threatened to have the marriage annulled if she didn't come home and finish her senior year of high school.

Under protest, Elsie returned, and Mama prevailed on Mr. Bedicheck, the editor of the local paper, to refrain from printing the notice of the license. He agreed, saying, "Why, I know that nice girl. She's on the debate team with Jake Pickle. I won't print it until you give the word, Mrs. Duff."

Elsie was allowed to date Jimmy within what Mama thought were reasonable limits. Fred came from Sweetwater one weekend and he said to me as he left, "Now, Manie, you let me know if you think Elsie is seeing too much of that f-f-fella. I think I know more about what is b-b-best for her than Mama and Papa do."

But how'd *I* know what was too much?

I came home on a Sunday afternoon in the late springtime to find Mama in tears, saying, "Well, she's gone." I'm afraid I was no big consolation to her.

Elsie had had her eighteenth birthday in December, and since married students were not allowed to go to school in those days, she dropped out of school. She and Jimmy took a room in a house between our house and town. Elsie and I had several classes together, so I, following Mama's instructions, told Mama when we had a theme, book report, or any assignment due, and Mama prepared the assignment for Elsie, and I took them to class and turned them in for Elsie. Elsie got her diploma when we graduated in May, but it should have had Mama's name on it.

On a certain morning during those weeks, Mama called to me from the backyard as I was getting ready to rush to school before the tardy bell rang. I found Mama at the bottom of the high steps at the back of the house where she had slipped and fallen. She was in considerable pain with a twisted ankle. I helped her into the house, then she insisted I go on to school before I was late. I was already late and when I went into Mr. Gentry's office, I said, "I need an excuse for being tardy."

He jokingly said, " What's the matter? Can't you think of one yourself?"

I was so upset by having seen Mama in pain that I burst into tears and said, "My mother fell down the stairs and hurt herself just as I was ready to come to school and I had to help her. That's why I'm late."

He was promptly contrite and expressed concern about Mama, and when he had sent me to class he walked over to the house to see if he could help Mama in any way.

After we no longer had a cow, Mama and Papa did away with the little barn on the back alley and had the garage moved from the side street to the place of the barn in the alley. Then they had a little store building built where the garage had been, facing the side street and the back of the schools. A couple of men had asked them to build this place of business because those men wanted to open a grocery store in the neighborhood. Mama and Papa must not have required the tenants to sign a lease, because after just a couple or three months those men moved their stock to another building in the neighborhood.

This left Mama with a nice store building right in her own backyard, so of course, being Mama, she opened her own grocery store, and being Mama, she installed a couple of long tables with benches in the back of the store and served lunches there to her family and anyone else, mostly schoolteachers who wanted to eat at school. The school teacher I remember best was Frances Melton, the daughter of "Miss Cora" of the "Cora, Dora, and Flora" trio.

All of us took turns in helping out in the store, but Berry more than the rest of us. He tells me that in the spring of 1932 some of the teachers in high school and junior high got up a petition to get Mama to run for the school board. They brought it to her at the store, but Mama refused, saying, "No. All my life I've made people believe I was a respectable woman. If you get me in politics they will find out what a reprobate and scoundrel I really am."

Mama used that as an example of the difference between *knowledge* and *faith*. The petitioners had faith in what she was, and she had knowledge of what she was.

Beryl and I both have recollections of Berry trying to boss all of us around during these few years. He was determined he was going to make all of us eat liver and spinach happily.

Elsie just absolutely refused to do so. I ate it, but not happily. Beryl stuck her spinach in her biscuit, then took it out in the backyard and threw it at the wall of the store building when Berry was in the store.

During those noisy interludes, Mama "kept the store" in the summer while Berry came in the house to eat, then Berry "kept the store" while Mama ate in peace and quiet with Papa when he came home at one o'clock. Nothin' dumb about Mama. She delighted in telling that she overheard me say at one time, "Mama isn't as dumb as she looks."

Besides being bossy, Berry was quite generous at times. He took me out on a country road and tried to teach me to fire a rifle. He became a member of the Book of the Month Club and shared the books with us. His copy of *Kristin Lavrensdatter* was the first adult novel I read that wasn't required in school.

The store was never a great money maker. The grocery part of the store had a credit business and the depression was really felt in our family when customers had trouble paying their bills. Berry ran in the house one day calling, "Hey, Mama, the neighbors paid their bill."

These good neighbors had had a run of bad luck. The father owned a string of cable tool rigs which he had been unable to put to work or to sell because the technology of the oil field was changing to rotary drilling. When he finally sold a rig or two, the mother of the family told Mama, "You were the only one of our creditors who didn't hound us for money."

Berry and Mama took $12.50 of that money and let me buy a new coat, the first brand new sto'bought coat I'd ever had. A beautiful taupe colored coat with beaver collar I'd received from Mary Noel had been irreparably scorched when a friend who'd borrowed it stood too near the gas heater. I was proud as all git out of my new brown tweed coat and wore it everywhere. While I was riding around in a car full of young people one rainy night, the rain poured in around the dashboard and soaked my lap, and the fine new coat shrank several inches in front, but it got worn by me for several years in spite of its uneven hemline.

Maybe one reason the store wasn't much of a money maker was that we not only got our school supplies from it, but the family used the groceries, particularly those that weren't selling very well. As part of a foods class, I had to prepare breakfast for my family. Saturday morning was the only time Mama and I figured we could get the family together at approximately the same time. She said, "I wish you could think of some way of using that can of fishflakes on the shelf. It's been there since we opened the store and is not apt to sell."

So one Saturday morning I fixed creamed fishflakes on popovers, and served a whole apple for fruit, the only time we ever had creamed fishflakes, or popovers, or a raw apple for breakfast. The rest of the family didn't let me forget that breakfast for a month of Sundays.

I had taken that home economics course in foods because, when I was a senior, I needed another course to fill out my schedule and Mama was still hopeful that I'd some day learn to cook, and besides that was about the only course in school I hadn't taken. I must have done well enough (Why not? I was a senior in a class of freshmen) because I was selected with two other girls to go to a state meet in home economics to be held in Lubbock. Since the school didn't provide transportation to such doings, at least for girls, brother Fred, at Mama's request, said we could use his car. He even brought it to Big Spring from Sweetwater.

The unpaved road up around Lamesa, between Big Spring and Lubbock, was such a quagmire that we couldn't go that way and we had to drive all the way to Roscoe, about ten miles from Sweetwater, where we let Fred out on the highway to hitchhike back home, then the teacher and we three girls drove to Lubbock via Snyder. In Lubbock the teacher and I stayed in the home of her brother and his family, and the other two girls stayed in homes opened by the hospitable people of Lubbock. It was a far, far cry from the bus and motel junkets provided by the school districts today.

In March of 1931, the Big Spring basketball team (boys, of course, we had no girls interscholastic teams) had gone to the state meet in Austin. To work up to that honored place, we played in Breckenridge, and I recall riding all the way to Breckenridge and back in a rumble seat (meant for two passengers) with three other students. The Breckenridge aunt of one of the members of our group welcomed about eight of us who dropped in unannounced and fed us a scrumptious chicken-fried steak dinner, again a far cry from today's excursions.

Some mother told Mama she didn't allow her daughter to go off on such trips, and Mama told me she said, "Why, Mrs. So and So, I trust my girls, don't you trust yours?"

When Mama told me she said that, it certainly kept me on my best behavior.

To get to Austin, some indulgent adult was found to drive a car full of girls down there, where we stayed about ten or twelve in a room in a big hotel, and we had a wonderful time. The Big Spring Steers lost the very first round (terribly overconfident) but that freed the boys to see the sights of Austin with us. That trip was the first time I ever saw the bluebonnets of Texas in bloom.

Mama was patient during all of this. We were supposed to be home by ten o'clock on school nights, eleven o'clock on Friday and Saturday nights. Mama and Papa had always gone to bed, but we had to let them know when we came in. We stood in the door between the kitchen and Mama's room, whispering over and over, "Mama, I'm home," a little louder each time, until we finally woke Mama.

"Why are you whispering?" she wanted to know. "So we

won't wake Papa," we replied loudly, thus completing the awakening of Papa.

As if that weren't enough, Mama said that sometimes after a particularly close game, we'd be so keyed up that even after we'd gone to sleep, we might let out a yell "loud enough to shake the rafters," according to Mama.

As I've said she was patient and didn't disown us, even though she may have been tempted to at times. One of the siblings received notice that he or she had a parcel or letter in the post office in Big Spring that must be signed for. Mama was downtown and decided to go to the post office to save her offspring the trip. The post office employee wouldn't let Mama have it, because he didn't know her and he didn't know if she was the mother of the addressee. Mama asked him, "Would you let Mr. Duff have it?"

"Oh, yes. I know Mr. Duff. He's in here often, so I would know he was their father."

Mama replied, "Well, let me tell you something, young man. I *know* they're my children, and he *thinks* they're his."

The postal employee answered, "Here, Mrs. Duff, you take it."

Yes, Mama certainly took care of her own.

CHAPTER 19

WE NEED TO MOVE

For Howard's first Christmas furlough from the Naval Academy, he and four or five of his classmates from the southwest rented a car and drove night and day to spend as much leave at their homes as quickly and as inexpensively as possible. This would be their practice for every furlough. On that first Christmas furlough, Howard properly impressed everyone with his midshipman's uniform and elegant social graces. Mama said, "All of my children know the right and proper thing to do. The others just don't put it into practice. I'm just glad that place has taught him to control that temper."

While Berry worked in Big Spring he stayed in the front bedroom and split his paycheck with Mama. Among his other jobs he did a little substitute teaching in Big Spring and Coahoma. Ann tells of him coming in griping about the dumb kids not knowing enough to leave out the comma when "and" was used before the last item in a series. "I hadn't started to school yet, and I thought he certainly was smart to know about that."

One May, Berry and Ben Anthony, another young man about town, were hired to drive a couple of cars to California by some man. They were to receive their expenses and a return bus ticket, but the employer said, "Thanks, fellows. Sorry I don't have any money to pay you. You're on your own now."

Berry: We had about a buck between us and I wouldn't have

dared wire the folks for help. We managed to get a five-gallon gasoline can, put our clothes in it and start walking toward Texas. Drivers stopped to give us a lift to our car "down the road," and only one of those drivers got mad when he found out our car was down the road in Texas. We made it back to Big Spring in record time, to find that Mama was instigating another trip for me as driver of a couple of young women who were going to the Great Lakes states and on to the East Coast.

When I got to New York City I visited Aunt Mary, Mama's youngest sister, who put me up in a room near her place of residence, and then she gave me a crash tour of New York City, including some of the theatrical offerings. I came back by Annapolis and Howard's classmates found a suitable uniform for me and taught me who, when, and how to salute and I stayed with Howard for a couple of nights before driving home with him and his classmates when they came to Texas for late summer.

When he got to Big Spring that summer, Howard tells me that we, Elsie and I or Berry and I, feeling sorry for him because his girlfriend was back in Sweetwater, fixed him up with a blind date with our friend Pauline Melton. They must have hit it off very well because Howard and Pauline have celebrated their sixtieth wedding anniversary.

During these years in Big Spring Mama decided she wanted to learn to drive a car, and Papa took her out on a country road to let her have a go at it. She reported, "I got along fine. We met three cars. One made a U-turn and went back the way it came, the second turned into a side road, and the third headed for the ditch, so I had no trouble at all in meetin' cars."

However, she did very little driving while we lived in Big Spring.

After our home economics trip to Lubbock Fred let me keep his car, a Plymouth sedan he had purchased in the past year, to use as my own in Big Spring for the last two or three weeks of school as my graduation present.

Few young people had easy access to a car in those days. Ted Phillips and Cecil Reed had a topless Model-T two-seater they had painted silver, giving it the name of "Silver Streak," and Pauline and Frances Melton had a Model-A Ford sedan, but after all, Frances was a teacher. Zillah Mae and Steve Ford had a coupe at their disposal, but it was a family car. There were no school buses and no parking problems because most of the students walked to school, although Big Spring, with a population count of 13,731 in the 1930 census, sprawled over a considerable area.

The Edwards youngsters got to bring their family car to school every day! They lived out in the country and had a family whose ages covered a span of years nearly as long as our family's. Besides the Edwardses, there were several families whose children ranged in age from Beryl to Berry: the Drivers, the Pickles, the Pattersons and the Dubberlys, to name a few. Elizabeth Edwards was in charge of their family car after her older brother graduated, and she helped me learn to drive. I would sit next to her and hold the steering wheel, and she even let me drive it by myself for a short distance.

One afternoon Beryl and I got in Berry's Model-T coupe parked in front of the house and I took us on a ride we will neither one forget. I meant to go only around the block, but our neighborhood was in one of those areas that didn't have simple and neat blocks. Besides, I couldn't stop the darn thing.

For you young people out on a space station, a Model-T had three foot pedals: clutch, reverse, and brake. The gas was a lever on the steering wheel. I pushed the brake and clutch in as hard as I could and I'm told now that pushing the clutch *all* the way in put the motor in a lower gear, giving it more power. At any rate, it didn't slow down, jut kept right on ginning along.

Fortunately, this wasn't going on at a very fast rate of speed. I'd begun to think I was going to have to drive it until it ran out of gas, when I spied a small pile of construction gravel and ran into that to effectively stop the vehicle. I hate to admit it, but a couple of high school boys standing nearby drove us back to the front of the house and we left the Model-T sitting there, really none the worse for our escapade, but that was the first time and last time I ever drove a Model-T.

Fred prudently took me in his car out to a country road and coached me in how to drive, stop and start, and a few little necessary and handy techniques along those lines. Imagine the courage it must have taken for him to leave his first car with a little sister who had no experience in driving. Texas didn't require a driver's license until three or four years later.

My friends and I had a high old time with that car for a few weeks and returned it to Fred, still whole if a little worse for the wear. We called it "The Sun" because of a Hit-of-the-Week record of the time, "Here Comes the Sun." I found among my souvenirs a receipt from a filling station signed by Papa, "Happy Graduation." It is for "gas, 55¢." I said, "I didn't know gasoline was fifty-five cents a gallon back then." Then it dawned on me it was for five gallons at *eleven cents* a gallon. There is another collection of tickets charged to Papa for "gas for daughter" and several "tire repairs, 50¢." They total $10.61.

I also found an invitation to our graduation among those souvenirs. Mama had written under my name on my calling card, "Elsie Duff Lee," and Elsie received graduation gifts just the same as I did. I had been acting as go-between for Mama and Elsie, and Mama told me to ask her if she wasn't ever coming home again. Elsie said, "She told me I couldn't come home."

Mama said, "Oh, I meant she just couldn't come runnin'

home to Mama every time she and Jimmy had a fuss."

So Elsie did come to the house several times before she moved with Jimmy to Henderson, in East Texas. The oil boom in West Texas had dipped considerably but was just getting started up in East Texas. Jimmy's father, for whom Jimmy worked, was in the construction business and he moved that business to East Texas.

One of the graduation presents Elsie and I received was ten dollars each from Mr. Winn, Papa's boss, the first time I'd ever had ten dollars of my own. Elsie's was stolen from their room, but I put mine to good use when six of us friends and Miss Kitty Wingo again managed to get Fred's car and go to Carlsbad Caverns in New Mexico for a great overnight trip.

I talked and daydreamed of going to exclusive and expensive colleges in the East, but the nearest I came to getting serious about college was at the time a recruiter of Baylor-Belton, later known as Mary Hardin-Baylor, a Baptist college and academy for women at Belton, Texas, came to the store to talk to Mama and me. She offered a scholarship and a job and had it figured out that it would just cost me twelve dollars, fifty cents a month to go to Baylor-Belton. Mama still said we couldn't afford it.

The lady replied, "But Mrs. Duff, it must cost you that much just to feed her here at home."

Mama said, "You'd be surprised. It doesn't cost any twelve-fifty a month."

Pauline Melton went to Simmons University, later known as Hardin-Simmons, another Baptist school in Abilene, and Dorothy Vandagriff and her mother, Miss Dora, moved to Lubbock where Miss Dora ran a girls' boarding house (Lovell Hall) and Dorothy started to Texas Tech. A few other members of our graduating class left for college, but in those dark depression days it was not an easy thing to manage.

Things were as slow as molasses in January in the fall of 1931. I couldn't find any sort of job. Louise Hayes, one of my friends in our graduating class, took a job in a filling station, a daring and unusual, but practical, move for that time. Mama arranged for me to go back to school for an hour a day to take accounting, and she kept urging me to use my shorthand to go over and take down the tales of old Mr. Mac.

Mr. and Mrs. McKenze lived in a pleasant, old, white pioneer home next door to us. Their grandchildren were about the age of Ida Rule, and I had very little occasion to visit with the old couple, but Mama insisted the old gentleman was full of wonderful stories. He had driven a freight wagon ahead of the Texas and Pacific Railroad as it was being constructed across Texas, and Mama said he enjoyed talking of some of his early day experiences. Ever since I've been old enough to have good sense, I've felt like kicking myself for not having gone over there and getting some of his reminiscences down on paper.

Howard tells me I wrote him (Howard) that I did ask the old gentleman, but I think it must have been Mama who asked him. Anyway, Mr. Mac is supposed to have said, "There's no need to be writing anything about me. I was no different from any of the other damn fools. The only difference between me and the others out here was that I had the good sense not to get myself killed."

Mary Gene Dubberly, my classmate and good friend, and I did get jobs at a variety store for a couple of Saturdays. Late one Friday night Berry called me from a deep sleep to come to the phone, grumbling, "Why can't your friends learn to call you at a decent hour?"

My caller was Mary Gene, who asked me to tell our boss she couldn't be at work the next day. I understood her to say she was going with her parents to East Texas where her uncle had been killed in an accident. I expressed my sympathy and asked if there was anything I could do. She said, "No, there's nothing."

Early the next morning Mama and Berry rushed in from the store and waked me with, "Who was that who called you last night?"

When I told them what Gene had told me, they said, "You misunderstood her. It was *her* mother and father who were killed in an accident while they were on the way to the uncle's funeral."

Gene's little sister had been seriously injured and she never fully recovered before her death a few years later, leaving only Mary Gene and her older brother, Hugh, in the family. Hugh took over Mr. Dubberly's job as County Clerk of Howard County. When I visited with Gene later, she did tell me that I had misunderstood her.

I believe that was one of the worst tragedies that happened during my youth. Our classmate Loretta Jenkins had been killed a few years earlier when some young people were playing with an "unloaded gun," and her funeral and the Dubberly's funeral were the only funerals I had attended since Little Boy died. I suffered the loss of Little Boy again at each of those times.

The autumn months were not a safe time to travel at night in Texas. Fall was cotton pickin' time and often on the highways were unlighted wagons or poorly lighted trucks loaded with fresh-picked cotton on the way to the gins.

Fred brought Sina Peavey, the young lady he would marry, over to meet us, and she still married him anyway. As Mama visited with her, they were talking about changing times and changing words, and I heard Mama say, "Why, if my mother were to hear us talkin' now, she wouldn't have any idea what we were talkin' about when we mention Kleenex, Kotex and Cutex."

We Need to Move

In November of 1931 Mama called Fred and told him that she wanted to use his car for a long weekend; she wanted Papa to drive her and the four girls down to Longview. Mama's sisters were to be at Aunt Noel's for a reunion, and Mama said, "I'm proud of my girls and I want to show them off."

Fred didn't quibble. We did have a nice visit, the first time I'd been back to Longview since we moved. Aunt Noel had dishes of chocolate candy to disappear in such a hurry that even I was embarrassed.

Mary Noel wasn't at home, but she called from Dallas where she was attending Miss Hockaday's School. I rode Mary Noel's old bicycle down Methvin Street, where the abandoned tracks from the old streetcars I remembered from my much younger days, were still exposed. Aunt Noel now had a second bathroom in her home, a lollapalooza with the first colored fixtures I'd ever seen.

Elsie came to Longview from Henderson, but she didn't stay long. I overheard her tell Aunt Noel's black cook that the next day was her first wedding anniversary and she wanted to get back to her husband in Henderson. I've wondered how lonely she must have felt that she couldn't talk with anyone else about her first anniversary.

About January, Fred told us that he and Sina had married and for a long time we thought they were married in January. Later, they told me they had already planned to be married that weekend we went to Longview, and Fred went ahead and let us take his car while he borrowed someone else's car to fulfill the plans they had already made. They didn't tell us they were married that weekend in November because he didn't want Mama to feel bad about borrowing his car.

Sina had a fine little blonde boy who made all of us think of Little Boy. Dub was the first grandchild and he was a joy to all of us as he grew into boyhood and adulthood.

Papa lost his job with Winn Produce Company and Mama announced, "We've just got to move somewhere so these girls can go to college." She was in touch with Miss Dora in Lubbock, and she and Papa began to seek earnestly for a way to support the family in Lubbock.

While this was going on, Papa and Berry took a truck down to the Rio Grande Valley for a load of green beans, string beans to Texans. On the way back the old truck wouldn't make it up one of the hills down around Kerrville, and they had to unload most of that truckload of green beans, then drive the truck up the hill, and go back and carry those bushel baskets of green beans one by one up the hill and reload. They finally made it back to Big Spring where they sold the beans for two cents a pound. That's one of the family's most-often-told depression tales.

It was on this trip that Papa stopped in San Antonio to see an old friend. As long as I could remember, we always received a Christmas card every year from some woman none of us children knew. Mama always explained, "That's YaPapa's old girlfriend. She's sent a Christmas card every year since we got married." Papa walked in the place where she worked and she recognized him after nearly forty years.

That summer, Berry went to Sul Ross State Teachers College in Alpine, Texas, and Papa managed a retail produce store located on the main highway of Big Spring. Selling tomatoes at six cents a pound, I worked in that store, too, from seven to seven, six days a week, with an hour for lunch, when I trudged up the hill to the house in heat hotter'n a firecracker, all for three dollars a week. With my first week's salary I bought a pair of shoes for $2.98, the only time I ever paid a whole week's salary for a pair of shoes.

Papa became occupied with making arrangements for us to move and he left the management of that store to the owner.

One afternoon I trudged up the hill to the store, swelled up with anger and tears because the owner of the store had fired me for no reason, at least that is what I thought. Howard, home on summer leave from the Naval Academy, was in the store visiting with Mama and he took off to tell that old man a thing or two. He did go down there and nearly got into a fight but I didn't get the job back, so the only member of our family left working there was our cousin Berry Murphy.

Mama and Papa completed a deal to rent a big house in Lubbock and we made plans to move to that place "where these children can go to college," as Mama had dreamed of for nearly ten years.

CHAPTER 20

TECH TAVERN

Papa's Bible shows that we moved to Lubbock on September 16, 1932.

Fred told a trucker we had a five-room house when he hired that man to come to Big Spring to move the furniture. Before the furniture was finally loaded, the man was heard to remark, "Five room house, my eye! This is the biggest load I ever got from a five-room house."

Again we used Fred's car, and during the packing and clearing out process, Mama told me to take a couple of boxes of books across town to the Mexican school. I did, but as I removed those books from the back seat of the car, I lifted out Fred's new hydraulic jack to get it out of the way, then just drove off and left it sitting on the curb. We never saw the jack again.

We arrived in Lubbock very late on Friday night, and Beryl recalls that all of us slept on the little patch of grass in the front yard until daylight when the truck of furniture arrived. Saturday was Ida Rule's birthday and Beryl and Lydia Ann managed for a couple of small sacks of candy, which they placed under her pillow as her birthday celebration.

Mama and Papa had leased a big, two-story, rectangular boarding house called Tech Tavern, located on Ninth Street. In the days before any dormitories had been built at young Texas Technological College, they planned to rent the upstairs rooms to college boys, serving three big meals a day for $25 a month for room and board. Mama worried about signing the lease and putting up her furniture as security for the rent, because she said, "I'd sure'nuf hate to lose my new frigidaire." Mama's first electric refrigerator was a General Electric, but for years most of us called all electric refrigerators by the generic term "frigidaire."

On Monday I drove the three younger girls to school, Beryl and Ida Rule to junior high, and Lydia Ann to the old Central Ward School. It was a beautiful, warm fall day.

Beryl: I was all gussied up in a sleeveless white pique sun dress, white sandals and no stockings and I thought I was pretty classy until I saw all the other girls in dark clothes with jackets, oxfords and hose. They *looked classy and I looked embarrassed.*

That summer, Berry had attended Sul Ross State Teachers College in Alpine, Texas, and he arrived in Lubbock some time later so ill with yellow jaundice that he could not attend the fall term of college. All of the young men boarders arrived in time to register on the first day of registration at Tech.

I recall many of those fellows: good-looking Fred, an engineering student, big and bashful Albert (called "Bull" by the rest of the fellows), and quiet and unassuming Joe, the banker's son, were all three from Eldorado, Texas; pre-med student Dyer (called "Butter" by his friends) and good-natured Harry were from Big Spring, and homesick Bill was from Coahoma, near Big Spring. I don't remember why we called Huffaker by his last name only; I just remember that Mama said he had a date with a different girl every night that fall, except one night he stayed home, but spent the evening talking to girls on the phone.

There was a quiet "older man," perhaps thirty or so, (the only one we called "Mr. Whatever-his-name-was"), who decided after a few days that the noise and exuberance of the younger men were not for him, and he asked Mama to return his month's rent. Mama had already used his rent to help pay her landlord and she thought that perhaps she wouldn't be able to rent his room at that late date, so she called the college to ask if she had to return his rent. They told her, "No, ma'am, that's why they pay in advance." That young man, whose name I have truly forgotten, stayed the whole year and seemed to enjoy life with us very well.

The list of boarders also included Jesse, a senior in the School of Agriculture; Edgar, who had a paper route; the Lippincott twins, and Woodrow. Woodrow had a milk cow stabled somewhere nearby, and he furnished us with milk for his room and board.

As far as I know, the fellows (Mama discouraged us from using the word "guy," said it was so common, cheap and uncouth) got along well enough together. I do know they had huge appetites. We had always been a rice'n'gravy family, but those boys could have eaten mashed potatoes and gravy three times a day. Mama didn't serve a great variety of dishes at any one meal, but she always served plenty of whatever she had. Mama had brought the remnants of the stock, including the school supplies, from the grocery store in Big Spring, but most of the perishables were purchased when Papa walked to the store once or twice a day every weekday and carried home a couple of big paper sacks full of groceries. None of the boarders had a car, and brother Fred's car had gone back to him after the first week or so in Lubbock, so anywhere we went, we walked or we rode the city bus at five cents a trip.

While Fred's car was still there, on our second Sunday in Lubbock we went downtown to put our memberships in the First Baptist Church, which was probably foolish because the College Avenue Baptist Church was only a couple of blocks from the house.

Although the buildings on the campus were scattered, walking was not a problem that fall because of the beautiful weather. The other places we lived had gone from hot summertime to a cold, damp winter overnight, but Lubbock had a long, protracted fall of pleasant days and cool nights, just right for me to wear some of Mary Noel's pretty suits and hats. But when winter came, it came with a vengeance. I understand the snow depth and low temperatures that December set a record that stood for many years after. Public schools were closed for several days, according to Beryl. College classes were not dismissed and I walked the long distance to the campus and the long distances between the Tech buildings in deep snow and cold, cold wind. I wore my hiking boots, but heaven forbid that we should wear anything as comfortable and practical as pants. I had an old blue rain slicker lined with flannel, which went over the coat purchased in Big Spring, and I succeeded in making it to all my classes. I had to, it was the end of the fall term and finals were in progress.

The house was comfortable enough, except for the downstairs bathroom. That bathroom, as large as the bedrooms, had no heat. We'd fill the tub with hot water and hope it warmed up the room a little. As each bedroom had its own lavatory, the only fixtures in that bathroom were a tub and toilet, and the rest of the big room was filled with two large trunks that Mama stored in there. As we went into the bathroom one day, we stopped short because there appeared to be a man lying on top of the trunks. Mama had arranged some of the linens on top of the trunks in the shape of a body, thrown a spread over it, and placed one of Papa's hats at one end, shoes at the other. She just wanted to liven things up around there, to shake us up, to get a rise out of us, which she certainly did.

To say that money was scarce that year is a masterpiece of

understatement. I have before me reproductions of advertisements from the *San Francisco Chronicle* showing prices for 1932: a Plymouth sedan, $535; prime rib roasts, seventeen cents a pound; eggs, nineteen cents a dozen; and butter, twenty-nine cents a pound, among many other low prices of that sort.

I registered for courses in Business Administration because that course of study involved the least registration money by a dollar or two. I took physics rather than chemistry because the lab fee was a dollar less, and besides, I could use our boarder Fred's physics textbook.

In an orientation class we were required to make a report of our personal expenditures for the semester, and all I could report was five manila folders at two cents each. The rest of my needed school supplies were taken from those brought from the Big Spring store. I could also report forty-nine cents spent for a blouse I'd bought because it had the first zipper I'd ever used. I was so embarrassed at my tiny expenditures that I lied and listed a few soft drinks at a nickel each.

In physical education we were required to buy a regulation pair of bulky black shorts that cost probably $1.50. I said to the teacher, "My mother says we can't afford those shorts. Is it okay if my mother makes some shorts for me?"

The teacher didn't believe they could be made any cheaper, but she didn't know Mama. Mama bought a yard of black sateen for 25¢ and made a pair of gym shorts that were the envy of my classmates. They were shorter and less bulky than theirs, and they fit me like a million dollars.

One of the social clubs (Tech didn't permit Greek letter organizations at that time) invited me to join, and Mama was distressed to have to tell me we couldn't afford the small initiation fee. "I want you girls to take part in social affairs until you are comfortable in any situation. I don't feel at ease at some society functions and I want to save you from that feelin', but we just don't have the money now." I was so surprised to hear that Mama wasn't the master of every situation, that I nearly forgot what I wanted the money for.

Berry: I came in one afternoon and Mama, almost in tears, said to me: "We're just goin' to have to get into your collection of Indian Head pennies. I need twenty cents for a couple of loaves of bread, and there isn't a nickel in the house."

I sho' hated to part with those Indian Head pennies, but we needed the bread and that was all there was to it.

It was a time of bartering. Virginia, a student in the School of Agriculture, had driven a string of horses from New Mexico to Lubbock where she worked her way through college by renting out the horses. The cowgirl traded a certain number of hours of horseback riding to Mama's friend, Miss Dora, in exchange for her, Virginia's, own room and board. Miss Dora, who ran one of the girls' boarding houses, parceled those hours out to her daughter Dorothy and two nieces, and had a segment left over which she traded with Mama (for me to use) in exchange for Mama's giving half a room to Miss Dora's nephew, Burgess. Do you follow that? Anyway, I got to ride horseback an hour a week all that year, and Burgess had a warm place to sleep, and Virginia, the girl with the horses, had her room and board, and no money changed hands.

Early in the fall Mama had had a woman helper. She was a widow who had one of the downstairs rooms and did the laundry and helped in the kitchen. Beryl tells me that the woman left because Mama thought she was getting too chummy with some of the boys. Berry and I had certainly never heard that story until Beryl told it recently. I always thought the woman left because the Willses showed up at the door.

The Willses (a pseudonym) were relatives of one of our boarders. Mama and Papa moved out of the one big room in the house and let the couple in need move in there, rent free. The Wills' little business had failed in another town and they had loaded their few belongings in a old jalopy and had come to our door.

This would be our first real depression Christmas, and we were living on the Staked Plains of Texas where there were absolutely no trees to be had for the cutting. Commercial trees were trucked in, I suppose, but we didn't have enough money even to inquire about the price of those. Mama had warned us that Christmas this year would be mighty poor pickin's.

While Mrs. Wills helped Mama in the kitchen, Old Man Wills scrounged around junk yards and wrecking yards for things he might sell. He found he could get glass from wrecked cars, cut it and put it together in some fashion to make counter pie-cabinets to sell or barter to cafes. Texas had recently passed a law requiring pastries to be kept under cover, and the market for pastry cabinets was good.

At any rate, Old Man Wills traded one or two cabinets to a cafe owner for a turkey (the first I remember us having) and another for a Christmas tree, which we decorated while we listened for the first time to Bing Crosby sing "Silent Night" on the radio.

I had Saturday classes and couldn't have a Saturday job, but Beryl, still in junior high, worked at Woolworth's on Saturdays and for the week before Christmas, at $1.15 for a nine-hour day. Mama always said we wouldn't have had any Christmas at all that year if it hadn't been for Beryl's generosity.

Beryl: When Mama said we wouldn't have much Christmas that year, I whispered that I could buy gifts from Santa with my big salary, and she said, "We'll see."

All November and December, Ida Rule and Lydia Ann and I would whisper and plan and say, "Oh, but that's a quarter gift!" I bought Lydia Ann a wall black board, for 50¢ cents, a child's ironing board, 25¢, and toy iron for 10¢. Papa got B.V.D.s, $1.00, and Mama got bloomers, 40¢, and a lingerie vest, 49¢. The other gifts were: for Berry a pair of socks, 15¢, and shaving lotion, 15¢; for Ida Rule, paper dolls and a bracelet, and for Rosemary hose, 49¢, and panties, 25¢.

I had all the gifts put back and I picked them up when I got off work Christmas Eve at 9:00 p.m. Loaded down with packages, I went to a garage a block from the dime store where I could ride home with a neighbor when he closed his business at midnight and save the nickel bus fare.

When I came into the house, only one light was burning, but the stockings were hung, and Mama and Papa had put out fruit and candy and what little things they had scraped up for us. As I put out the last gift, I looked up and there in the doorway were Papa in his split-tail nightshirt and Mama in her big white flannel nightgown. They smiled and said, "Merry Christmas, Mrs. Santa."

For me, it was just about the best Christmas ever.

Howard had come to Big Spring for Christmas leave, and while he was visiting in the home of Miss Cora and Pauline, he was stricken with a bad case of the flu and was too sick to return to the Naval Academy on time. He had brought to Big Spring the car in which the other Texas boys at the Academy traveled and had no way of getting it to Cisco where the next nearest midshipman was spending the holidays. Mama sent Berry to Big Spring to take the car to Cisco for Howard.

Recovered from his illness, Berry started to the Agricultural School of Tech in the winter term of 1933.

Berry: I gave Mr. Gaskin, the business manager at Tech, Papa's shotgun as collateral for my registration fees. Dean Leidigh gave me a job pruning trees in that big windbreak across the west side of the campus. I pruned every one of those Chinese elm trees for 15¢ an hour. That was a lot of trees, but

Dean Minnick tells me those trees are still there. And I repaid Mr. Gaskin and got the shotgun back.

On Saturday afternoon shortly before the spring term ended, Lydia Ann, about ten years old at the time, was running barefoot down the hall and got a terrible splinter in her foot. There wasn't a carpet or rug in the whole house. Mama called upstairs to Dyer, the pre-med student who had worked several summers in a doctor's office, to come down and help her get the splinter out of Lydia Ann's foot. Sounds like a good idea, but Dyer and some of the other boys had hauled a case of beer by rope up on the roof of the front porch, and brought the beer into the upstairs room where they were having a high old time. They wouldn't have dared to bring it in the front hall and up the stairs. You understand that beer in the house was against all rules—Federal (prohibition was in effect), state, and most important, Mama's.

Dyer told me that when he heard Mama call him, he washed his mouth out, first with water, then with toothpaste. "I must have used a tube of toothpaste and I had a mouthful of it when I went downstairs. I kept my head ducked down over Lydia Ann's foot so Mrs. Duff wouldn't smell that beer, and nearly choked on that mouthful of toothpaste. I helped her as much as I could with Lydia Ann's foot, but I never knew whether she smelled the beer."

They were unable to get all of the big splinter out, and two or three days later, Mama and Lydia Ann walked all the way to West Texas Hospital and had a doctor take care of the foot for the big fee of two dollars, then walked home again.

Howard graduated from the Naval Academy, but not all graduating First Classmen were given a commission as an Ensign in the Navy. Due to the economic conditions of the time and a severe disarmament cutback in the Navy, it was decided to commission only the top fifty per cent of the class, and

Congress was asked to authorize the granting of Bachelor of Science degrees to the whole class. The measure passed Congress with only one dissenting vote--that of the House Member who had appointed Howard.

Howard got busy and studied harder to assure himself that he would be in the top half of the class and Mama sat on the davenport in that little front hall of Tech Tavern and listened to the broadcast of the graduation ceremonies on the radio. As Howard's name was called and President Franklin D. Roosevelt handed his diploma and commission to him, Mama embroidered an "N" for Navy in the central piece of a quilt she was making in the Flower Garden pattern. Mama was as proud as all git out of Howard.

I had my name on a list in Dean Mary W. Doak's office, hoping for some kind of job, and although I had typed a graduate student's thesis on Walter Lippman, nothing really came through until school was out. The wife of one of the professors wanted someone to go with her and her two small children to Georgetown for several weeks, and Mama, of course, made arrangements for me to go.

Mr. What's-his-name, the boarder who was older than the rest of the young men, asked Mama, "How much is she going to be paid?" Mama said, "Oh, they'll just feed her and I won't have to. But she'll see some more of the country."

That boarder, bless his heart, said, "Seems to me she ought to be paid something, no matter how little."

But I wasn't, and I was gone for several weeks. Elsie, with her year-old son, Jimmy, came home for a visit about the time I left, and the boarders had left for the summer. Elsie spent most of the summer with Mama, and Mama said later, "I knew something must be wrong with that marriage. You couldn't have got me to stay away from YaPapa that long when we'd been married that short a time."

Berry went back to Alpine for the first part of the summer, but he returned and entered the last summer term at Tech.

Soon after my return from Georgetown, I went on another trip to East Texas with Shirley Mansell to help her with her small daughter, Patsy. Berry had met Dr. Chris Mansell and his wife, Shirley, some months earlier, and all of us in the family had babysat for Mrs. Mansell that first winter and would continue to do so for several years to come. While Mrs. Mansell stayed with Dr. Mansell's family in one East Texas town, I went via bus to Longview to see Aunt Noel and Mary Noel, then on to Henderson to see Elsie. I joined Mrs. Mansell again and we returned by way of her beautiful old home in northeast Dallas, where she had been reared by her father and mother, Dr. and Mrs. John Lomax. Dr. Lomax had been a banker in Dallas and had later become a professor at the University of Texas and a well-known collector and recorder of American folk songs.

Mrs. Mansell introduced me to Neiman-Marcus and big city shopping. She advanced the money ($7.50) for me to buy a white genuine suede jacket I yearned for. When I got back to Lubbock I kept the jacket hidden from Mama for some time because I knew she'd say we couldn't afford that extravagance. She did. In fact, she had a conniption fit.

We came home from Dallas through western Central Texas and stayed a short while on the large Calloway ranch. My horizons were certainly broadened that summer.

Mama always said we moved as often as a Methodist preacher. While I was in East Texas I heard from Mama that we were moving again, this time to another house in Lubbock. I didn't get in on any of the work of packing and moving. I just drove up to the new house and walked in for the first time at 2118 18th Street. It was to be Papa's home for the rest of his life, and Mama's for approximately twenty-five years.

CHAPTER 21

MORE CRISES FOR MAMA

The house I entered that summer day in 1933 had six small bedrooms (three of them on the second floor under the eaves), a small kitchen, living room, dining room, no clothes closets and one bathroom. When appraisers were examining the house a few years later, Mama overheard one of them say, "Rome may not have been built in a day, but I'll bet this house was." The rent was much less than that at Tech Tavern, however, and Mama planned to rent the downstairs bedrooms to a few of her former boarders. Papa had a job managing the butcher shop of Mr. Logan's lunch room and store across 14th Street from the junior high school, and Mama, in addition to serving breakfast and supper to her boarders at the house, would prepare noon lunch at Mr. Logan's place to be served to a horde of junior high students, as well as to mama's family and boarders.

A couple of weeks before the fall semester began, Mama arranged for Dr. Mansell to remove my tonsils so that I'd be ready for school in September. He said he couldn't take them out for nothing, he'd have to charge me a dime. He came by the house on a Sunday and gave me a shot of some kind, and a little later Mama and I rode the city bus to town and walked up five or six flights of stairs (the elevator of the Myrick building didn't run on Sunday), I sat in a chair and the doctor cut out my tonsils. As simple as that. He told us to wait there in the office for an hour or so before we went home; he was going duck hunting. Mama, remembering her experience with Elsie's excessive bleeding, asked him what she should do if I began to bleed too much. He replied, "Call Dr. Standefer," then left. After a couple of hours, Mama and I walked down those flights of stairs and caught the city bus back to our neighborhood. I spent about a week recuperating in the east bedroom upstairs, taking a lot of kidding about taking so long to get over a simple tonsillectomy because I was an old lady of eighteen, whereas most other family members had had their tonsils out when they were much younger.

I recovered soon enough and went back to babysitting for the Mansells, working to repay them in a small measure for their kindnesses. School was to start soon and Mama and I studied the Tech catalogue, looking for ways to save any money we could. There was an optional medical fee of $2.50 which I almost didn't pay, saying, "The only illnesses I've ever had were sore throats, and now that my tonsils are out, I shouldn't be bothered with a sore throat ever again."

Mama said, "Oh, go ahead and pay it. It's better to be safe than sorry."

It was the best bargain we ever made. Four days after school started, I was at a rush party at the Lubbock Hotel and began feeling worse and worse. I went home early and the next morning I said to Beryl (we shared the west bedroom upstairs), "Tell Mama my heart hurts every time I take a breath."

Although I had no cold or cough, Mama called Dr. Mansell, who told her she'd better call the school doctor because I might have to go to the hospital. That year Lubbock Hospital had the medical contract with the college, while Dr. Mansell practiced medicine at the West Texas Hospital. The school doctor came and listened to my chest and told me to turn over so he could listen to the back. I said, "It hurts too much for me to turn over." He went downstairs and I heard him tell Mama that he couldn't find anything wrong with me, and he thought I was just faking an illness to keep from going to school.

I heard Mama say, "Doctor, that girl hasn't missed a day of school for years because of illness. She's looking forward to this year and there's no reason for her to want to miss school. Besides, she's not one to put on any act. I've had one child with an abscessed lung and I know that there's something seriously wrong with her."

"Well, Mrs. Duff, you'd better call your family doctor because I can't find anything wrong with her."

Dr. Mansell came, listened to my chest, asked a few questions, told me to turn over, and I pulled the excuse that it hurt too much. Dr. Mansell was a big man and he just reached down and turned me over. When he had listened to my back chest, he went downstairs and I heard him tell Mama she'd better have the Lubbock Hospital send an ambulance for me. On a beautiful fall day, the ambulance took me and Mama to Lubbock Hospital, where I was soon being x-rayed and settled into a room.

The x-rays showed my chest was so full of infection it had pushed my heart over to the other side. After the school doctor had pulled such a boo-boo, the Lubbock Hospital certainly gave me VIP treatment. I was ensconced in what the nurses called "the bridal suite," a large corner room with easy chairs and a private bath. It usually cost the huge sum of $10 a day and the nurses said that ordinarily only doctors' wives could afford it, but that $2.50 medical fee covered it for fourteen days. As sick as I was, I remembered something in the Tech catalogue about if an extended stay worked a hardship on a student's family, arrangements could be made to extend the fourteen days.

Mama went to see Dean Mary W. Doak and President Bradford Knapp and arranged for the rest of my stay to be covered by that $2.50 fee. Ann told me recently that Mama also got a refund on my registration fee because it was obvious I wouldn't be able to continue in school that semester.

Mama stayed with me night and day. The hospital brought in a cot for her for $1.00 a night, but she got very little sleep. I suffered severe night sweats and she had to change my pajamas and bedding about twice each night. For several weeks she had to hold my head while I vomited so much we thought my very intestines were coming out.

The daily visit of the surgeon in charge of me was quite a production. First a student nurse came in and checked that the room was in order, then the head floor nurse came in to check everything again (heaven forbid that the doctor should see a speck of dust or a wrinkled bedspread). Finally, the doctor, with his assistant, the head nurse, the head floor nurse (again) and even a couple of student nurses, stepped in briskly, glanced at my chart briefly, patted me on the head and departed for the next patient. One morning Mama slowed him down long enough to ask him if something couldn't be done about the vomiting, and he said to the nurse, "Cut out the citrocarbonate."

They left off that medicine and the vomiting stopped, but I had lost so much weight by that time a silver bracelet with the Naval Academy insignia on it that Howard had given me, and that previously had fit snugly about my wrist would slip over my elbow.

Every two or three days Mama went with me into the operating room where my pleural cavity was aspirated by the insertion of a big hollow needle which Mama said was about the size of the crochet hook she used constantly as she sat by my bed. My condition would improve for about twenty-four hours, then the infection would start building up again and the aspiration would have to be repeated. Finally, after more than three weeks of that, the doctor admitted that the treatment wasn't working and he'd have to perform major surgery. Mama asked him what his fee would be and understood him to say "Two-fifty." Mama said, "Doctor, there's no chance on earth of our getting $250."

He replied, "You misunderstood me, Mrs. Duff. With the student medical fee discount, it will be $62.50."

Mama said, "Well, we'll get that much somehow." Brother Fred came through with the money.

The doctors took me back to the operating room and performed a rib resection and inserted an empyema tube, all with only a local anesthetic. This means they cut out part of a rib and inserted a tube into the pleural cavity. We teased Mama that she was in the operating room with me to tell them how to do it, but I later saw among Howard's things a telegram Mama had sent to him in San Diego where he was stationed as a naval officer: "Operation tomorrow. Pray for her."

Later, I worried that the scar from the operation would show if I wore a backless swimsuit or evening dress. Mama said, "If you're going to show all that skin, what difference does a scar make?"

Lois, a nineteen-year-old student nurse, was very good to me and for me. As she pushed me on the stretcher to the operating room day after day, one or the other of us would say something the other thought extremely funny, and we would go down the hall and into surgery laughing like we were on our way to a picnic. Mama said later, "There you were, sick as all git out, and the nurses and other patients looked at you two like you were out of your mind."

For several weeks I was not allowed to have visitors, but I saw my Sunday School teacher standing in the hall outside the door, weeping. I said to Mama, "What's she cryin' about?"

Mama replied, "She doesn't like to see you sick." It made me realize for the first time that there was a possibility of dying, but I also remember thinking, I don't want to die now, but I'm not afraid to die.

Although he was not my doctor, Dr. F. M. Malone, who was on the staff at Lubbock Hospital, stopped by to see Mama. I never knew if he came as a representative of the hospital or as a representative of the First Baptist Church. He was pretty much "Mr. Baptist," an outstanding layman and leader at our church. When he asked if I were being treated all right, if we had any complaints, Mama said, "Why did you ever build this place so close in town? There's a manhole cover out there in that busy intersection that makes a terrible racket every time a car passes over it, and there are a jillion cars that pass over it day and night."

He replied, "And when we built this building, we were asked why did we build it so far out in the country?" But within a little while the manhole cover was quiet.

A few days after the operation, I was moved to a less elegant room and Mama didn't need to stay with me day and night. I could have visitors occasionally and Shirley Mansell was one of those who came often. She introduced me to *Reader's Digest* because I was too weak to hold a larger magazine. Shirley told me such funny tales of her experiences at Goucher College in Baltimore that I'd laugh so hard I'd start coughing. Then she brought me George Bernard Shaw's *The Intelligent Woman's Guide to Socialism and Capitalism*, which certainly offset the humor of Shirley's tales.

Miss Ruth Pirtle, a speech teacher at the college, was a surgery patient in the hospital while I was there and many faculty members came to see her and stopped in to see me. Miss Anno Jo Pendleton, one of her visitors and another professor of speech, told Mama I had been an excellent speech student the previous year. Mama said, "You mean Berry, don't you?" Miss Pendleton replied, "Oh, Berry was a good student, but Rosemary was an excellent student." Mama said I never let her forget that she had just naturally assumed that Berry was a better student than I.

Three Tech students, including Matt Hitchcock, a football player, and Lois Adair, a sweet freshman girl, died of pneumonia in that hospital while I was there, and remembering them makes me think of how many thousands of lives have been saved since that time by antibiotics.

When I was about to be discharged, I asked my new friend Lois, the student nurse, what I could tell folks when they asked where I'd been. We thought of several crazy, ridiculous answers, then she looked at my chart and said, "You might just tell them you had 'double pneumonia with pleural effusions, changing into empyema, calling for a rib resection and the insertion of an empyema tube.' That oughta keep 'em quiet."

After nearly six weeks in the hospital I returned to the house and settled into a single bed in the corner of Mama's small bedroom. The young men boarders had earlier considerately found themselves other places to stay inasmuch as Mama was snowed under with caring for me. Mama kept in touch with some of those boys for years and I dated some of them occasionally through the rest of my college years.

The doctor had told me to return to his office daily to continue to have my pleural cavity irrigated with Daikin's solution. He said that was a disinfectant that had been widely used to treat the soldiers of World War I who had been gassed in the trenches. Somehow, it didn't seem right to be riding the city bus with that big tube taped around my mid-section, and Mama and Papa found a car to purchase. He bought an old Chrysler—I think a 1925 model—built long before any streamlining was ever a gleam in an auto designer's mind, and it had a horn that went "ah-ooga." Papa paid for it and the family really give it a workout for the years we had it.

Ann: Some years later the old Chrysler was sitting out in the driveway, overgrown with morning glories. Mama told Pop to get rid of it and he sold it for $12.50. It was last seen headed for East Texas with the back seat loaded with a bunch of coon dogs.

Elsie's second baby, Barbara Jean, had been born in Henderson on October 11th and Elsie had brought the brand new baby and eighteen-month-old Jimmy to Lubbock so she could help Mama. One afternoon when Elsie drove me to the hospital I told her to come back about three o'clock and wait outside for me. I was sitting at the examining table, ready for the doctor to make his sudden appearance, when I heard him talking to someone in the next room: "I tried to get you to have that operation a year ago. Now it's too late, it wouldn't do any good." I heard the murmur of voices and then a woman crying. After a short while, the doctor came in to see me and was obviously upset. Without saying a word he picked up the syringe contraption used for pumping the solution into my pleural cavity, and soon the walls of the room seemed to me to move up and down and in and out.

I said, "I feel funny."

The doctor said, "You're not going to pass out on me, are you?" I did.

I regained consciousness lying on the examining table, and heard the doctor say to the nurse, "I've told you, you just can't pump that solution in too fast." As if *she* had been the one to do it. I had difficulty for a time thinking of simple words, but that passed after an hour or so, but I had to stay in the doctor's office for such a long time that Elsie, waiting in the car outside, finally came in to see if I'd gone home some other way. It was so late when Elsie and I arrived at the house that Mama was really worried.

One afternoon while I was in the bed in Mama's room,

I heard the most heart-stopping wail come from the house up on the west corner across 18th Street. We saw a police car at the curb and two officers standing at the door with the distraught woman. They had had to tell her that her little boy had been killed when he was struck by a truck as he crossed 19th Street to return to Dupre Grade School after lunch. The child's head had been so badly mangled that before identification could be made, the first and second grade teachers had to call the roll to see which boy had not made it back from lunch.

My recovery seemed interminable. While I was taking it easy around the house that fall, Shirley Mansell's younger brother, Alan Lomax, came to see me. I knew he was involved with their father, Dr. John Lomax, in collecting folk songs around the country for the Library of Congress. They had already discovered "Leadbelly" (Huddie Ledbetter), a Negro who spent most of his adult life in prisons. Once he was pardoned because of his singing, and the Lomaxes had recorded many of the old folk songs that Leadbelly knew, including "Good Night, Irene" which later made the Hit Parade.

I heard more about Alan from Shirley as she described some of his activities that varied from the norm of our comparatively small town, conservative lifestyle. While he was visiting with me, we decided to go for a walk, and he said, "Let's walk in the alleys. Alleys are much more interesting than streets. You can tell more about people who live in the houses from their alleys." He was right, but it is probably the only time I deliberately went for a walk down the alleyways.

We can't remember just when Elsie returned to her home in Henderson, but it must have been before Thanksgiving, or the following incident never would have happened.

A short time before Thanksgiving Day, Mama was working

at Mr. Logan's lunchroom when she had some sort of attack. She thought it was a heart attack; the doctor said it had to do with menopause, which we called "change of life," and I've wondered from something Mama said many years later if it were a miscarriage. At any rate, she was brought home and put to bed, the only time I can remember her being confined to bed except for childbirth, until that time. She was not allowed to get out of bed even to go to the bathroom. It's small wonder that she had some sort of collapse after the strain she had been through, but all of us were worried silly.

When Thanksgiving Day arrived, Berry had gone somewhere for the weekend, Fred and Sina didn't come up from Sweetwater, and of course, Howard and Elsie were far away. The four of us girls, Lydia Ann, Ida Rule, Beryl and I, and Papa sat down to Thanksgiving dinner of burnt pork chops and underdone sweet potatoes (called yams by the produce departments today). If there was anything else on the table, we don't remember it. The four of us girls got the giggles. Why, I don't know. The contrast between that meal and other Thanksgiving dinners, the release of tension from the long autumn, the realization of the ridiculousness of our helplessness when Mama was sick--whatever the reason, first one then the other would snicker or giggle, then stifle it. Another would follow, then another until we couldn't hold it in.

Papa, who must have been frantic with worry about Mama, slammed down his knife and fork and said, "Ta! Ta! Ta! It's a disgustin' shame that four big girls are so good-for-nothin' they can't fix any better meal than this!" And he arose and stalked away from the table and went to sit by Mama's bed.

Then we really broke up and laughed until we nearly fell out of our chairs. I suppose we eventually recovered and cleaned up the kitchen, but Beryl, Ann, and I all remember Papa's disgust with his good-for-nothin' daughters.

We realize now that if Elsie had been there, she would have prepared a wonderful meal.

At last the small tube was removed from my chest on Christmas Eve and it was, I thought, just a matter of getting my strength back and gaining some weight. I was tired and petered out all the time and some doctor prescribed a tonic that made me gain seven and a half pounds in seven and a half days, but it also made my face break out so much that Dr. Mansell gave me an x-ray treatment to clear it up. They finally x-rayed my lungs again and found that I had "a spot on my lungs," a euphemism for tuberculosis. Mama thought I would have to go to a sanatorium in San Angelo or El Paso, but the doctors prescribed long hours of bed rest and no exercise involving the chest muscles. When I started back to school for the spring semester, I had to spend twelve hours a day in bed and that can surely play havoc with a sophomore girl's social life, but at least I didn't have to take Physical Education that spring semester.

When April came, I started taking sun baths on the scraggly Bermuda grass in the unfenced back yard under the direction of Dr. Mansell, who was a dermatologist. I started out with thirty seconds on front and back and increased it thirty seconds a day, always between 10:00 A. M. and 2:00 P. M. By the time I got up to fifteen minutes on each side (the time limit the doctor set for me) I had a beautiful tan and I was soon pronounced cured.

Fred's wife, Sina, had had empyema when she was younger and she told me, "It took me as long as two years to get over it."

I said, "Well, it's not going to take me any two years!" But it did.

CHAPTER 22

OH, I MISSED THE MOUNTAINS

While Mama and I were occupied with my illness, life was still going on at 2118 18th Street.

Ann: I remember that fall of 1933 as a time of very real worry and concern as I entered the high fifth grade at Dupre Grade School in our new neighborhood. I later had to miss a half-year of school because I had a "bad shoulder." Pop said it was caused by my turning cartwheels, but the cause was never determined. A chiropractor might have solved the problem with one visit, but Mama said we couldn't afford it. After I missed half a school year I was able to go on with my other activities. I was in Girl Scouts with Mrs. Mansell as my leader and I went to the old junior high school on 14th Street and later to Lubbock High School down in the next block from 2118.

Ida Rule had another year of junior high before she entered Lubbock High. She made many friends and was kept busy by Mama with babysitting jobs. She reported one young mother scolded her when Ida Rule said to the youngster, "Lay down."

That mother said, "Don't say 'lay down' to her, the correct grammar is 'lie down.'" Ida Rule was so embarrassed at having her grammar corrected that she was one of the half dozen people in the world who used "lay" and "lie" correctly.

Beryl entered Lubbock High School that fall of 1933 and had a much more active social life than any of the rest of us sisters. She worked many Saturdays at Woolworth's to pay for her involvement with the SubDeb Club and her other activities. At one time she thought she just had to have a new pair of shoes, her old ones were of suede which was wearing off and getting shiny in spots. Papa said, "Tommyrot! There's nothing wrong with those shoes that a good brushing wouldn't help."

He took the shoes, over Beryl's protests, and brushed them hard and long until he made them shiny all over! Beryl had a conniption fit.

Berry had returned from Alpine and entered the late summer term at Tech, then enrolled for the fall semester.

Berry: I began working at the Lubbock Cotton Oil Company from four to twelve P.M. for 22.5 cents an hour and worked there all the fall of 1933, splitting my paycheck with Mama. Mama said we had clocks set at three different times around the house: Tech time, cotton oil company time and correct time.

Berry had made friends with young business and professional men his own age and was much in demand to fill in at bridge games. It was while playing bridge that he met Dr. Elizabeth West, not only a good bridge player, but head librarian at Tech. Dr. West offered him a job in the college library for forty cents an hour if he could maintain a B average in his grades. He worked in the Tech library that spring semester of 1934, and the better hours enabled him to revive his social life and to make a little extra money promoting dances at the old Tech gym. My friend Emily Davis reminds me of a time he invited her to a home where he was to play bridge, then he had to go to work, leaving her there to play contract bridge with a bunch of experts when, at that time, she knew how to play only auction bridge.

My own memories of that spring semester include being chauffeured to school by Mama in the old Chrysler on very cold mornings—the only time I ever rode to school. My dating life, if any, had about gone down the drain, but I made friends with many young women, three of whom--Frances McKee, Idell Bacon and Emily Davis—I still consider long-distance friends fifty years later.

At the end of the spring semester of 1934 when I had been pronounced cured, Mama sent me to Sweetwater to spend the summer living with and working for Fred and Sina. Fred had changed jobs and had opened a nice place called "The Sandwich Shop" on the highway on the east side of Sweetwater. The local bakery made special loaves of sandwich bread about seven inches square for us. Fred had a menu of sandwiches only, about twenty or thirty different kinds. There were booths and a counter inside and curb service outside. Fred, Sina, and I worked along with Wendall, the chef, and a more experienced waitress whose name I do not recall.

We didn't open until nearly noon so we got our recreation in the morning, going to the skating rink, going to Lake Sweetwater and that sort of thing. Prohibition had been repealed in the fall of 1933, but only 3.2 beer was legal in Texas—in Sweetwater, anyway—and we served that, as well as soft drinks. I don't remember that I was paid any wage, but at the end of the summer I believe Fred sent me home with enough to pay my fall registration fee.

It was a fun job and I enjoyed it. The only night of the week that I was free was Thursday when Fred gave me the money to go to Bank Night at the movie. This was a weekly event in nearly every town where names were drawn and the winner was awarded twenty-five dollars, or maybe even fifty dollars. That was considered a terrific amount of money in 1934, and the place was packed on Thursday night because you had to be present to win. The one Thursday that I missed, my name was called! You couldn't convince me the management didn't know I was out of town.

Berry had called from Lubbock and asked me to come home and look after Lydia Ann, who was to have an emergency appendectomy, and Mama was down in East Texas. Fred sent me on the bus or train to Lubbock and I went straight to West Texas Hospital to be there when Lydia Ann was returned to her room from surgery. This was before the days of recovery rooms, and I stood by Lydia Ann's bed with tears running down my face, holding the basin while she was miserably sick. Mama had been called (she was the one who told Berry to call me), but she had to ride the bus nearly all the way across the state, not knowing whether Lydia Ann was all right or not.

When Mama arrived, she took over and I went back to Sweetwater. Mama and Papa had opened another little grocery story—where else?—across 13th Street from the back of the junior high building where they planned to serve hot lunches to the school children when school started. When Lydia Ann was ready to be discharged, Mama arranged to have the surgeon "take out his bill in trade" at the store. The hospital didn't want Mama to take Lydia Ann home until a note was signed for the doctor's bill. Mama just said, "I've made my arrangements with the doctor. I hope you'll take good care of her because I'm leaving her here," Mama started walking out. The hospital quickly made plans for Mama to take Lydia Ann with her.

When I told Fred I was going to have an F.E.R.A. (Federal Emergency Relief Act) job that school year which paid fifteen dollars, he said, "Fifteen dollars a week is pretty good. You ought to be able to get by on that."

"It's fifteen dollars a month, Fred, but it pays twenty-five cents an hour and that ain't hay," I replied. "I'm glad to have it."

I worked a couple of hours a day for Dr. J. O. Ellsworth, head of the Department of Agricultural Economics, and became familiar with a whole new jargon of the agricultural industry.

Dr. Ellsworth was the first Mormon I had ever known, thus broadening my world a little more.

Because I had missed that year of Physical Education and because I still could not take a fun P.E. course like tennis, I took what we participants called a "toe-wiggling class." I couldn't use my chest muscles, some of the girls couldn't use their abdominal muscles, and those recovering from broken legs or feet were slowed down in that area. But Miss Johnnye Gilkerson, the instructor, did a masterful job of finding something that each of us could do, although about the only thing we could all do at the same time was wiggle our toes.

Beryl: In that summer of 1934 I went over to the store after our noonday dinner at the house so Papa could go home for dinner. Sometimes I stayed there while Papa took a nap at home, and business was so slow I would get unbearably sleepy. I stretched out on one of the lunch tables and tied a string from the doorknob to my ear so I'd wake up when someone came in the door. A customer told Papa he caught me that way once, the string just slid off my ear without waking me.

I also delivered groceries for the store in the old Chrysler, and once Papa made me change a flat tire in the rain "so you'll learn how," he said. I haven't changed a flat tire since.

The office of Assistant Dean of Women at Texas Tech became vacant during our early years in Lubbock, and Mama went to the school and talked to Dean Mary W. Doak and Dr. Bradford Knapp about getting the job for herself. She told me, "I presumed I could do as well in that job as anyone else (I don't doubt that she could have) but they said they had to have someone with a college education, preferably someone with a degree. Well, someone out there suggested I put down on my application that I'd been to that school in Bowling Green, Kentucky, where my older sisters went. It's closed now, out of existence, and there'd be no way of checking on it, and I was tempted to do that, but I thought better of it. I thought it wouldn't be the right thing to do, so that took care of that job possibility."

Berry: I had become interested in the wool and sheep business and thought I'd like to go to the University of Wyoming at Laramie because they had the only course of study in the country in that particular field. I'd worked in the library at Tech for the twelve weeks of summer school in 1934, but at the end of that time I went to Sweetwater and worked for Fred for a couple of weeks while he and Sina took a trip. He paid me twenty-five dollars and when I went to the bus station to buy a ticket to Lubbock I saw a sign reading, "Round trip to Denver, $15." I bought the ticket to Denver, thinking I'd go to Laramie and if I couldn't make arrangements there, I could come back to my job at Tech and classes there. Tech was opening late that fall because the new dormitories were not quite ready.

I stopped by Lubbock while Mama got my clothes ready, and she sent me off with her blessing and a full lunch box. I arrived in Laramie with $5.49 in my pocket and went to Dean John A. Hill's office where he offered me an NYA (National Youth Administration) job at the stock farm for fifty dollars a month. Dean Hill signed my note to register, and I did enroll at the University of Wyoming where I worked and studied all that year and graduated the next summer, 1935.

Mama and Papa began serving lunch at the 13th Street store when school began in the fall of 1934. I walked down there from college, Beryl and Ida Rule walked over from high school, and Lydia Ann walked over from Dupre. The little place was full of junior high students, as well as a few teachers. We didn't have much of a menu. Mama served one big dish and dessert, and if you cleaned your plate you could have seconds. I'm sure she had a variety, but the two things I remember are spaghetti and meat loaf with rice'n'gravy.

Mama Pays the Grocery Bill

One noontime two young girls, daughters of two of the doctors who were taking out their bill in trade, began acting up, and Mama called them down. One of those girls said, "You can't talk to us that way. Do you know who our fathers are?"

Mama said, "Yes, I do. I know both of them and I'm bigger than either of them, and I can spank them, too, like I'm goin' to do you if you don't settle down."

The girls quickly settled down.

It was in that store that the Great Fried Pie Operation took place. Every morning about four o'clock, Mama and Papa fired up the old Chrysler with much noise as they went to the store where they proceeded to make as many as twenty or thirty dozen fried pies. Mama made the dough, rolled it out and cut it into circles using an oatmeal bowl as a guide. She placed dried fruit which had been stewed the afternoon before on a circle of dough, folded the crust over and pressed the edge with a fork to fasten it together. After it was fried in peanut oil, then sprinkled with sugar, each pie was placed in a little wax-paper sack across which Papa had written in his fine Spencerian handwriting, either "Apricot," "Peach," "Apple," "Mince" or "Pineapple." Then Papa brought Mama to the house to rouse the children and whatever boarders were living there and feed them breakfast. In the meantime, Papa delivered the pies to many of the working men's little eating joints in the community, where the pies were much in demand at ten cents each.

Then he picked up Mama and they were back at the store in time for the before-school customers, and Mama began to prepare the lunch she would serve her customers at noon.

The old car and Mama's and Papa's clothes were saturated with the smell of the hot peanut oil in which the pies were cooked. To counterbalance that disadvantage, a plus from the operation was that for a long time Mama had a wonderful shower gift for all the brides of our acquaintance: a half dozen big flour sack dishtowels from the great amount of flour used to make the pastry.

Mama had a young woman to help her at the store part of the time. It is small wonder, because Mama still had a houseful of work to be done at the house. In the winter the washing was done in the kitchen with the dasher washing machine and two tin washtubs on apple boxes crowded into the already crowded kitchen. The water faucets at the sink had been modified to hold a shortened garden hose, and the tubs were filled from the sink and the hot water tank in the closet under the stairs. In the summer the washing machine and tubs were moved to the detached garage and a long garden hose used to fill the machine with hot water from the kitchen, and the rinse tubs were filled from the outdoor hydrant. Mama got a little help from her own girls, but nothing compared to the work she did. She also still sewed for us. I remember some very attractive dresses she made for me, which I just took for granted as my natural right.

During these years when Mama was on her feet so much, she was afflicted with what she called "the heebiejeebies." I believe the medical profession today would call it "involuntary muscle spasms" or some such technical phrase, but when Mama tried to relax in the evening after a hard day her legs would begin to twitch and move until she'd say, "I'll just have to go to bed, I have the heebiejeebies." She used it that way so much I thought it was a professional medical term.

She used it at other times occasionally: "That child playin' in the street gives me the heebiejeebies." "He's so sneaky I get the heebiejeebies just bein' around him," or "This hojang gives me the heebiejeebies."

Although my dictionary tells me it is a slang word coined by Billy De Beck in his comic strip *Barney Google*, Mama told me it was a word from her childhood, used by her mother and the black people around in her mother's childhood.

Howard resigned from the Navy (he was now in the Naval Reserve) and came to Big Spring where he and Pauline were married on December 23, 1934. I went to Big Spring and attended the quiet but beautiful wedding ceremony at the home of Pauline and Miss Cora. They left by train immediately after the ceremony for Fort Worth where Howard had a position with Lone Star Gas Company.

Berry wrote that he wished I could come to Wyoming. When my friend Emily Davis told us that Miss Grace Padley, a Lubbock High School teacher, was looking for someone to drive with her to Denver where she planned to go to summer school, Mama grabbed at the chance. President Franklin Roosevelt had "called in the gold"—whatever that meant—and Mama patriotically turned in a gold pin her long-ago boyfriend had given her and received fifteen dollars for it.

My tale is that I left Lubbock with a ride to Denver, fifteen dollars, and a box of fried pies for Berry, and supported myself in Laramie that summer, earned twelve credit hours and paid my way home on the bus with enough money left to register at Tech in the fall of 1935. It was a wonderful summer and I began a lifelong love affair with the Rocky Mountains.

The train fare from Denver to Laramie was two dollars and fifty cents, and Berry met me at the Laramie station. Berry had told me to bring my coat, and I planned to take a little spring topper I had when Mama said, "Berry doesn't know you have that coat. He means that heavy gray tweed he gave you."

I felt like an idiot lugging that heavy coat through the heat to Laramie, but on June 23, my first Sunday there, I was snowed on when I walked to church. I quickly wrote Mama to send me a wool suit, a wool skirt and my hiking boots. Enclosed in the package with them was a front page of *The Lubbock Avalanche-Journal* with the headline, "Temperature

Hits 115."

The weather wasn't the only thing that was different. The campuses of the two colleges were very different, everybody except Berry and me had a Yankee accent, jobs were easier to get in Laramie than in Lubbock, and NYA jobs paid more in Wyoming than in Texas. My classmates in a political science class explained that Wyoming was essentially a Republican state and the Administration was trying to win Wyoming over to the Democratic side, whereas Texas was so solidly Democratic there was no point in trying to woo them.

On the strength of a new position he had for the coming year as a Vocational Agriculture teacher in the high school at Moorcroft, Wyoming, Berry had purchased a 1929 Ford and in it we explored the surrounding countryside from Denver to the Snowy Range.

Mama wrote that she wanted to get into Berry's collection of Indian Head pennies to send us money enough to go the Frontier Days in Cheyenne, but Berry said, "No way!" We managed to see Frontier Days, however, and Sally Rand, the fan dancer, was the entertainer the afternoon we were there.

Berry wanted me to stay at Laramie for the coming school year, and after his graduation ceremonies, I began to make plans to stay in Wyoming. Since the dormitory where I had stayed the second half of summer would be closed, a friend arranged for me to rent a room from Judge and Mrs. Tidball, and my stay of two or three weeks with that nice family was a delightful conclusion to a wonderful summer.

Mama wrote that I had received word from Tech that I could have an NYA job (NYA jobs had replaced FERA jobs) working for Dr. W. C. Holden the coming year, and I found that because the University of Wyoming wouldn't accept some of my Tech credit hours, I would be unable to graduate in one more year.

So I bought a bus ticket from Laramie to Lubbock and headed south. My wool suit and heavy coat felt great when I left Laramie about midnight in early September, but they became an extra burden the farther south we went, and I thought I would melt before we got to Raton, New Mexico, where the bus driver informed me that the heater had been inadvertently left on after the cool night. It was good to see a Dr. Pepper sign in the bus station at Denver, and to taste that southern drink again. My bus was fifteen minutes late in arriving in Amarillo late at night, and the bus to Lubbock had not waited. I had to spend a couple of my precious dollars staying at a crummy little hotel near the bus station.

I arrived in Lubbock just in time to register for the fall semester at Tech. I was glad to see my family and friends and to put my feet under Mama's table again. It was great to see the wide open spaces on the Tech campus and to hear friendly student voices calling, "Hi, y'all," "I cain't get the cou'ses I need," or "Are you fixin' to registah?" But oh, I missed the lovely Wyoming campus and the mountains in the western sky.

CHAPTER 23

LIFE AT 2118

I began my final year at Texas Tech soon after my return from Wyoming. My NYA job with Dr. W. C. Holden, professor of History, Anthropology and Archeology, was quite informative. Most of my work was done in the study of the lovely adobe home he and his wife, Olive, had built to demonstrate the practicability and comfort of a home built from the natural materials available in the area.

Dr. Holden and several other men had been on an ethnological expedition to the primitive Yaqui Indians in northern Mexico the previous year, and Dr. Holden kept me occupied writing the reports made by him and the other scientists who accompanied him. From Dr. Holden I acquired an interest in oral history and local history that has never left me.

Mama and Papa continued the Great Fried Pie Operation and the junior high lunchroom and grocery business all of that year and into the next.

My academic life, as well as my social life, prospered. Berry bought for me a classy evening dress of black satin that fit like a million dollars. Its white faille jacket with high buttoned neck and tight-fitted sleeves made it appropriate for less formal occasions, also. It was my first brand new, sto'-bought formal that hadn't come from Mary Noel, and I loved it. Mama made a white fur muff for Beryl and me out of Papa's old Masonic apron, and because muffs were the rage for a couple of years, Beryl and I took turns struttin' our stuff in sure'nuff style.

The day after my graduation from Tech, Berry, who had returned from Wyoming in the early summer, drove me and my friend Frances McKee, and my current boyfriend to Dallas to the Texas Centennial celebration. Mama couldn't stand to see a car going anywhere that wasn't packed jammed full, so she had us take Ida Rule and Lydia Ann to see Fred and Sina in Coleman. Where Fred and Sina put us I don't remember, but the six of us spent the night with them, then minus Ida Rule and Lydia Ann, drove to Fort Worth the next morning to have lunch with Howard and Pauline before we went on to Dallas where the boyfriend took his departure from us.

After enjoying the Centennial celebration for a couple of days, Berry, Frances, and I drove nearly all night to get back to Lubbock, and Berry soon left for Clovis, New Mexico, to work for the U.S. Department of Agriculture for a few months. This was during the time of the Dust Bowl, and Berry reported that practically every farmer he interviewed said, "If that fella just west of me wouldn't plow his land, we wouldn't have these dust storms. That's where all of the dust storms I get come from."

Beryl recalls the Dust Bowl days as a time when she and Ida Rule had to sweep the dust out of the house every evening about dark. The wind blew all day, covering everything in the house with dust, but the wind usually died down about sunset.

All of us remember the black dust storms—blackouts, black dusters—whatever you might call them, when a huge wall of black dust rolled in, most generally from the northwest, and usually with very little wind, at least much less wind than we had on other days. As it covered the sky and earth, everything went completely dark, no matter what time of day it was. At those times we couldn't see the porch light about three feet from the glass in the front door. Many people reported their chickens went to roost, even in the middle of the day.

I did a lot of babysitting in my college days, and one of the children I sat with was a sweet little boy, severely disabled. He had the body of about a six-year-old, but I'd surmise his mind was that of about six-months old. He was sweet and easy to handle; we just fed him, talked to him, then put him back in his crib. He was accustomed to going to sleep when it was dark, and when those black dusters rolled in, he'd snuggle down in his crib and go sound asleep.

Babysitting was not the most lucrative job in the country. I was often paid twenty-five cents for a whole evening's work, occasionally thirty-five or fifty cents, and once when I stayed until two o'clock in the morning of New Year's Day, I got a whole seventy-five cents. That's not per hour, my dears, that's for the whole evening's time, and I was glad enough to get it.

Salaries were comparable at that time. When we returned from Dallas, Mama had heard of a place for me to apply for a job. I got that job at a telephone company—not the big one that served Lubbock, but in the main office of a smaller company that served small towns surrounding Lubbock. I went to work every day in the Myrick Building and used my fine college degree in Business Administration to sit there and separate toll call tickets for all of fifty dollars a month.

On one particular day when I rode the bus home from that office for lunch, Mama and I were the only diners at the table. Lydia Ann and Ida Rule were in Coleman, Beryl was in Henderson, Berry had gone to his new USDA job, and I suppose Papa was at the store on 13th Street, which they were still operating. We had fried ham and little new potatoes-in-jackets with lots of butter. Mama reported it was the first time in more than thirty years when she'd had only two for lunch.

Beryl had graduated from Lubbock High School that spring of 1936 and soon after that she went to East Texas with her friend Mollie Davis and Mollie's parents. When she returned from visiting Elsie in Henderson, she reported to Mama how Elsie was being treated in her marriage, corroborating what I had said after I'd visited Elsie a couple of years earlier. Mama took my first month's paycheck and sent it to Elsie, telling her to get herself and the children on home. Elsie managed to get to the train with what pitifully few belongings she had without confronting her husband or his family, and she and almost-three-year-old Barbara Jean and four-year-old Jimmy arrived in Lubbock to be a part of the household for the next six years.

Ten years later when my own small daughter, Rosemary, and I spent three weeks with Elsie in Lance Creek, Wyoming, while my husband looked for a place to park our trailer in a town with no trailer parks at the time, I offered to pay Elsie for our room and board. "Don't be silly," she said, "You helped me out when I needed it and this is the first time I've had a chance to repay you."

Before Elsie even arrived in Lubbock, Mama applied for a job for her at Woolworth's Five and Ten Cent Store. The manager told Mama he didn't like to employ mothers of young children because they had to miss work so often to look after their children. Mama stared at him and said, "Do you presume to think that I can't look after those children?" Elsie got the job and worked there for awhile, then later she worked for some physicians at a clinic before she went to work in the office of the West Texas Gas Company.

Mama visited with her neighbors who were the 13th Street store's customers and she heard about nearly every job opening in town. Towards the end of my first month in the telephone office, she sent me downtown to apply for a job she'd heard about at the law office of Bledsoe, Crenshaw and Dupree.

Mama said, "Without any stenographic experience, you'd better tell them you'll work for nothin' just to get the job."

Which I did. Mr. Dupree told me he didn't want secretaries who had bright painted fingernails or who smoked. Neither of those practices were a part of my lifestyle, so I got the job.

A year or two later when Henri Sue Still came to work with me, lovely, colored fingernails were a part of her well-dressed appearance, and she smoked cigarettes, but as long as she worked there, when she wanted a cigarette she had to go the restroom down at the end of the long hall on the second floor of the old two-story First National Bank Building where the office was located.

Of course, all three lawyers smoked incessantly, but that was different: They were men.

I got the job and was paid $25 for that first month's work, and after that I was paid $50 monthly for the rest of the year, then raised $25 a month for each year after that until I reached $125 a month. I believe I received $150 for a few months before I left six years later. By that time a younger lawyer, James H. Milam, had joined Charles C. Crenshaw and George W. Dupree, and the firm was known as Crenshaw, Dupree and Milam.

Although I worked much unpaid overtime, especially when the courts were in session, the lawyers were generous with cash gifts at Christmastime, and they were forgiving of my tardiness due to bus schedules. The salary seems small today, but six-ounce Cokes were five cents at the soda fountain of the drugstore downstairs in the bank building, and although we had no scheduled breaks, the other stenographer and I never had to make or serve coffee, a practice that had not become a way of life at that time.

Mama wanted to apply for my old job at the telephone company. I told her, "I agree that you could handle it with no trouble, but you'd have to sit in that same chair eight hours a day, and I don't think your poor ol' hip joints would take it." Since she was bothered by a form of arthritis that was aggravated by prolonged sitting, she had to agree, but reluctantly.

Mama's connection with the law firm was quite limited. When Elsie came home to stay, Mama had me arrange for her to see the lawyers about suing for divorce. (The lawyers didn't charge us a fee.) On the opening day of the term of court for which the divorce hearing was set, one of the lawyers called me from the courthouse and said, "Tell your mother to keep the children in the house, at least in the backyard today. Their father was over here at the clerk's office early this morning, making threats."

Mama did keep the children under close supervision all that day and perhaps the next day or so, but their father made no further appearance. As a matter of fact, Elsie never heard from him again.

A few years later the Schantz family, our good neighbors across the alley, wanted to take in laundry to make enough income to survive. They weren't going to put a sign in their front yard; the customers wouldn't come to the house. Mr. Schantz would go to their homes to pick up their laundry, and the clothes would be hung in the backyard to dry. Nevertheless, some of the residents in their block on 17th Street objected to what they thought would be a disruptive business in the neighborhood.

Mama told me what to tell Mr. Crenshaw to tell his golfing buddy and client, H. L. Allen (father of Ida Rule's good friend Dorothy Allen), who was vice-president of the Texas-New Mexico Utilities Company: "My mother said to tell Mr. Allen and Senator Nelson, too, that if they didn't leave Mr. Schantz alone she's going to start buying her electricity from the city and she's going to vote for _____(whoever was running against Senator Nelson for the State Senate). Mama says she's the only one who'll see those clothes hanging in their backyard, and it won't be any worse than Mama's backyard."

Something worked. Mr. Schantz continued to go and pick up laundry, wash it in a machine in his garage, and Mrs. Schantz ironed it in the house, and nobody noticed any difference in the neighborhood.

We had other good neighbors on our own block. The three lots west of the house were vacant, making a handy shortcut as we walked to college or to the 16th Street bus stop. In the house on the other side of us were several neighbors through the years, but my best memory is of the Walkers, whose son, I. D., was about Ann's age.

Beyond the Walkers was a family with a boy and a girl about the ages of Jimmy and Barbara Jean, and Mama found herself doing a great amount of free babysitting for that young gadabout mother. The old grandmother in that family died during these years, and Mama was disappointed when the young mother asked Mama to babysit that boy and girl during the funeral. Mama babysat, of course, but she had planned to take Barbara Jean and Jim to the funeral because she thought it would be an excellent chance for them to learn about death.

Next door to that family lived the Davises (but not the family of my good friends Emily and Mary Ann, who lived on Main Street). Across the street from the Davises lived Mr. Matthews, principal of Lubbock High School. The Matthews' lovely home was of Spanish design, next door to the brick home of Dr. Jones, a dentist, and his wife.

Directly across the street from us lived the Colliers, whose five children ranged in age from Norma, who was Ann's age, down through Jimmy and Jean's generation. Years later, when Mrs. Collier came to see Beryl at the time of Gene Barnett's death, we three sisters (Beryl, Ann, and I) marveled that Mrs. Collier hadn't changed one little bit, we recognized her immediately. Later we figured that she'd probably been no more than in her late twenties or early thirties when we first knew her, but because we were unmarried and in our teens, we thought she was an old married lady and she was, of course, "Mrs. Collier."

Next door to the Colliers lived the Tysons, who were about the age of Mama. Mrs. Tyson died of cancer during our years of living at 2118.

We had lived at 2118 for a few years when the loan company from whom we were renting offered to sell Mama and Papa the house for $1600, with a $500-down payment and a note for $1100 payable at $16 a month. It's no wonder the company wanted to get rid of it. The floor was just about six or eight inches from the ground, not enough crawl space to look after the water pipes, but not flat on the ground to protect those pipes from the cold air. For all of the years we lived there, if the temperature was predicted to go below freezing at night, Mama said, "Get your baths early. YaPapa is goin' to shut off the water at nine o'clock." To put it mildly, it was not a very well-built house.

In those times that were so slowly moving out of the depression, a big part of my law firm's business was representing parties who were having to refinance their homes, or representing companies who were troubled with many defaulted loans. Mama's old home place, her parents' farm, had been converted by Uncle Tad into a lovely residential addition and as the money from the sale of the lots in the oil-booming town of Longview had been divided between Mama and her sisters, it enabled Mama to get the down payment to buy 2118.

Then Papa put a crimp in the plans. He thought $500 was

too large a down payment for that purchase price, and he took it upon himself to look for another house, and even went so far as to tell a real estate man he would take a three bedroom place on 17th Street for $3,500 because he could get it for the same $500 down payment.

As its monthly payment would be thirty-five dollars, I hit the ceiling—to Mama, of course, not to Papa. I said to her, "Ye gods, Mama, we're having a hard enough time paying the sixteen dollars a month rent now. How could we ever manage a payment of thirty-five dollars a month? And with only three bedrooms, how'd we ever be able to get any money from boarders?"

As Ann says, "You get to say, if you're gonna pay," and a big part of my salary was contributed to the family coffer.

Later Mama told me, "I went to that real estate man and told him I'd never contradicted Mr. Duff before and I hated to do this, but we simply couldn't afford that house. He was pretty nice about it."

So 2118 was purchased and for another twenty years Mama received some financial support from the house. As a little money trickled in from her father's estate they were able to remodel it, adding clothes closets, an upstairs bathroom, and another bedroom upstairs in two dormers built on the back wing of the house. A coat closet was built into the downstairs hall by the telephone, making it a good place to step into to have a little privacy for telephone conversations. Two downstairs bedrooms were made into one large bedroom with a good closet across one end. This large room was known as Mama's room, although at times she rented it out while she moved into the smaller room in back of the kitchen. The straight facade of the house was changed to accommodate an enlargement of the dining room and a little sheltered entrance for the front door, nearly doubling the size of the east room upstairs.

In the living room the old tan wallpaper was changed to white wallpaper, making Beryl very happy. She wanted "white walls and Venetian blinds" so very much that we thought one of the characters in a book *If I Have Four Apples* had been patterned after her. Our whole family had identified with that novel, which was based on the financial struggles of a family in hard times, but one of the young female members of the fictional family wanted nothing as much as she wanted "white walls and Venetian blinds."

The glass doors of the built-in bookcase in the living room were removed and became the windows of the new bathroom upstairs, but the mantel for the false fireplace remained in the living room, and the little kitchen was not enlarged. Perhaps some cabinets were built high over the benches of the tiny eating area, and the seats of those benches were hinged to make more well-used storage space. When Elsie went to work for the gas company, she bought Mama a more modern cook stove, much to Mama's distress because, Mama said, "That old stove we bought in Big Spring was good enough. Now I have to bend over to use the oven."

Through the years the backyard was fenced, the Bermuda grass spread to its limits, and the few Chinese elm trees provided a comfortable summer room. In the days before even window air-conditioners Mama and Papa put a bed out there and on some of the hottest summer nights they slept outside, coming into the house about daylight.

Mama discovered Mr. Gunn, a carpenter and jack-of-all-trades, who could translate her housing wishes and desires into a pretty accurate rendition of what she really wanted. When Howard and Pauline and their children, Karl and Eleanor, moved to Bremerton, Washington, in 1939, they came through Lubbock with a car and a truckload of furniture, and Papa went along with them to help in the building and rebuilding of houses on a project they had bought near the Naval base at Bremerton. Papa stayed with them until the first of December and Mr. Gunn, who followed them later, worked for Howard an even longer time.

Ida Rule graduated from Lubbock High School in 1937 and she and Beryl were both in Tech that fall. Berry moved to Fabens, Texas, near El Paso, in the fall of 1936 to teach Vocational Agriculture, and there he met Aileen Felty, whom he would later marry. Beryl went to Fabens at Christmastime and met Aileen, but in June, 1937, Aileen married Berry anyway.

Berry brought Aileen to Lubbock in August to introduce the rest of the family. Howard and Fred came up also, and we have snapshots of the whole family, except Papa who was sick in bed, taken in the backyard of 2118. I went back to Fort Worth with Howard, and Fred rode as far as Abilene with us. As we got underway, Fred chuckled, "Brother Berry always said he wouldn't marry someone with a family as b-b-big as ours, but that young lady is a good-ol' girl with a family every b-b-bit as b-b-big as ours." She has put up with Berry and the rest of the Duffs for fifty years.

Christmases at 2118 leave pleasant memories. Perhaps we never again had such a lean Christmas as we'd had at Tech Tavern. Fred and Sina and their son, Dub, were usually there. Sina's father had died and Fred saw how his death had put an end to the old family home, so he was determined to come home each Christmas if he possibly could as long as Mama and Papa still had a home. Fred always bought Dub a whole lot of fireworks for Christmas and we all enjoyed the display.

Howard and Pauline came out when Karl was a year or two old. Berry and Aileen and their children were usually there. One Christmas Berry had said he was going to stay in his own home at Christmas, but on Christmas morning after they'd opened their gifts and faced the day without the usual hojang of Mama's house, they packed up and drove to Lubbock in time for Christmas dinner. Aileen brought a delicious dessert she'd made for their dinner, but Berry said, "Mama, aren't we going to have ambrosia? We always have ambrosia."

When Mama remembered that occasion, she'd say, "I'll bet Aileen could have killed him." But Mama fixed the usual ambrosia for our Christmas dinner. Mama's ambrosia was simply pieces of fresh orange mixed with canned pineapple and coconut flakes.

Mama usually made a yellow cake with caramel icing, a coconut cake (white cake with white icing piled high with grated coconut), a devil's food cake with icing, and her form of fruit cake, which was a pretty simple spice cake with raisins. She always made lots of homemade fudge (no short cuts for her) and divinity candy. It is small wonder that she didn't have time to read the Christmas cards she'd received until Christmas Eve night.

Years later I asked Berry, "Wonder why we never thought to take Mama out for dinner on Mother's Day, or Christmas or Thanksgiving—any of those times we were all together? I can remember the kitchen full of dirty dishes after each of those huge meals."

He said, "She probably wouldn't have let us. It meant a lot to her to have her family together at her table."

Finances had improved a little and we were able to buy Christmas trees as the years rolled along. One tree was so old the limbs just drooped so much the decorations slid right off-- until we held the branches up by tacking the tinsel rope to the wall on each side of the tree.

Another year Papa came home so proud of his bargain tree. He had paid thirty-five cents for what surely must have been a tiny and misshapen branch lying on the floor of the tree market. Because it was practically impossible to decorate, Elsie, who always made a bigger deal about the decorative side of Christmas than the rest of us, fumed and faunched, but not to Papa. She insisted she was going to throw it away and get a nicer one. Fred told her, "Just c-c-calm down. Pop bought that tree and he's mighty proud of his bargain. It's his house. When you get your own house, you can choose your own tree."

We survived the Christmas of the pore, scraggly tree. When Elsie married, she always did have a beautiful tree and a beautifully decorated home. But no matter what kind of tree we had, the collection of familiar balls and decorations used year after year made us say, "That's the prettiest tree we ever had."

One Christmas Eve afternoon the lawyers told me I might as well close up early. I took advantage of the free hour or so to go to the beauty shop. I'd had a bad cold which I thought was cured, but sitting under the dryer brought all that inflammation in my head to a common point in my ear, and I rode the bus home suffering with a terribly painful ear. I walked in the front door of 2118 crying with the pain, "My ear hurts."

Mama said, "Oh, you poor thing. We must get you to the doctor right away." She found Dr. Standefer still in his office late on Christmas Eve, and Mama even called a taxi for me to take down there, that's how urgent it was that I get there before he left his office. Dr. Standefer opened an abscess in my ear. Although I was able to ride the bus home, that is one Christmas I'd just as soon forget.

But I don't want to forget those pleasant pre-Christmas meals when Ann and I would sit at the table as it was cleared and sing every Christmas carol we knew, with our fingers playing the tune on an imaginary keyboard on the tablecloth. The rest of the sisters thought, for some reason, that we were just killing time until the dishes were washed, but Mama said, "YaPapa always has wished that he could get a piano for this houseful of girls to learn to play."

Although we now had more room at 2118, we never had enough money for any extras, such as pianos or for anything else that wasn't absolutely essential to survival.

CHAPTER 24

THOSE BOARDERS AT 2118

As the house became more comfortable, Mama and Papa closed the 13th Street store and discontinued the Fried Pie Operation, and Mama boarded girls, both Texas Tech and Draughon's Business College girls, and working girls. Ann recalls how pleased she was when she realized Mama would be home every afternoon when she, Ann, came in from school.

Some of those boarders that we remember best included Anita Seay, Mary Anna Wood, Shella Head, Lavella Vaughn, Burma Ney Hargis and Winifred Piner. Mama's tenants were from various places around Texas, but Anita Seay later married Roy Bass and settled in Lubbock after World War II, and Beryl kept in touch with her through the years. Winifred Piner had been Beryl's classmate in Big Spring, and Beryl kept in touch with her in Big Spring. The rest of us wanted to nominate Winifred to play the part of Scarlett O'Hara in the movie *Gone With The Wind* because she was the only person we knew with a waistline as tiny as Scarlett's and because her eyes no nearly matched the description of Scarlett's that we decided author Margaret Mitchell had Winifred in mind. However, the producers of the movie weren't lucky enough to see Winnie.

We had a couple of quite large girls whose names I have forgotten. This was in a time when most young women were pretty trim and slim inasmuch as we didn't have access to fast foods, French fries and the like, and not having much motorized transportation at our disposal, we walked off all the calories we ate. One of those chubby girls (who always said she was going to Hollywood to be a movie star) would get up from the table where she had eaten very little, go to the telephone in the hall and call 19th Street Drugstore to deliver a couple of hamburgers or sandwiches and a malt or ice cream soda. Her aggravating habit prit'near drove Mama to distraction.

It isn't that Mama didn't feed us well. As she said, "It isn't fancy, but it's plenty." We had a pretty good variety, making well-balanced meals. Although she served salad by the large bowlful--Waldorf salad, grated carrots and raisins, all varieties of cabbage salads, green salads and wilted lettuce—Mama was partial to individual salads: sometimes only lettuce and sliced tomatoes, at other times pears or peaches with either cottage cheese or grated cheddar, bananas with peanuts on top of the salad dressing, and occasionally sliced oranges alternated with sliced onions.

There was always a big bowl of stewed dried fruit on the table, usually apricots. One of the boarders had a habit of clearing her plate, piling it high with stewed apricots, and after eating all of those apricots, she'd eat, in addition, the dessert Mama served.

There was always dessert, often cakes of different flavors. Beryl tells me we were never allowed but one piece of cake. I don't remember that, but Mama did tell me at one time, "YaPapa got so aggravated when we'd eat a whole cake at one meal (Mama had extra large pans for her layer cakes). YaPapa thought a cake ought to last for two meals, at least. He didn't mind how much meat we ate, that was okay, but he sure'nuf thought a cake should last for two meals, no matter how many it served."

Mama served more cakes than pies because as she said, "I

can make a cake that will serve twelve or sixteen in the same length of time it takes me to make a pie that will serve only six, at the most eight. When I have to make several pies, a big cake is cheaper and quicker.

Mama could take some leftover battercake batter and add a little of this'n'that and come up with a pretty good chocolate sponge cake, which she served with a vanilla sauce.

She served all sorts of puddings: banana, rice and bread puddings to name some of them. Ice cream was made in the electric refrigerator in those days, and she early on used pudding mixes, as well as gingerbread mix. It seems to me that for a period of time her favorite Sunday dessert was butterscotch pudding covered with whipped cream and frozen, then served on a slab of made-from-scratch angel food cake.

Beryl tells me Mama often said, "It doesn't matter what you serve 'em, just give 'em hot homemade rolls and they won't even notice what else you serve." The bread Mama served her boarders, however, was biscuits, cornbread (she insisted it was against her law to serve cornbread after one o'clock in the afternoon) and white bread and sweet rolls from the bakery.

The bakery truck stopped by regularly to see what Mama needed, but for most of the other supplies Papa trudged to Furr's on 19th Street and brought home two or three large sacks of groceries, once or twice a day, or as often as they were needed. Years later when that Furr's celebrated some anniversary, probably its twenty-fifth, Papa told them he'd been trading with them since the first day they opened, and in recognition of his faithfulness they gave him a nice assortment of groceries. My siblings who were around at the time tell me that for some unknown reason this irritated Mama. She is quoted as saying, "He oughtn't to have mentioned that to them."

When Papa brought home something that met with the girls'

approval, whether a certain brand of canned peas or a new package of cookies, he was so pleased that we liked it that he'd bring it day after day, until we were ready to holler "Uncle!" We learned not to be too enthusiastic about any particular purchase or else we'd have to eat it so often we'd get burnt out on it.

Papa helped in the kitchen and often was the dishwasher. Beryl and Elsie complained that his dishwashing methods didn't meet their sanitary standards, but they didn't fuss to Papa and they didn't take the dishwashing chores away from him.

Although Mama claimed, "For a large family, I really didn't use a lot of meat," we did have a large variety of the cheaper cuts of meat: hamburger in all disguises, and chicken fried steak, smothered steak, roasts, stews, and beef and vegetable soup, which, with the addition of okra, became Mama's style of gumbo. She served us as well all cuts of fresh pork and chicken in every form, except broiled. I can't remember Mama's ever broiling any meat.

She served liver and onions frequently, and occasionally boiled a beef tongue. This was always served cold and sliced, and I was surprised when I had it served warm with noodles in a cafe because I thought it just naturally came in cold sandwiches with Mama's chow chow on it. I could always give Elsie a special treat when she visited me in Wyoming by serving boiled tongue to her because, although she liked it, like most people I know today, she wouldn't prepare it.

For years Mama's favorite way of fixin' vegetables was with a cream sauce. When I returned from Wyoming I mentioned that those people up there ate carrots with nothing but butter on them, and that's the way we ate cooked carrots from that time on. Most green vegetables, green beans, cabbage, mustard, collard and turnip greens, were cooked a long, long time and seasoned profusely with bacon drippings or salt pork.

Mama boiled them in lots of water and that seasoned water was known by us as "pot likker" which was often enjoyed, particularly by Papa, with cornbread crumbled into it. Years later when I was served some sort of Chinese soup in an exotic restaurant, I exclaimed, "Why, this is nothin' but Mama's mustard greens pot likker."

Through the years I still had trouble with various attachments to replace that tooth I'd lost when I was thirteen, and the attachment I had at this particular time precluded my eating corn on the cob. Papa couldn't manage it either and he had a sharp knife by his plate to cut the kernels from the cob. When he finished with the sharp knife, I used it to cut the kernels from the cob. One of those chubby girls boarders said, "Pass that knife to me when Rosie is through with it."

Someone asked her if she had an attachment that prevented her from eating corn on the cob, and she said, "Oh, no, but if Rosie cuts her corn off the cob, I thought that was the way it was supposed to be done."

Everybody hooted, but that impressed me with the fact that other people watch everything you do.

One of the boarders helped Mama in the kitchen for her room and board. Mama's friend, Mrs. Fannie Gee, asked her why Mama's own girls couldn't do that and Miss Fannie had trouble believing Mama when she said, "They don't have time."

When Mrs. Gee spent a longer period of time around the house, she got the idea. My working days were long and busy. Mama said I just came in from the bus and hurdled the table at lunchtime, as it took most of my lunch hour to ride the bus and I couldn't afford to eat downtown. Besides, I didn't want to miss anything.

Beryl had a busy, active social life in college where she was working and majoring in Home Economics. Ida Rule didn't stay in college very long; we cant' remember if she finished her first year there, but she soon quit, much to Mama's distress, and went to work in an abstract office downtown where I saw more of her than I had previously because our paths crossed often in the business world. Ann graduated from Lubbock High School in 1940. She was busy with her babysitting jobs, as well as an active social life, and besides, as I've mentioned somewhere earlier, Mama still didn't want to make Ann do a lot of housework because she said Ann'd be looking after Mama and Papa after the rest of us were gone.

Perhaps all those girl boarders didn't stay at 2118 at the same time, but the five or six who shared the upstairs with Mama's four girls at one time (Elsie and her children stayed downstairs). also shared the one bathroom at the same time. That bathroom had a small closet with several shallow shelves, so that each girl had a spot to keep her toilet articles and clean towels.

It was not only a matter of keeping clean and beautiful, but every night we each felt that we had to wash out the underwear we'd worn that day and leave the garments drying overnight on our individual towel racks. Mama washed our linen: "All right, you girls, I'm washin' today, get those sheets and towels down here if you want me to wash 'em." She'd also wash the girls' washable clothes, too, if they got them downstairs on time, but we all had to do our own ironing, of course.

Most of the time, Mama was interested in our boarders, their friends—male and female—and she usually stayed abreast of the current slang phrases, popular songs and culture. Like most of any older generation, she thought our music was awful and had no memorable tune, but once when Mama had used some current slang phrase and later was singing "Flatfoot Floogie with the Floy-floy" (probably to show us how silly it was), one of my friends said, "I envy you your mother. My mother wouldn't know what your mother was talking about, and she never even heard that song."

Mama involved several of us in plotting to keep Fay (a pseudonym), one of the boarders, from running off to get married. Mama thought she was too young, that she should finish school, that her parents would be devastated, and that the young man "had no substance," Mama's way of saying he wasn't worth diddly squat. She called Fay's mother in a town nearly a hundred miles away and told her what was going on. The mother said she'd send her husband to Lubbock right away. We managed to keep Fay waiting for the young man for a couple of hours until the stepfather arrived. All he had to say was, "Let 'er go. I reckon it'll be the best thing she could do for herself."

Besides the live-in boarders, Mama also served meals to schoolteachers and others in need of a convenient place to eat. One of the schoolteachers was a beautiful young woman who, we understood, had been raised in a wealthy home with plenty of servants. Knowing this, we were duly impressed by her considerate habit of taking her own dishes to the kitchen after each meal—a habit the rest of us didn't have.

Miss Watson and Miss Clark were high school teachers who ate lunch with us for several years. They gave Mama a divided relish dish in a beautiful and practical Early American pattern of crystal as a Christmas gift one year, and for the next several years, the whole family gave Mama many pieces of that crystal, enough to serve sixteen at one time, with many larger serving pieces.

Edgar Heald had lived with us at Tech Tavern, and he and his brother, Ronald, were at 2118 much of the time in the very early days on 18th Street. Edgar worked his way through college by delivering newspapers and was most adept at riding his bicycle with two huge sacks of newspapers, folding and throwing as he rode along. Ann reports that, some years later, he came by in his military officer's uniform to introduce his bride to Mama, and Ann heard Mama say to the young lady, "You have the finest husband in the world there."

Mrs. Mary Young came from Oklahoma to open a decorator's shop on 19th Street, and she and her son took their meals with Mama for some time. As Social Security was still pretty new at the time, Mrs. Young was the first person I'd known who received benefits from Social Security after the death of her husband.

Most of the boarders were gone in the summer and Mama took advantage of their absence to indulge her love of travel. In the springtime of one of the early years at 2118, she went to a reunion of her sisters in Monroe and they traveled to one of the early Pilgrimages in the historic old city of Natchez, Mississippi.

Berry's first son, Berry Noel, Jr., was born in 1938, and Mama took little Barbara Jean with her and went to Fabens to "give Aileen a hand with the new baby," as she expressed it.

Beryl: In 1938, Mozelle, one of my classmates at Tech, said her father, a retired widower in a small town near Lubbock, would take us to California so we could go to the University of California at Berkeley. I called Mama at Fabens to tell her about my desire to go and she said, "I reckon I can sure understand that. I always wanted to go away to school. You tell Rosie I said to let you have the money you need. Have a good time."

I did both of those things: asked Rosie for the money to get me started and I had a good time. My experiences out there would make their own book.

Mama urged me to go to California to come home with Beryl and her party. I rode to Berkeley with Mr. and Mrs. Crenshaw and their daughter, Ann, and came home with Beryl,

Mozelle, and Mozelle's father. When I got there, I found Beryl had yellow fingertips from eating too many carrots, just about the cheapest thing available when she and Mozelle fixed their meals.

The back of the rear seat of the Plymouth sedan driven by Mozelle's father, would lift up, and the three of us girls—two of whom were quite tall—slept with our feet sticking into the luggage compartment of the sedan. The father slept on the ground beside the car, except the night when we spent the night in Yellowstone Park, and there he jumped into the front seat and slept draped over our several make-up kits, because a bear had come nuzzling around his face as he slept outside. This was another of those trips that was quite an experience.

On New Year's Day of 1939, Tech played in the Cotton Bowl at Dallas, and most of the girls who had returned from Christmas vacation went to Dallas. I managed to find a ride down there with a bunch of young fellows, and stayed with Beryl, Joyce Craven, Ina Bacon and several other of their friends in the Adolphus Hotel. We were so crowded that we put mattresses on the floor and some of us tried sleeping on box springs. After an exciting day at the game, I sat up on the train all night and arrived in Lubbock just in time to go to work. The other girls went on to the house in time for breakfast, and as they went through the kitchen, they are reported to have said to Mama, "Hey, what're those fellows doing in our dining room?"

Two young men had gone to work for the City of Lubbock as firemen, living and working in the 19th Street Fire Station just a block south of 2118. Mark Long, a long-time fireman at that station, had called Mama. "Mrs. Duff, could you feed a couple of young single men who've gone to work over here?"

"Of course," Mama had answered. "Send 'em over."

Those men later reported that that was the sorriest-looking, most beat-up bunch of girls coming into the dining room that morning they'd ever seen, and girls just seemed to keep coming in. Those young fellows, Hank Williamson and Bill Scott, took their meals at Mama's house for the next couple of years.

After they began eating at the house, they later told me, the first time they distinguished me from any of the other girls, I came in at midday dinner, sat down and, after looking over the table, grumbled, "Spinach and liver! What is this, a boarding house or a hospital?"

The first time I distinguished Hank from Bill happened because Hank could talk intelligently about the rapid lowering of the underground water table in the South Plains area around Lubbock from which the city got its water supply. This was one of Mr. Dupree's favorite topics, and since Hank had worked for the Water Department of the City of Lubbock before he began to work at the Fire Department, he knew what I was talking about.

Hank bought a 1936 blue Ford Tudor sedan soon after going to work for the Fire Department. He told me it cost $400, with fifty dollars down and twenty-five dollars a month payments at two or three percent interest. (*Per cent* was correctly spelled as two words in those days.) On Hank's first Sunday off (The firemen were on duty for four twenty-four-hour days, with three hours off for meals, then were off for twenty-four hours), he asked me to go to the movie one Sunday night.

"You sure'nuf haven't been around here very long, have you? Or you'd know Mama don't 'low no Sunday night movies 'round here!"

"Then how about going for a ride?"

"Mama doesn't want us riding around during church services. Says if we can get out then, we can just go to church. Stay here and we'll play Peggity (or whatever board game was set up in the living room at the time). Then when church is over, we can go for a Coke."

And that was the beginning of the courtship that made me into the proverbial landlady's daughter who married the star boarder.

CHAPTER 25

I WISH I'D TAUGHT YOU TO COOK

In the summer of 1939, I planned to make a tour with Miss Ruth Pirtle and some of the students of the speech department at Tech. We were going by chartered bus to New York City to see several Broadway plays before returning via Washington, D. C., to Dallas. When I told Mama that Hank planned to take his vacation and meet me in Dallas so I could go down to Kemp, in Kaufman County, to meet his family, she said, "This sounds serious—goin' to meet his family."

It *was* getting serious but I didn't see how I could walk out and take my contribution to the family budget with me.

I thought I'd not be able to keep working because we were not far enough out of the Depression and the economic climate when many employers would not hire married women.

After going via Niagra Falls and Toronto, we arrived for a wonderful week in New York city. There we saw some great shows, including *Hellzapoppin'*, Tallulah Bankhead in *The Little Foxes*, and Frederic March and Florence Ellredge in *The Immigrant*. We thought we were watching Raymond Massey play the role of Abe Lincoln until we went backstage to get his autograph and found we had been watching a stand-in. We took in all the attractions of the 1939 World's Fair and there saw Eleanor Holm, the great swimmer, and Bojangles Robinson, the black dancer. We went to the Cotton Club, to Harlem and to Chinatown, and to a very big hotel where one of the Dorsey brothers' band was playing. There wasn't much we missed, from a boat ride around Manhattan Island to the first smorgasbord most of us had ever seen, and the Rockettes at Radio City Music Hall.

Mary Anna Wood, one of the boarders at Mama's house, arranged for her brother, Mark, to call for me at my hotel. He escorted me on a double-decker bus ride and a ferry boat ride to the Statue of Liberty.

Mama had contacted her sister, Aunt Mary, who took me to dinner in Greenwich Village. Forty years later when I saw Aunt Mary when she was in a nursing home in Monroe, I reminded her of that occasion and asked her if she remembered that time.

"Of course," she said in her soft voice, "I remember you're the only person I ever took to dinner who refused a cocktail."

We went to the big department stores, and in Saks a salesgirl took us up to the employees' recreation area on the roof where we hoped to find a Lubbock young lady, an employee of the store, who was on her lunch hour, but we missed her. As walked down Fifth Avenue we saw Paul Whiteman leaving a men's clothing store. There was no mistaking him. Oh, that too, was quite a trip.

I returned to Lubbock to find that Beryl planned to marry Gene Barnett, with whom she had been going for some time. Gene was a fine young man, a graduate of Tech where he had been a star football player, but more important to Mama, he was a Baptist. He was going to teach Vocational Agriculture in Memphis, Texas, and plans were underway for their wedding. In keeping with the practice of the times, a big announcement party was held in our home, and Beryl was later feted and showered by her many friends. Young women today are amazed to hear that she was married in black, with a wide-brimmed black hat.

"You were supposed to have a basic black dress and I sure couldn't have two dresses, so black it was," she says.

The wedding was finally held on September 9th. Beryl tells me that it was planned earlier, and even later, but both of the other weekends Gene had to take some pigs to a fair or a stock show or some such affair, and after all, "Pigs is pigs and first things first."

Hank and I stood up with them— we could hardly be called attendants—in the chapel of the First Baptist Church downtown on Main Street. This was really the old sanctuary before the big tabernacle-style auditorium was built next door. Beryl and Elsie had gathered armloads of flowers the evening before from the Tech flower gardens, and the place looked as pretty as possible.

Beryl and Gene left immediately after the ceremony for Memphis, without a reception or supper, or any further festivities.

A year or so earlier when my friend Emily Davis did not plan to have a reception after her wedding ceremony in her parents' home, Mama told her, "You really ought to have a reception afterwards. It's such a let-down when the couple drives off and there's not much left to do." Mama always thought dishwashing could be of therapeutic value.

When Beryl and Gene came back to Lubbock, either for a visit or passing through, Beryl tells me that Mama always sent them on their way with a fifty-cent piece to buy hamburgers and pop on the way home.

Beryl and Gene usually came for Christmas because Beryl insisted on being at 2118 when the presents were opened on Christmas morning. How could you possibly have Christmas the night before? Santa Claus came during the night, so the whole kit'n'caboodle of us would have to get up about four o'clock in the morning to open presents, then Beryl and Gene, and later their little boys, left immediately for Melvin, Texas, to have Christmas dinner with Gene's big family. Some of those earlier Christmases, when there wasn't a defroster on their car, Beryl rode along holding a lighted candle near the windshield to keep ice from forming thereon.

Mama kept after me to get together some sort of hope chest. She'd bought two Double Wedding quilts for Elsie and me when we lived in Big Spring, but I think that was to help out the woman who made them, as much as for our hope chests. She practically forced me to buy a maple bedroom set, and then she sent me to another store to buy a second-hand loveseat for six dollars. That loveseat has been reupholstered several times and slipcovered more times than that. When she was visiting me in Casper, Wyoming, Mama made a slipcover for it in one afternoon, and when that was worn out I used it as a pattern to make more. The comfortable old piece of furniture is still in use in my living room today.

I had undertaken to learn to knit, but somehow I didn't quite catch on and I was left with some dark red wool yarn on hand. Mama announced she and Miss Dora would crochet a granny afghan for me with that red thread for the background--no matter that all the other afghans ever made had a black background. According to Mama I could buy a few packages of yarn so they could get started, then a package or so as they needed it to keep going. "You'll never miss the money," she said, "and it'll give us something to work on all this winter."

Well, they picked Thanksgiving weekend to get started, when Mama's boarders and Miss Dora's boarders had all gone home, and Miss Dora invited her cook at Lovell Hall to help, as she, too, wasn't busy. Every time the phone rang in the law office that weekend it was Mama telling me, "We need some more yellow and blue. And maybe you'd better get some green, too." Whatever colors they needed. They soon ran out of red and that was added to the requests. Anyway, I took home wool thread twice a day to keep them crocheting, and although it was only ten to twenty-five cents a package, that afghan used up about twenty-five dollars' worth of thread in one long weekend. That sounds pretty reasonable nowadays, but that was probably my week's salary at the time. That warm red afghan has been an integral part of each of the many places I've lived since then.

In 1939 we were becoming more conscious of the black duster clouds of war quietly rolling over the world, quietly, that is, for those of us in our little corner of the world. The Neutrality Act, passed by Congress in 1935, had met with the approval of nearly everyone I knew, at least those of us who paid any attention to it at all. Without television, with our interest in radio limited to the good music of the big bands, and our perusal of the newspapers limited mostly to local events, the conflict in Europe seemed far away and unrelated to us except as material for good movies, books, and *Life Magazine*. The most common attitude was expressed in the phrase, "So what's *that* got to do with the price of cotton?" meaning "What does that have to do with us?" or as other people might say, "So?"

We paid attention, however, when Hitler and Stalin entered into a nonaggression treaty in August of 1939. Mama was busily involved with Beryl's wedding plans when the news of Germany's invasion of Poland reached us. Tears came into Mama's eyes and she said, "It's a terrible thing to think that where there was a free and separate country one night, there just isn't a country the next day."

Things were getting closer to home when a client of the law firm asked the lawyers for help in contacting our Congressman to see if he could get any information about the client's daughter who was a passenger on the liner *Athenia* when it was sunk by torpedoes in September of 1939.

We generally couldn't see any reason for us to go to little Finland's aid when Russia attacked her in the fall of 1939. The Finns were holding their own very well against the numerically superior Russians, and we hadn't lost anything in Finland, as we argued with Mrs. Young, the boarder who thought we should be involved. But it was sobering and tragic when the Russians overran Finland, after massing their forces in one gigantic effort.

As tension in the world increased in 1940, Berry and his family moved to Garden City, Texas, where he would serve as County Agent of Glasscock County for four years.

President Franklin Roosevelt declared a National Emergency in 1940 and the National Guard was made a part of the Regular Army. A widowed client of the law firm came in to ask if anything could be done to keep her only son, who was in the National Guard, from going on active duty.

On September 3, 1940, Howard went back into active service to take training in degaussing and mine sweeping operations. Degaussing was a method of demagnetizing ships by encircling them with an electric cable to combat the dreaded magnetic mines of Hitler's navy.

Radio news broadcasts came more often, or we began to listen to them more frequently and with more concern.

On September 16, 1940, the draft law was passed, requiring men between the ages of eighteen and thirty-five to register. They would be called as needed for a year's service, although an amendment had been tacked on to the law preventing the sending of drafted men to any area outside of the United States. Hank had a comparatively low number, and he decided to volunteer, to get his year over with instead of putting our hopes of getting married on hold with the uncertainty of knowing when he would be called.

Since Hank had left his car with his family in Kemp, Jim Milam let me use his car to take Hank to the railroad station where he and about thirty other young men from the area left by train in January, 1941, for Ft. Bliss at El Paso. Privates made $21 a month in those days, and after basic training Hank was promoted to Private First Class, with the great salary of $51 a month.

With the noted efficiency of the Army, Hank, who had never been a great horseman, was placed in the U.S. Cavalry (which was still horse cavalry at the time). I guess the Army thought all Texans were cowboys, because others who went in with him were placed in the horse cavalry, too, even including Charley Maedgen, a banker.

Jim Milam went into the service in March of 1941. An experienced, practicing attorney, he had been turned down for a commission in the Judge Advocate General's department because of sinusitis, but he was placed in the Infantry as an enlisted man.

That summer I visited my old friend, Louise Douglas, in El Paso. She had married Dr. Ben Hutchinson, who was also stationed at Ft. Bliss, and Ben reported that the Medical Corps also often placed doctors in areas other than their specialties.

Immediately after Jim Milam left, I entered the hospital with a streptococcus infection in my vocal cords. Penicillin hadn't come to our part of the country yet, but the sulfa drugs eventually helped to cure me. Elsie, who had been going with Bill Scott about as long as I'd been dating Hank, had gone to Sherman, Texas, to meet Bill's family. While there she had an emergency appendectomy, and Mama rushed me out of the hospital to the house so she could go to Elsie because she was sure those doctors in Sherman would have to find out the hard way that Elsie was a bleeder. Elsie got along fine, but I didn't. I had left the hospital too soon and had to go back for several days before Mama returned home.

I wonder how Mama ever kept track of her children and their various illnesses, travels, and jobs. She read how Rose Kennedy, wife of Joseph Kennedy, Ambassador to England, kept a card file of her numerous children to keep up with their vaccinations, illnesses, schools and activities. Mama said, "That's a good idea, I've just waited too late to start."

Barbara Jean's tonsils were removed soon after they came to live with us. She, too, bled extensively, but she swallowed the blood until she threw up with great force during the night, covering one wall of the room. Fortunately, Mary Anne Davis was spending the night with me and with her car we were able to take Mama and Barbara Jean to the hospital.

Jim, at another time, had an erysipelas infection on his face. Before antibiotics, Mama, Elsie, and I took shifts sitting by him all night, keeping hot packs on his face.

One spring found Barbara Jean and Jim each with three different childhood diseases, probably measles, chicken pox and mumps, but they never had them at the same time. One or the other of them was in the bed back in Elsie's room for all of three months or more.

Lydia Ann had a tooth pulled, but the extraction didn't relieve the pain. In fact, it kept getting worse and since Mama couldn't stand to see any of her children hurting, she called the dentist who said, "Just give it time, it'll quit hurting soon."

When the pain became excruciating for Lydia Ann, Mama called our old dentist in Big Spring, then had Hank drive them down there. That dentist x-rayed and found that the tooth next to the extraction had abscessed. He treated it, and Lydia Ann—and Mama—soon had relief.

Elsie had a wisdom tooth pulled and suffered such pain that Mama asked the dentist, "Did you break my girl's jaw?" His reply was, "Do you suppose I did?" Elsie recovered eventually but I believe it required the help of the medical doctors for whom she worked at the time.

I got a pyracantha thorn under a fingernail, and after doctoring it all night, I fainted (for the only time in my life) at Mama's feet the next morning when I came down for breakfast. Ann and I both recall that Ida Rule had a history of medical problems, but our memories are vague about what they were. Ida Rule had a more difficult time finding her niche in a life that Mama could control. Mamá was so distressed when Ida Rule dropped out of college, and even then Ida Rule gave Mama worries for quite a while. She went to work in Amarillo and later worked for the government in Texarkana. She eventually returned to the fold and was a big help to Mama in her last days, and vice versa, because Mama was a help to Ida Rule who was in her terminal illness when Mama died.

Those are just some of the illnesses I can recall without really trying. Mama said, "I can handle them if they'll just come one at a time."

In June of 1941, Mama went to Garden City to help Aileen when Berry and Aileen's daughter Geraldine was born. Mama insisted that Berry take Aileen to Big Spring early, which, as Berry and Aileen tell me, turned out to be a very good idea because the rains came that night and they would never have been able to make it later over the muddy roads before the baby was born.

Mama enjoyed visiting at Berry's home and was there so frequently that I once fussed at Berry for taking Mama off, thus depriving me of chief cook and bottle washer. Mama took Jim and Barbara Jean with her one time to Garden City, and since both children had never really been in the country, they were reluctant to get out of the house.

When Howard and his family came through Lubbock in July of 1941 on their way to Elizabeth City, North Carolina, they showed the first home movies we'd ever seen. Some of those pictures were of the beautiful Northwest, and some of them had been made in Lubbock, as they had been moving to Bremerton. In Elizabeth City, Howard would take command of a ship when it was completed at the shipyards there and then commissioned. They would stay there before going to Miami for his tour at a sub-chasing training center. Later he took his family back to Bremerton in 1942 when he went on sea duty.

In that long, hot summer of 1941 I stood at the bus stop on 16th Street talking with a young black woman who had spoken of the latest news in the paper: Hitler's invasion of Russia. "What does it mean?" she asked. "Who do we want to win between those two mean men we've never heard any good thing about? Will the winner come over here and try to take over our country? Who'd we be better off under—the Germans or the Russians?"

That is a good example of the feeling that pervaded the country. I tried to assure her: "We don't have to worry about either one of those nuts coming over here, but if we had to make a choice, I reckon the Russians would be better for your people than the Germans. That Hitler has a screwball notion that he wants to get rid of everyone who isn't white Anglo-Saxon."

Hank was sent to Fort Brown, way down in the Rio Grande Valley at Brownsville, then back to Fort Bliss, from which place the whole Eighth Corps was sent to Louisiana for a couple of months of maneuvers in the piney woods and swampy river bottoms of that state.

The law firm needed Jim Milam's signature on a certain legal paper, so Jim's fiance, Kathryn Malone, and I volunteered to take it to Louisiana, no charge at all for the service, of course, just the use of Mr. Crenshaw's car and gasoline. Arrangements had been made by mail and telephone for us to meet Jim at the Washington-Youree Hotel in Shreveport on a Friday afternoon. It seemed to Kathryn and me that the whole U. S. Army was in Louisiana at the time. Jim found through some headquarters where Hank's outfit was, but we couldn't travel down that way because all the roads in the central part of Louisiana were closed to civilian traffic. Jim had brought with him from his outfit Greer Estes, a young lawyer from West Texas we had known in the law business. While the four of us were waiting until traffic was allowed on the roads south, we drove east to Monroe to call on Aunt Elsie in her beautiful country home. Mama had drawn a map of directions to Aunt Elsie's plantation, which was so far removed from the hullabaloo of the traffic around Shreveport that it seemed to be in a different world.

Red-headed Aunt Jessie, who was visiting Aunt Elsie at the time, said to the young soldiers with us, "Do you have any important, rich generals over there just lookin' for a nice widow lady like me?" It was said in such a soft voice—not only the voice of a southern lady, but the soft voice of the deaf—and was so incongruous that we had to laugh.

When we were able to travel on the roads, we drove south from Shreveport and after a few inquiries by Jim we stopped in what was an apparently empty country road. When Jim walked over into the woods and found Hank, Hank was surprised enough to see Jim, but when they came up to the car and he saw me, Hank was speechless for probably the only time in his life.

We found a hospitable farmhouse in the area that had opened its doors to servicemen's families and stayed there for the night. At the end of their twenty-four-hour furlough, we left the fellows with their respective units, then drove through the piney woods of deep East Texas and dropped in on Hank's family to spend the night. The next day we stopped to say hello to Tom Milam, Jim's brother in Dallas, then drove until late at night to get to our respective homes in Lubbock and Plainview. That, too, was quite a trip.

When I told Mama that Hank and I had decided to get married when he could get a furlough, she said, "Somehow I'm not real surprised." The thing that surprised her was my reluctance to tell her.

Mama had sensed for some time that I wanted to marry her boarder, and she was anxious to make enough money to keep the household going without my help. She said, "I'd take that Lewis Hotel Training School correspondence course in hotel housekeeping if I could afford the tuition."

I offered to pay the tuition, and in a time long before older women were returning to school, after she was well into her fifties, Mama finished the course during the next year.

Our wedding date was set for Hank's furlough in October. Mama said, "You need to get yourself some housekeeping things together. You should select a silverware pattern."

When I told her Hank and I had already bought a nice set of sterling—we'd each chipped in two dollars a week for the last couple of years—she was flabbergasted. She said, "You don't know how many times I've started to just go down to the jeweler's and get a set and charge it to you to make you buy one."

"One's aplenty, Mama, one's aplenty."

We planned for the ceremony to be held in the little living room of 2118. The bakery that had delivered bread and other baked goods to Mama all the years we had been in Lubbock provided the cake for only $7.50 (to Mama). Someone else whom Mama had helped out brought a spinet piano and left it in the corner of the dining room. Mama borrowed a lovely candelabra for the mantel from Mrs. Douglas in Big Spring, and a silver tea service from someone else. I think she really enjoyed planning the whole affair.

Years later, I was bragging to Ann about what beautiful large baskets of flowers I'd bought for each side of the fireplace for only $12.50. "Kiddo," she said, "I hate to tell you this, but you just rented those flowers. After you and Hank left and most of the guests were gone, the florist came and took those flowers over someplace else."

Oh, well, the house looked pretty good anyway. Aileen's sister, Helen Lakey, who lived in Lubbock, had brought bucketsful of beautiful fall flowers. The long dining room table was shortened into a circle, and the old davenport and library table were moved out of the living room to the backyard in order to make room for the two dozen or so guests we invited. We hoped for a nice day so the furniture wouldn't get rained on, but at the same time we wanted a cloud just before the 5:30 P. M. ceremony so the candles would be more effective.

Everything worked out very well. Ann's friend, Jean Casey, brought her camera and took several good pictures, using the first flash attachment we'd seen. Mama took four-month-old Geraldine over to Mrs. Schantz so she wouldn't disturb the festivities.

The ceremony was so short I'm not sure it was legal, but we'd asked the preacher for it because we thought Beryl's ceremony had been quite long. They tell me that Hank and I argued over how to cut the first piece of the wedding cake, but the marriage has lasted forty-five years anyway.

After a short wedding trip to New Mexico, Hank and I planned to take his car back to his folks, and Hank could ride the train from Dallas to Fort Brown. Mama said, "Well, good. You can just take me by Abilene and you two can stop at Fred and Sina's for the night."

Now we hadn't planned to go by way of Abilene, but one didn't argue with Mama! We didn't spend the night at Fred's, however, we told them we were going on to Mineral Wells, but we spent the night in a motel in Abilene.

I returned in a few days to the big upstairs room filled with wedding gifts, but I didn't pack them away because, as I told everyone, "Hank will be out of the Army in January."

Congress passed a law extending the one-year draft to the duration of the emergency, and for the first time I wrote a letter to our Representative, George Mahon, and told him what I thought about their lousy plan for keeping my husband in the Army while there were so many men who hadn't served their year yet.

On the Sunday afternoon of December 7, 1941, I packed away my wedding gifts when we heard over the radio of the Japanese attack on Pearl Harbor, a place we'd never heard of before that time. The Japanese had succeeded in doing what FDR had been unable to do: get the American people united one hundred percent.

Dub, the son of Fred and Sina, is quoted as saying, "I'm glad I'm still in high school—they won't be calling me." He thought of that statement a few years later when he was a Marine in the Pacific. He told Ann he spent most of his time opening beer for the officers.

I wonder if Mama realized that December afternoon the effect the war would have on her family: Howard was already in the service and would stay for many years; Hank would be in for four more years, serving in Europe for a couple of those years; Fred would become a Civil Service personnel officer for the Army in Alaska; Gene Barnett and Berry would each try very hard to get into the service; Bill Scott had been declared 4-F because of a bad ankle he acquired playing football at Tech, and he had already left for Louisiana to go to work for Halliburton Oil Well Cementing Company, a part of the oil industry so essential to national defense.

In Hank's outfit, as I suppose happened in all the Armed Forces, on Pearl Harbor Day the men were put on 24-hour alert, which meant they had to get rid of all superfluous clothes and equipment (including Christmas gifts held for families) so that they could be ready to go anywhere on 24-hour notice.

The Saturday before Pearl Harbor, his troop had discharged fifteen or twenty of the National Guard men whose one-year duty had been completed. Those men who stayed at the base waiting for the final paycheck on Monday had their discharges cancelled, but those who had left the base were not allowed to return to the outfit as most of them wanted to do.

A few days before Christmas, Mama phoned me at the office to tell me that Buck Price, one of the firemen, had told her of a group of young men who were going to Fort Brown to see a buddy, and they'd give me a ride if I wanted to go. Mr. Crenshaw gave his blessing, and I told Mama which of my clothes to get ready for me so I could leave after work for Fort Brown.

It's a "fur piece"—about 700 miles via San Antonio—from Lubbock to Brownsville, but we drove straight through. I spent almost a week in a hotel within sight of the flag flying at the fort. Hank could get off the base from six at night until six in the morning, and except for Christmas Day, when I ate at the mess hall, I had the days to myself.

This was the first Christmas I'd spent away from home with all the noise, excitement and companionship of a big family, and in spite of the beauty of Brownsville, with massive hedges of poinsettia flowers in bloom, it might have got me down if I hadn't fixed up my own Christmas tree. For seventy-five cents I bought a two-foot white tree, and at the same time I purchased some narrow red ribbon, a sack of tiny red and green gumdrops and red twine. I tied a little red bow on the end of each branch, and using my needlepoint needle, I strung the gumdrops into tiny individual "balls" and hung them all over the tree. Early on a morning right after Christmas, after Hank had said good-by, I prepared to take the twenty-four hour bus trip back to Lubbock. I hated to leave Hank and I didn't like having to leave that pretty little tree in the empty hotel room. I knew I'd never see the tree again, and things were pretty chancy for anyone in the Army that December of 1941.

In the elevator I asked the operator if he knew any children who didn't have a Christmas tree. In a heavy Spanish accent he said, "Si. Mine." When I told him about the one I was leaving in the hotel room, he asked if we could go get it before someone else did. The tree rode down in the elevator with me, and as I left, I said, "Tell your children, 'Merry Christmas.' That's the prettiest tree I ever had."

Hank had applied for OCS (Officer Candidate School) the day after Pearl Harbor, and after I was on the way home he was interviewed with several other young men. He soon found that he had been accepted for OCS at Ft. Riley, Kansas. He left immediately and he has quite a tale to tell of his trip from Houston to Dallas on a special train bound for a Texas A&M game at the Cotton Bowl.

After a hurried overnight visit with his parents in Kemp, a cousin drove him to Dallas to rejoin his fellow OCS candidates so he could arrive at Ft. Riley at the same time they did.

Bill Scott transferred from Louisiana to Lance Creek, Wyoming, in the early winter, and when Elsie joined him in February, they went to South Dakota to get married without a three-day waiting period. Because Mama felt that Bill deserved to start his married life without any children underfoot, she kept Jimmy and Barbara Jean in Lubbock until school was out. Mama later saw some of the firemen from the 19th Street Station and said, "Send me some more single men boarders. I still have two unmarried daughters at home."

Mama moved out of her big bedroom to let her new boarders, Dr. DeLauney, a professor of physics at Tech, and his wife, Keenzi, and two small children have that big room, while Mama and Papa moved into the smaller room in back of the kitchen. Dr. DeLauney had been a Rhodes Scholar and while he was on vacation from Oxford he went to French Morocco in North Africa where he met and courted Keenzi (the name, they told us, meant "Little Goat" in Arabic). Eventually he had her come to New York City where they were married.

Keenzi was a citizen of France and they talked French between themselves. When Dr. DeLauney held up a radish and spoke to his little boy, I asked him what he was saying. "I told him 'it's round, it's red, it's good.'"

At dinnertime I once tried to be sophisticated, mentioning *hors d'oeuvres*. I kept repeating it in my Texas accent and tried to explain to Keenzi what I meant. She finally said, "I don't know what you're talking about, but the word you're saying means "garbage." Maybe that's what we're talking about when we say *hors d'oeuvres*.

When Keenzi heard us talking about Elsie and Bill going to South Dakota to skip the three-day waiting period, she asked what we meant. When we explained that most states required a three-day wait between the issuance of the license and the actual ceremony, she said, "We didn't have to wait."

Dr. DeLauney said, "Yes, we did."

"But we went right from the boat to City Hall and were married in a civil ceremony there."

"No," he said, "we were applying for a license there. The priest married us three days later."

She exclaimed, "You mean we weren't married when we left City Hall?" And they cut into excited French as she left the table in a huff. The rest of us tried to keep straight faces and Mama changed the subject.

When the DeLauneys had lived back in the East, they had painted a large map of the world on one wall of their apartment as they tried to keep up with what was happening in the turmoil of the times. To show the emotional climate of our society that suspected nearly anyone of being a Fifth Columnist, their successors in their former residence reported them to the FBI as possible spies. Asked to come to the police station in Lubbock and talk to an FBI agent, the DeLauneys explained it was a matter of interior decoration and interest in world affairs that had placed the map on the wall, and they were told to forget it.

In the summer of 1940, Hank and I had been to a secluded resort in the beautiful mountains outside Denver that was operated by an interesting old character named Fritz. When I told Keenzi that Fritz said the Germans and the French people loved each other and would get along fine if other countries would just leave them alone, Keenzi hit the ceiling. "There's not a word of truth to that. The French hate the Germans."

When I repeated that Fritz said that you couldn't believe anything the American newspaper printed and that President Roosevelt was a Jew interested only in having Jews rule the world, both of the DeLauneys—and Mama—insisted I should go down and tell that FBI agent this tale.

I did, and told him, "There may not be a thing to it. I'd hate to cause them any trouble because they're a nice old couple, and that shortwave radio may be just a hobby, and all those Germans who come out from Denver on Sunday afternoons are probably just interested in a little beer and polkas."

The agent assured me that if there was nothing to the story, no problem would arise. "It may be they've already been reported, investigated and cleared, and everything is fine."

I never did hear anything further about it, so I suppose it was my overactive imagination taking charge.

The incident was indicative of the times, however. Dr. DeLauney and other members of the Physics Department had built a small structure in back of the Science Building at Tech, with instruments in it to study the static electricity generated by sandstorms in the area. Built with copper nails, it was of no use to anyone but that Physics Department, but one morning the staff found that little building vandalized and wrecked. It was suspected that the damage had been done by a spy or someone who had thought that the building had something to do with the war effort.

Hank finished OCS after three months (his class was the last class trained as horse cavalry) and had a short leave before he would be assigned to a permanent outfit. Since we didn't know if he would be sent overseas or some other place where it would be impossible for me to go, he returned to Fort Riley by himself, and left the car with me to drive to the to-be-assigned station if it were possible for me to go there.

As I drove north by myself, I foolishly picked up a hitchhiker. I had stopped for a couple of soldiers, which was the patriotic thing to do at the time, but this young civilian jumped in the car first. He was a small fellow who said he had been going to Tech, but he'd left because he didn't like the faculty or the school, or anything else about the college. When I asked him what he majored in, he said, "Electricity."

Now I began to suspect something was rotten in Denmark, because no one majored in "Electricity." Electrical Engineering, perhaps, or Electronics, or some more professional sounding title, but no "Electricity." He sounded a little more weird all the time and I soon stopped at a large, busy service station and told him this was as far as he was going with me. He got out with no argument, and I wrote Mama about this experience after my arrival at my new home. The first letter I received after I left Lubbock was from Dr.

tell him all I could remember about the man. The small size of my passenger harmonized with the small footprints found at the wrecked building, and his attitudes and ramblings seemed to qualify him as a suspect.

I wrote Dr. DeLauney all I could remember about the young man, but I'm afraid it was not enough to be of much help.

Keenzi had tried to teach me to knit and this time I learned a little better. After I arrived at my new home I asked Mama to get from Keenzi the instructions for making a baby bonnet I'd seen Keenzi knitting. I still have those instructions *for Petit bonnet bonne femme* written in Keenzi's unusual script, using "wool" for "thread," and spelling "purl" as "pearl." This was a little improvement because when she taught me, she always said, "with the wool in back" or "with the wool in front" for knit and purl. In Mama's handwriting on the side of the first page is: "This took us both 30 min to translate to Eng. I knew no knitting terms, she no Eng. For it."

Mama had finished her correspondence course, and while she took some on-the-job training at one of the hotels in Lubbock, she asked Sina to come stay with Jimmy and Jean (Elsie was in Wyoming). One Saturday I worked through my lunch hour and went home in the middle of the afternoon to find Sina sitting at the big dining room table which was loaded with dirty dishes. She was madder'n a wet hen (the only time I ever saw Sina angry) because everybody had left after dinner and left her there with the table and kitchen to clean. Berry and Aileen had been there, and Beryl and Gene were there for dinner, too. Ida Rule was already in Amarillo working at the time, and I don't remember where Ann was. I didn't blame Sina for feeling put upon, and I tried to make Jimmy and Jean clean the kitchen. We didn't do such a bad job, either, but Mama really chewed me out because "we didn't bring those children there to do the housework for this hojang."

Fortunately, Hank had been assigned to the CRTC (Cavalry Replacement Training Center) at Fort Riley, Kansas, and had found us an apartment in Manhattan, Kansas. I asked Mama for her recipes for cornbread, hamburgers, chili, and spaghetti (you can see I expected to live on ground beef), packed the car and prepared to leave about the middle of the day, because I was going by Wichita Falls, Texas, to spend the night with my long-time good friend Idell Bacon, who was teaching there. Mama walked to the car with me and said, "I'll tell you what I told Beryl when she got married."

I expected some great words of wisdom, and perhaps they were: "Read a good book every week. Don't let your mind go to waste."

As I started to leave, Mama bent and kissed me—perhaps for the only time in my adult life—and said, "Oh, my, I do wish I'd taught you to cook instead of getting a college education."

CHAPTER 26

GRANDMA, WE DIDN'T HARDLY HAVE TO BEG YOU

When she completed her on-the-job training as a hotel housekeeper, Mama got a job as head housekeeper for a large hospital in New Orleans. Ann tells me that Papa cried because Mama was going off, but of course, she went anyway.

After a few months at that institution Mama became housekeeper, with a large crew of maids under her, at the big old historic DeSoto Hotel in New Orleans. Papa had a job as purchasing agent for the dining rooms of the hotel and they seemed to enjoy living in the rather elegant suite of rooms furnished by the DeSoto.

Ann: I rode the bus to New Orleans that Christmas of 1942 to spend the holiday with Mama and Pop. Ida Rule came down from Amarillo where she was working.

I had rented Mama's room out to Walter Isom's family who were living in one crowded room and they, with access to the whole downstairs of 2118, thought I was pretty special. Both Reese Air Force Base and South Plains Glider School had been opened at Lubbock and places to live were at a premium. The upstairs rooms had been rented out, too, and I moved into the dorm that fall. Ida Rule generously sent me many lovely gifts from Amarillo: coats, sweaters, robe, underwear. How she could afford it, I'll never know, but she was able to hold some pretty good jobs in her day.

Mama Pays the Grocery Bill   291

That was about the time Howard sent me a monetary gift and I wrote him so quickly to thank him that he sent me another. This was my first adult memory of Howard, because he'd left home when I was so young.

Ida Rule and I had a good time in New Orleans and we all enjoyed that package of cakes you sent. It arrived on Christmas Eve.

In our tiny basement apartment in Manhattan, Kansas, I felt so sorry for Mama and Papa because they were away from all their family at Christmas (I didn't know Ida Rule and Ann were going to make it) that I got busy one day and, in an oven with no thermostat, baked three cakes to match those big cakes Mama usually made at Christmas, iced both layers, and in my one saucepan, popped some corn to use for packing material. I walked to town and got the package in the post office just before the deadline for Christmas mail. I was so petered out that I haven't made three cakes at one time since then, because that was such a hectic day with no electric mixer, no large mixing bowls, no cake mixes and such other conveniences.

Ann continued to live in the dorm as she went to Tech and graduated in August of 1943. She kept the rooms at 2118 rented out, usually to the wives of soldiers or airmen at one of the two military installations in Lubbock, and sent the rent money to Mama in New Orleans.

I was expecting my first baby about the first of June and wanted Mama to come to Manhattan and "give me a hand" as she put it, but she wanted to keep working until the first of July when she could be able to get a paid vacation. I could understand that, and I managed to have the baby without Mama's help, but I was certainly upset when I found she had left New Orleans in the middle of June for some reason.

Howard: In the summer of 1943 I had just assumed command of the USS WILLIAMSBURG, later to become the

Presidential Yacht, when Mama came to the Norfolk to visit me. She took a taxi to the Naval Base and was brought to the head of Pier 5, where we were moored. I was unaware of her arrival and was not there to greet her as she started up the officers' gangway. The sentry stopped her, saying, "Sorry, Ma'am, that is for officers only."

Mama replied, "Son, the Captain of this ship is my son and I'll go up where I please." And she did.

It was a hot summer day, and after working hours, I took her to the Officers' Club for a cool drink. I thought she would order a lemonade and I was never so surprised as when she ordered a beer. And she further surprised me by telling me that the doctor had Papa taking a jigger of bourbon each night before bed to reduce blood pressure.

Papa took that liquor as medicine, just as he had been ordered by the doctor. He'd all but hold his nose and gulp it down in one swallow and his sons could say, "Pop, you're supposed to sip it. You're supposed to relax to bring your blood pressure down." But to Papa it was medicine and he took it like medicine.

After Ann graduated from Tech in August (with a B.A. in English) she went to Lance Creek, Wyoming, to visit Elsie and to get a rest. After sleeping for a couple of weeks, she helped Elsie move with Bill and the two children to Lamont, Wyoming. Soon after that Elsie drove her to Rawlins to take the train to Tacoma, Washington, to visit me. We had moved to the Fort Lewis area earlier in the summer and Ann was a lot of company for me as I lived with my baby in a house on beautiful American Lake while Hank was on maneuvers in Oregon. Ann and I, with the baby, drove up on Mr. Rainier on a foggy weekday in October, and we certainly did get stared at. An Army ski unit was in training on Rainier and we were in the first civilian car that had been on the mountain in several weeks and we were the first females those soldiers had seen in a long time.

When Hank's outfit was transferred to Camp White near Medford, Oregon, Ann and I packed our belongings in the black Ford and headed in that direction. We were so excited the first time we saw the Pacific Ocean, you'da thought we were Balboa himself. We stayed in a motel right on the beach, with blackout curtains and everything, and we imagined a Japanese attack beginning at our room.

Mama worried about Ida Rule. She knew Ida Rule was in the Portland area, but she couldn't get in touch with her, so she left Papa in Garden City with Berry and Aileen. While Papa worked for the Rationing Board of Glasscock County for three months, Mama visited Beryl in Memphis and then she headed for Portland. She never did find Ida Rule, so she came down to Ashland, Oregon, and spent Christmas with us. While she was there we drove to Crescent City, California, and I have a snapshot of us having lunch by the side of the road. Mama was a firm believer in taking her lunch with her when she traveled.

When I lived at home, Mama served oatmeal and cocoa for breakfast, it seems to me, every winter morning of our lives. In Ashland, Mama insisted that we buy a big box of oatmeal ("How can you fix breakfast without oatmeal?" she wanted to know), and every morning she fixed oatmeal for breakfast in a quantity that would have fed her boarding house. I said, "Mama, don't fix so much oatmeal, there are just three of us." Hank ate at the Army camp and Rosemary still ate Pablum.

"I want to use up the whole box before I leave because I reckon you won't cook it after I'm gone," was her explanation.

"If that bothers you, why don't we just dump the rest of it out uncooked, and save us a lot of trouble." Of course, she wouldn't.

Mama said she would fix Christmas dinner for us, "But

you'll have to get me a sack of coal, because I'm not goin' to spend all my time puttin' that fast-burnin' wood in that stove." (This place, and on American Lake, were Ann's only experiences at cooking with wood, or with wood as the only source of heat.) We got a sack of coal and Mama, as usual, fixed us a scrumptious Christmas dinner.

Soon after the first of the year Mama and Ann returned to Lubbock, and Ann went to work in the office of Texas-New Mexico & Oklahoma coaches on February 1, 1944.

Elsie and her children were living in Lamont, Wyoming, under most unsatisfactory conditions: kerosene lamps with no kerosene for sale in the community, the children going to a one-room school, a house right on the highway with unsavory characters prowling around, but worst of all, Bill was gone constantly on oil well cementing jobs all over the state. Mama wrote Elsie to come home until a more decent place could be found. Elsie took the children to Lubbock and lived for a while until Bill was transferred to Casper. Incidentally, she found that in transferring from that one-room school to the Lubbock schools, which were supposed to be some of the best in the nation, Jim and Jean were ahead of their classmates in every subject.

Hank was transferred to Camp Maxey, Texas, in the late spring and we came through Lubbock on our way to his new place of service. Mama called Berry, Fred and Beryl and their families to come and welcome me back into what they considered civilization. Mama had a way of calling all the brothers and sisters together when any one of us was passing through or coming for a visit.

Berry had just moved to Sonora where he could be County Agent of Sutton County. When Berry and Aileen came to Mama's they nearly always asked her to go home with them, or to go on whatever trip they were launching. Sometimes she had to be coaxed, but often she didn't need much persuasion. Perhaps it was at this particular visit that, according to what they tell me, she didn't need much coaxing, and as they prepared to leave, their young daughter, Geraldine, said, "Grandma, we didn't hardly have to beg you this time."

That phrase pretty well describes Mama and her love for travel. She was never loath to go anywhere at the drop of a hat. She claimed she could get ready to go to Timbuctoo, or at least New York City, in ten minutes, until she heard someone say it wasn't necessary to brag about that, because if you got ready to go anywhere in ten minutes, anybody could tell that by looking at you.

Hank left the car with me in Lubbock while he took the bus to Camp Maxey, and Mama rode with me to Kemp where she caught the bus on to Longview and Monroe.

My little girl, Rosemary, and I lived in one room of a lovely home in Hugo, Oklahoma, for a couple of months that summer while Hank was at Camp Maxey. He was off duty most of the nights, and we stayed there until he was sent overseas about the end of June. (We had been awakened by sirens one morning in early June, and Hank murmured, "Those poor devils," thinking of the local firemen. We learned later the occasion was D-Day in Europe.)

Rosemary and I had to stay in Hugo a week or so after he left, waiting for hard-to-get tires that had already been ordered under the authority of the Rationing Board. When his father saw Rosemary and me as we entered their home unannounced, his face contorted as he realized, "Henry's gone." We were not allowed to mention any Army troop movements until they had arrived at their destination.

In the late summer Hank's sister Virginia drove with me to Lubbock. In those days before we had air-conditioned cars, and with the war time speed limit of 35 miles per hour, the last few hours of driving straight west into Lubbock were murder. We arrived hotter'n a firecracker to find Papa, bless his heart, had proudly fixed us a good supper of pork chops and whatever else might have been more appropriate on a cold winter night. Mama was gone on some more of her travels.

Rosemary and I settled into the dining room of 2118. It had been converted into a nice bedroom with the addition of a big closet in the corner. Some of my friends whose husbands were overseas also were in town, and we survived.

Merle Forrest came to be Ann's roommate at the end of the fall semester of 1944 and would be around for the next couple of years. When I asked Ann which of the rooms at 2118 was their room, she replied, "Merle says we stayed in every room upstairs—whichever one was clean or not rented out, we used it."

Merle and Ann were fun to have around, never a dull moment as we contended with rationing stamps and shortages of those things we thought essential to our comfort and well-being.

Ann corresponded with two boyfriends overseas, using V-Mail. I called one "the Catholic" and the other "the Baptist." V-Mail was a form on which to write a short letter. The one-page letter-envelope combination would be reproduced in a reduced size and sent airmail to an Armed Forces address. This process saved lots of weight and took up much less space than ordinary mail. In order to save time, Ann typed her notes, using a carbon copy for the same message to each solder (why not? It was going to be reproduced anyway) and then typed in the address on each note. The only trouble was the carbon didn't reproduce in the copying, and one of the young men received V-Mail with just his address and no message. I can't remember if it was the Catholic or the Baptist who received the non-message, but Ann said the other one would have caught on to what was happening.

Ann had another gentleman friend who lived and worked in Washington, D.C., and from whom Ann received a lovely bouquet of three dozen beautiful roses on some occasion. The young man called her soon after and she thanked him enthusiastically, saying, "But three dozen? Nobody ever received three dozen roses—I thought a dozen was the limit."

He asked her to repeat what she'd said, and about thirty minutes after the conclusion of their telephone conversation Ann received two dozen more roses from the florist. The young man had ordered and paid for five dozen roses, but somewhere along the market chain of command, someone had decided that three dozen was enough, probably thinking that no girl would ever say "Thank you for three dozen roses."

My brothers and sisters and I are a little vague about Mama's activities for the next ten years. She continued to work and travel and be concerned about her family, but we are not in total agreement of which job was when, or which trip was made in what year. For instance, we don't remember exactly when she went back to work at the DeSoto Hotel in New Orleans. She was gone from Lubbock at Christmas, but Ann thinks she was in Sonora and had Berry drive her to Lubbock on Christmas Day because "I don't want to be away from Ann on Christmas Day."

Rosemary, then eighteen months old, and I went to New Orleans to see her in January of 1945. I drove to Sonora to see Berry and Aileen, and after a nice visit with them, Rosemary and I rode a bus to Del Rio (we were the only English-speaking passengers on the bus) and took a Pullman car to New Orleans. Mama and Papa had a lovely suite of rooms in the hotel and we enjoyed a good visit.

Anita Seay, one of our former boarders, had married Roy Bass, who was stationed in New Orleans with the Navy, and

Anita gave me a good tour of the French Quarter and New Orleans in general. Mama and I also saw the sights. She took me to a play and we went to church together, and I met some of the friends she'd made in New Orleans.

One frail little Frenchwoman, a permanent resident of the hotel, offered Rosemary some wine when we were visiting in her room. Mama knew I was persnickety about what Rosemary ate and drank, so she whispered to me, "Keep calm, the old lady just thinks everyone drinks wine as we take it for granted that everyone drinks water." That was the same woman who asked Mama if she were Catholic, and then asked her what she was. When Mama said, "Southern Baptist," the lady answered, "I understand they're quite numerous around about."

Rosemary had a sore throat while we were there, so Mama ordered milk toast from Room Service, because her suite had no cooking facilities and she couldn't fix it for her as she had treated all of her own children. I was properly impressed with the elegance with which it was served and silver serving dishes for the toast and hot milk.

My enjoyment of the visit was tempered by my anxiety about Hank. The daily newspapers were filled with news of the Battle of the Bulge, and I knew Hank's outfit was located in that area of Belgium and Luxembourg. It turned out that he was right in the middle of the Battle of the Bulge, but was unhurt.

I returned to Del Rio by train, where friends from our Fort Riley days got me back to Sonora and I drove on to Lubbock, after stopping for a short visit in Abilene with Fred and Sina.

Some time while Mama was in New Orleans, Ann flew down there. She tells me, "It was my first real, live airplane flight. I borrowed forty dollars from you, but I paid you back, so relax."

Berry took leave from his County Agent job and went to Boston with the United States Department of Agriculture for wool research. Aileen and their two children, Berry Noel and Geraldine, came to stay in Mama's big room in Lubbock. I visited Elsie in Lance Creek that summer, stopping by Claude to see Beryl before Joe was born, and when I returned, Aileen and the children had gone to Boston and Mama and Papa were at 2118.

As I said, it's a little difficult to keep up with the comings and goings of Mama and Papa and their family for some time. Papa had worked at an ice house in Lubbock during these years, and he also had a job in the Quartermaster Corps at one of the air bases in Lubbock.

Beryl reminds me that Mama worked at the Lubbock Hotel at one time. I believe she worked at a hotel in Midland for a while, too. She said one prospective employer said her resume showed she changed jobs too often to suit him. He was looking for a more permanent employee.

Ida Rule married K.R. Marshall in 1944 and they worked in various places in Texas.

Fred was in Alaska, where he worked as a Civil Service personnel supervisor for the branch of the Army that was building the Alcan Highway, and when Dub graduated from high school and enlisted in the Marines, Sina joined Fred in Dawson Creek.

I was in Kemp when the news of FDR's death and then later the news of V-E Day reached us, but I was in Lubbock on V-J Day in August. At that time Hank was a Captain in the 9th Division stationed in Schweinfurth, Germany. He later returned to San Antonio, where he was discharged in October of 1945. Elsie and her children came to Lubbock from Wyoming to see Hank and were there over Hallowe'en. They brought the Yankee practice of trick-or-treat with them. Our family was not familiar with this, and neither were most of the neighbors, and Jim and Jean reported that people gave them money, some as much as a dollar. The kids thought they had a good thing going.

Hank, Rosemary, and I lived in the ex-dining room of 2118 until the next summer. Mama had rented a couple of upstairs rooms as a small apartment to a woman with several big boys, some of them returned soldiers. Their sleeping arrangements were such that they put a mattress on the floor each night to take care of the overflow. One night when they dropped the mattress on the floor above us, Hank awakened with a jerk and nearly jumped out of bed. He said it was the same sound as a bomb landing nearby.

Hank brought a souvenir bottle of wine back from Europe and presented it to Mama. He tells me that one afternoon when he entered the house after work he heard laughing and talking in the kitchen and thought the house had been taken over by the girl boarders again. "I stepped to the kitchen door and there sat your mother and Mrs. Vandagriff just killing that bottle of wine. Those two ol' ladies were laughing and carrying on like a couple of teenagers, but they were sure having fun."

Some time during these years while I was living at the house, Mama was returning from a trip to the northwest and to Wyoming to see Elsie when she stopped in Colorado Springs, and through the YWCA, found a job as a cook in a wealthy household. She wrote to me that she wanted to sell the house and to dispose of all the belongings in it, and she told me to see about taking care of the matter. I wrote her that if she wanted to close the house she'd have to come home and do it herself because I believed that it would kill Papa to have to get rid of 2118 and to pack up the collections of a lifetime.

She also told me in that same trip to send her electric mixer to Elsie; Elsie had given it to her, Elsie didn't have one, Elsie would use it more than I did, and she (Mama) wouldn't be needing it any more. I was willing, but did you ever try to pack up a large mixer with glass mixing bowls? I dillydallied around so long looking for a suitable box that by the time I had the mixer ready to mail, Mama had come home again. She said she didn't last long in that job because she didn't cook fancy enough for that family.

That experience seemed to make her more content to confine her money-making efforts to babysitting jobs. Mama had taken over the babysitting jobs that her daughters had graduated from, and when she was in town she was always kept busy, either babysitting babies or older people who could not be left alone, and she became one of the most popular babysitters in Lubbock. Some women wouldn't leave the hospital with a new baby unless Mama was free to take care of them. A year or two later, she was at our apartment in Rock Spring, Wyoming, when a woman called from Lubbock to reserve her time for some special occasion months away.

In July of 1946 Berry and his family moved to Ft. Collins, Colorado, where Berry went to work as Extension Sheep and Wool Specialist for the State of Colorado. Hank and I had bought a small house trailer and we left Lubbock about the same time and Hank went to work for Halliburton Oil Well Cementing Company, stationed in Rock Springs, Wyoming.

Soon after we were settled in the backyard of a local family (because there were no trailer parks in Rock Springs at the time), Mama and Papa came to see us. They had been to see Howard and Pauline, I suppose, or maybe to see Aunt Jessie in San Francisco, because they came from the west. I knocked myself out fixing a big pot of soup and a lemon meringue pie for their lunch, but they had eaten lunch at a short stopover in Green River, about thirty minutes before arriving in Rock Springs. It might have been just as well, however, as the lemon pie was a disastrous failure. Mama proceeded to tell me what I'd done wrong, but the cause of the failure of the recipe that had worked so successfully for me in Manhattan and Lubbock was the high altitude. I hadn't yet learned about changing recipes so they'd work at high altitudes.

Upon her arrival in Rock Springs, Mama announced she wanted me to drive them to Salt Lake City to see the sights. We'd take the pot of soup I'd made and heat it up on the way. As I've said, one didn't argue with Mama. I had to wait until Hank's first Halliburton paycheck came in later in the afternoon so I could get some cash (Hank was away on some oil field job), then we left in the late afternoon and spent the night in a rustic tourist camp somewhere along the road, where we heated the soup over a wood stove. Mama had long since found that places to stay overnight were cheaper away from towns.

We enjoyed seeing the sights of Salt Lake City, then old Fort Bridger in Wyoming before our return to Rock Springs. The next day I drove the folks to Casper (we went off and left our lunch that day) and Elsie met us and took them with her to Lance Creek.

That trailer in Rock Springs wasn't the most elegant home in which to entertain visitors. Besides being so small compared to today's travel homes, I cooked on a gasoline stove, heated with diesel fuel, used the restrooms of the filling station owned by our landlord, carried water for our use, and climbed down a ladder into the landlord's basement to use their washing machine or take a shower—twice a week when their coal cook stove heated the hot water tank. I'm not griping, I'm just telling it like it was. I was so happy to have a place of my own that I honestly don't remember complaining.

But we didn't have much money. Veterans could receive on-the-job training assistance if they made two hundred dollars a month or less; Hank made two hundred and ten, of which more than half was paid out for trailer payment, trailer space rent, insurance, and payment on a lot we'd bought in Lubbock before we found we couldn't get materials for building a home in the post-war economy.

During the war when items that were not essential to the war effort were not manufactured, merchants let customers sign up for those items to be first in line when they were again made after the war. I think Mama signed up everywhere for everything: record players, electric mixers, vacuum cleaners—whatever. She wrote me that she had purchased a record player that we could have for something over a hundred dollars. I told her that we not only didn't have room for it, but we didn't have the hundred and something dollars. She replied that we could find room for it and could pay her when we did have the money, no hurry. She sent it anyway, and it wasn't two or three months before she wrote to please send her the money, she'd let us have the record player when we wanted it, and the least we could do was let her have her money. It aggravated me—we hadn't been able to buy any records for it yet—but we found the money somehow and sent it to her. We did enjoy the record player for several years, but technology changed and long-playing, different speeds came out and the old record player soon became obsolete.

As time passed we truly didn't hardly have to beg Grandma to travel. I have a picture of her sitting on a log with young Berry Noel and Geraldine on either side, silhouetted against Old Faithful Geyser erupting. Berry tells me that on one trip he and Aileen returned to their motel after seeing the Passion Play in the Black Hills and found Mama eating watermelon in the dark because she didn't want a light to wake the children.

In 1947 Gene Barnett moved to Jayton, Texas, and when Beryl was unable to find a place there to live, she and her two boys spent much of the summer in Lubbock before their third son, Robert, was born. Soon after Robert was born, they moved to Plainview, where Gene was Vocational Agriculture teacher in the school system until his retirement thirty-four years later.

That fall I flew to Lubbock to await the birth of my second child.

Beryl was in Lubbock frequently to be treated for severe arthritis.

Ann was living at home, and Fred and Sina's son, Dub, was at 2118, going to Tech as a veteran of the Marine Corps, and I got a glimpse of how student life had changed in ten years. Dub was in the School of Agriculture and he reported to the family that Berry had become well-known as a wool specialist in the nation. It was about this time that Berry received a letter from Europe addressed to "Berry Duff, Wool Specialist, USA" and it was delivered to him in Fort Collins.

Mama had rented a couple of the rooms upstairs as an apartment to a young woman and her little girl. That beautiful young woman had lived in California where her marriage to a well-known man in the movie industry had been ended by a famous movie actress. She and the little girl did have the same name as the man in her story and he was married to that actress, according to the fan magazines.

The house was pretty full and Mama and Papa were both busy babysitting. On Hallowe'en night they were both out on babysitting jobs and left me sitting in the living room to protect the house. Although I was only a few feet from the open front door, some tricksters stole the front porch light and left the hydrant in the front yard running full blast and I didn't even know it.

The next year Beryl decided she wanted to get her degree, so with Mike, Joe, and Robert she lived with Mama in the fall of 1948, and while Mama babysat the little boys, she attended classes at Tech and got her degree in Home Economics. Beryl's graduation concluded the immediate family's student days at Texas Tech, although Ann would work there in a responsible position after Mama's death, and several of Mama's grandchildren have attended Tech through the years; Terry Miller, and Mike, Robert, and Craig Barnett, to name some of them. The family has established in Mama's memory the Ida M. Duff Memorial Scholarship for qualified graduates of Sweetwater High School who want to attend Tech.

Mama wrote that with Rosemary starting school next year I should come to Lubbock for a nice long visit while Rosemary could be away during the spring weather. We didn't go to Texas every year, but as I said, one didn't argue with Mama, and at the end of his vacation Hank left me, the two children and the car in Lubbock for about a month's visit which extended to nearly three months.

On Rosemary's sixth birthday Mama wanted to have a big party and invite my old friends and their children. When I got up that morning and kept complaining of a bad stomach ache, mama sent me to the doctor, and that afternoon some of my friends hosted the party while Mama was in the operating room supervising the removal of my appendix. Some of those friends are rumored to have said as they washed all those china dishes, which Mama insisted on using even for children's parties, "And to think I have an electric dishwasher at home to do this."

Beryl took Rosemary home with her and Mama looked after eighteen-month-old Dick during my stay in the hospital. When I was dismissed, Mama sent me home with our friend Dorothy Vandagriff Cone until I was able to be on my feet.

Ann planned to marry Houston Miller in July. Houston was a widower with two young children, Terry and Judy. He and Hank had known each other since their CCC days.

For you young people out there on that space station, the

Civilian Conservation Corps was one of FDR's most successful programs for overcoming the hard times of the depression of the 1930s. In it were enrolled unmarried men between the ages of seventeen and twenty-three in need of employment. They lived in camps all over the country, working in National Forests, the prevention of soil erosion, flood control and similar projects. They were under the administration of two governmental agencies: the War Department, which was responsible for providing food, clothing, housing, medical and dental care as well as education. Enrollees were paid thirty dollars a month, of which twenty-five was sent home.

The Interior and/or Agriculture Department was responsible for the designation, planning and supervision of the work projects. Although the educational program was voluntary, an average of 89 percent of all enrollees attended classes approximately three nights a week, and this enabled many men to find better jobs and some to go on to college. The CCC's impact upon the country and three million men can still be seen today in trees, fences, parks, dams and the successful lives of most of those men through the years.

Houston's aptitude for mechanical drawing had been enhanced by studying architectural drawing while in the CCC. He later completed a course from ICS and made a career as a successful building designer, designing and supervising the building of many homes and buildings in the booming post-war economy of the South Plains.

They planned to be married in July, and since the doctor wouldn't permit me to drive my car until after that time, I asked Elsie to come down from Wyoming to attend the wedding and then drive my car back to Wyoming. Ann and Houston were married on a Saturday afternoon with similar arrangements to those that had been used for my wedding eight years earlier.

The next morning in church I'm afraid Mama didn't listen very closely to the sermon. She thought that with all those flowers in the house, and with that borrowed tea service, and with most of the girls here, and the house nice and clean, "Why don't we just have another party?" She, Beryl, and Elsie fixed some fancy refreshments and we did have a big afternoon party when all of our old friends who were in town dropped by for a little visiting. It was the last time I have seen some of those friends.

Ida Rule returned home after an unsuccessful marriage and Mama sent her to stay with me in Casper, because I was the one sister her husband didn't know and he wouldn't be able to find Ida Rule there with me. She did stay with us for almost a year, during which time she had a pretty good job in Casper. Her boss was active in politics and sold her tickets to a dinner to hear Albin W. Barkley, Vice-President under President Harry Truman. She took Hank and me to the dinner and it was the first time I'd heard a master politician speak. He spoke for over an hour, and I don't believe he stopped to catch his breath, but he had the undivided attention of every person at the large gathering, although I can't remember a thing he said.

Ida Rule was a lot of company to me and became attached to our baby, Fred, who had been born that spring. Mama wrote Ida Rule to come back to Lubbock because a former employer had called, wanting her to come back to work, and she returned to Lubbock a short while before Ann's baby, Scott, was born. Ida Rule had a good position as bookkeeper for Western Pipe and Steel Company and helped Mama and Papa pay the grocery bill for the next several years.

Mama came to Newcastle, Wyoming, when Elsie's daughter Barbara Jean was married. Someone was playing a tape recorder (the first I'd seen) after it had been left running in the midst of the festivities. Mama, in the next room, said, "Who's that back there makin' fun of my southern accent? Nobody I know talks like that." It was Mama's own voice that she heard played back.

Three or four years later, Elsie and Bill took Barbara Jean and her little girl, Vickie, to Lubbock, and we have a four-generation picture of Mama, Elsie, Barbara Jean and Vickie Sue.

Mama and Papa were visiting Berry and Aileen in Broomfield, Colorado, when Papa suffered a stroke. I drove down to see him while he was in a Denver Hospital. Berry and Aileen's youngest child, Bryan, was only about a year old, and they lived with their two teenagers on a farm in Broomfield north of where Berry worked for U.S. Testing Company in Denver.

I marvel how Aileen coped with all the work she did and at the same time put up with the brothers and sisters descending on her one or two at a time. Papa went back to Lubbock by train and was bedfast at 2118 until his death about nine months later.

I took my three children down to Lubbock a few weeks before he died in the spring. He was on a bed in Mama's room and seemed to enjoy my sitting by his bed and talking to him. A Lutheran church had been built next door and when the organist came to practice the Sunday music, that good woman left the windows open so Papa could listen to the old hymns she found that he loved so much.

Elsie had been down for a visit a short time before I was there, and Beryl's husband, Gene, and Ann's husband, Houston, gave Mama help when they could, but Ann was Mama's mainstay and helper during this time. Beryl was helpful, too, but she was teaching, and Ida Rule was very supportive, but her job kept her busy.

It was on this trip that my children and I saw our first television programs.

After Papa's death Mama went home with Fred and Sina for a visit, but she soon sold the old house at 2118 and she and Ida Rule lived together in a smaller, newer house. That first one was too far from a bus line to suit Mama and they later moved to another house nearer a bus line, although Mama insisted on keeping her driver's license current until her death.

During these few years she had various grandchildren visiting her. She and Ida Rule came to Casper and brought my two oldest, Rosemary and Dick, back to Lubbock for a visit in the summer after our youngest child, Lucy, was born. Geraldine was in Lubbock, too, that summer. Ann's daughter, Judy, tells me Mama and Berry Noel, Berry's son, drove Ida Rule's car with the three of them to Natchez and New Orleans, and that Ida Rule also took Judy on a good many trips.

No, Geraldine, we didn't hardly have to beg her, because she continued to travel. Mama went to the northwest to see each of Howard and Pauline's post-war babies, Larry and Marjorie. She came to Casper each time when my last two babies were a few weeks old, saying, "I knew you'd be havin' cabin fever. I feel so sorry for you girls because you don't have Mahaley to help you out."

One of those times when she arrived in Casper from Cut Bank, Montana, she said, "I spent the summer with Elsie in Cut Bank, all four days of it."

On one of our summer trips to Lubbock, Mama had Hank drive us to Wichita Falls to see Fred, who was in the hospital. We went in Ida Rule's car because it was air-conditioned, the first air-conditioned car I'd driven.

Mama had had a liver problem for some time, and she was finally operated on in a military hospital in Wichita Falls. Fred and Sina lived in Wichita Falls, where Fred was in charge of Civil Service personnel at Sheppard Air Force Base. Howard, at that time a Captain in the Navy, was the senior member of the National Naval Reserve Inspection Board, stationed in Omaha, which was the location of the Headquarters of the Naval Reserve Training Command. He had a monthly allotment sent to Mama, and I understand it was because of this she could be treated in the military hospital. The doctor assured Fred there was nothing wrong except "she has cirrhosis of the liver, but she's lived with it forty years and can live with it another forty."

We moved from Casper to Sterling, Colorado, in the summer of 1956 and I felt so much closer to Lubbock that the first long weekend the children were out of school in the fall I drove through the first snowstorm of the season to go to see Mama.

Later in the winter was the last time I saw Mama on her travels. She was in Wheatridge, Colorado with Berry and Aileen, and Hank and I, together with our two-year-old Lucy, drove down and spent the afternoon with her. Elsie, who at that time lived in Riverton, Wyoming, was in a hospital in Billings, Montana, to have exploratory surgery. Mama was just determined she was going to fly to Billings to be with Elsie. Mama was in a quite frail condition by this time, and I argued with her that she'd have to stay in a room near the hospital, and what if she should get sick away from anyone she knew except Elsie, who was herself in the hospital? She said, "But she's my own child and I think I ought to be with her." She didn't go to Billings, but reluctantly flew back to Lubbock.

The next summer I took my three youngest children to Lubbock for a visit.

Ida Rule had had a mastectomy a couple of years earlier, and plastic surgery had to be done to get the wound to heal. The family had written me that they teased Mama that she couldn't tell the doctors how to do the operation because she'd had no experience with plastic surgery.

When I went down in the summer, Ida Rule had just been

discharged from a Wichita Falls hospital where she'd received a further series of treatments, and she and Ann had gone on vacation to the deep South. It was a time of grief and heartbreak for Ann as she had been told Ida Rule had not long to live, but she kept up a cheerful attitude, because Ida Rule had not been given that prognosis.

I left my two young boys with Beryl and her boys, and Lucy and I had a nice visit with Mama. Mama spent much of her time resting in her old "strawberry bed," but she was able to come to the table for meals or sit in the living room visiting with her callers. Ann had found a young woman to stay in one of the rooms of the house and help look after Mama. While she may not have been the very best help in the world, she relieved Ann of some of the housework and chores.

When my children and I returned from a short visit with Hank's parents, Ann and Ida Rule had returned. I had a short visit with Mama and Ida Rule, then drove on to Beryl's place in Plainview on my way back to Sterling. That last afternoon I spent with them, Mama and Ida Rule were involved with finding a safe haven for a young woman and her child who were seeking shelter from an abusive husband and father.

Berry and Beryl and their spouses were there frequently, and Elsie went down in the winter to help Ann.

Mama was taken to the hospital a few days before Christmas. We had just moved back to Rock Springs and I was at a Christmas party when Beryl called me to tell me Mama was in the hospital. On New Year's Day I arrived by train at Amarillo, to be met by Ann's son, Terry, who took me to Lubbock.

Ann told me the doctor had said, "Mrs. Duff always thought she had a heart problem, but that old heart has just kept beating along when nearly everything else has stopped."

I sat there by Mama's bed all that afternoon of New Year's

Day and Ann told me the last thing Mama said was, "Who'll look after Rulie?" When Ann assured her that she, Ann, would do that as she had been lovingly caring for Rulie and Mama for months, Mama seemed to relax.

One day into the new year, Mama died. She had done well in helping to pay the grocery bill.

AFTERWORD

THE GOSPEL ACCORDING TO MAMA

Ida Rule died a couple of months later. When Elsie and Ann closed the home of Mama and Ida Rule, Mama's heirloom walnut dresser was sent to me, and in the top drawer I found Mama's old Bible with several mementoes representative of the two precepts which were so near and dear to her heart: love of family and love of God.

Some of these mementoes include a small picture of her oldest sister, the address of an old friend in Monroe, a newspaper copy of the poem, *When The Works All Done Next Fall,* with two lines underlined:
> *I'm going to a new range, boys;*
> *I hear the Master's call.*

A newspaper clipping tells of Little Boy's death and funeral, and another clipping from a Fort Worth paper has a picture of Howard in uniform. It begins: "Lt. Cmdr. Howard C. Duff, son of Mr. and Mrs. B.N. Duff of Lubbock, has been awarded the Legion of Merit for meritorious performance of duty as Commanding Officer of the *USS Flaherty* in a submarine attack on April 24, 1945."

There is also a tiny pamphlet compiled by Beryl's pastor entitled "Sure Salvation for the Souls of Men."

Printed in 1886, the old Bible is frayed and well-used, but it is not marked with pen or pencil as many of our Bibles are. Mama didn't have to do that. She taught the Bible to her children through practice rather than through preaching.

I am unable to recall hearing Mama quote any Bible verse before I was an adult. Not very many years before she died, Mama said to me, "When I remember what I went through to get all of you children clean, out of the house at the same time and to church on time—, it wasn't easy, I'm tellin' you. And for what? Most of you don't care whether you go to church or not, and some of you don't even worry about getting your own children to church."

"Cheer up, Mama," I said. "Think how we might have turned out if you hadn't done all that for us. We may not be the best church members around, but at least we haven't done anything to disgrace you and Papa."

"True," she replied, "but I take more comfort from the Bible verse that says 'Raise up a child in the way he should go and when he is old he will not depart from it.'[1] It's that phrase 'when he is old' that I hung on to. I just pray that those of my children who are weak in their faith in their middle years will live to be old enough to return to the way they were raised."

It was a surprise to me to find that the word used in that verse in the King James Version is "train" instead of "raise," but in the language of Mama's time and place she didn't "train" or "rear" them, but as the TV commercials say, she did it the old-fashioned way: she "raised" her children. I suppose there is a slight difference in meaning, but Mama wasn't into etymology, she was into raising children.

Mama taught the Bible through example, by putting into practice rather than verbalizing, the verses that set a standard for selfless living. My very earliest memory is of going with Mama to the missionary society meeting at a home with a wonderful terraced lawn, just made for us children to roll down the hill.

In another early memory I am sitting in a chair just outside the kitchen door—out from under her feet—asking Mama, "What's this word?" for nearly every word in Hurlbut's *Story of the Bible*. This was in my fourth year when I learned to read with Mama's help. Imagine the patience she must have had to leave the big black iron cook stove to come help me so very frequently as she went about the task of preparing supper for her rapidly growing family.

She never quoted to me "Thou shalt teach them diligently unto thy children, and shalt talk of them when thou sittist in thine house, and when thou walkest by the way, and when thou liest down and when thou risest up."[2] She didn't quote it, she just did it.

We were taught a bedtime prayer ending with "Bless Mama 'n' Papa 'n' Mahaley 'n' Grandma and all my brothers and sisters . . ." and then we added any pets, friends, teachers or whomever. It may not have been the greatest prayer, theologically speaking, but it taught us of the nearness and accessibility of God and the closeness of family. She didn't have to read to us "Thou art near, O Lord,"[3] she just demonstrated that He was.

When I was about eight years old I was asked to say a "piece" for the Sunday School Promotion Day program. Mama saw to it that I had the poem memorized and that we arrived at the empty church well before Sunday School started so that she might have me practice saying it loud enough to be heard at the back of the church. Now I was the Number Five child and there were two younger than I was; we had to come to church in a horse-drawn buggy from the house in the country; Mama left Sunday dinner already prepared and the ice cream freezer full, and we were all breakfasted and in clean clothes. It just exhausts me to think about getting to the church on time under those conditions, much less ahead of time. But Mama did it, Sunday after Sunday. She did have a poem cut from a magazine

Afterword—The Gospel According to Mama

giving a mother's thoughts in worship service. In it the mother thinks of all the things she did on Saturday evening and Sunday morning to get the children to the church on time, and the last line of each verse was "God won't mind if I doze during the sermon, will you, God?"

On a certain miserable, icy morning in Longview, there were only sixteen persons at church and thirteen of them were from our house. Yet I never heard Mama say, "We are 'Not forsaking the assembling of ourselves together, as the manner of some is.'" [4] She just assembled us together with the rest of the congregation.

She never quoted "Remember the Sabbath Day, to keep it holy."[5] She just did it. The whole family was at church every Sunday morning and evening, and in the earlier years, on Wednesday night—Prayer Meetin' Night—too. I had finished college and was helping to support the family before I had the nerve to go out on a date on Wednesday. During my growing up years we might not have had to go to Prayer Meeting, but we couldn't go anywhere else on Wednesday nights.

When I was at 2118 for an extended visit when my second child was born, I told Ann I'd been to a movie one Sunday night. Ann, then a young career woman helping to support Mama and Papa, exclaimed, "Girl, you *have* been away from home a long time if you can say out loud around this house that you went to the movie on Sunday night. Best not let Mama hear you."

During my childhood, Mama served as Treasurer of the church. It was at a time and place when part of the Treasurer's duties consisted of going from door to door, reminding the members of their responsibilities for the finances of the church. I am sure that the nature of Mama's position didn't make her the most welcome visitor as she trudged from home to home, but she continued to "Serve the Lord with gladness."[6]

She served Him in other ways, too. At her funeral in Lubbock, several women told me she had been the best Sunday School teacher they ever had. Fifty years after we lived in Big Spring, a woman from there told me that Mama was the best Sunday School teacher she could remember. Mama didn't think she was doing anything special; she just kept "doing the will of God from the heart: with good will doing services, as to the Lord."[7]

I overheard Dr. Dimwit (the name is changed, obviously) start to make a critical or derogatory remark about Mama's pastor. Mama drew herself up to her full, not inconsiderable height, and interrupted, "Doctor, I never let anyone criticize my doctor, and I don't allow anyone to criticize my pastor, either."

The good doctor stammered, "You're absolutely right, Mrs. Duff. I was completely out of line with that remark." They remained friends as well as patient and doctor, but Mama had demonstrated in a practical way the verse "Against an elder receive not an accusation."[8]

Mama told of another time at a prayer meeting—or some sort of fault-confessing (or fault-finding?) meeting—one of the women present told the pastor that he had a habit of talking out of the side of his mouth that irritated her so much she couldn't pay attention to what he had to say. Mama said the preacher just looked stunned, and the gathering was very quiet for a second or two. Mama spoke out, "Brother Mac, you can preach the Word from the side of your mouth better than any other preacher I ever heard speaking from the front of his mouth." After a round of hearty "Amens," the congregation relaxed.

She carried this attitude into the secular world, too. I cannot remember that she ever criticized any of our schoolteachers. I cannot believe that she never found fault with any politicians or public officials, but if she and Papa criticized them, ti was some time when the children were not around. I took this practice for granted when I was growing up, and I was certainly scandalized when my world broadened and I heard other parents who were critical of local, state and national politicians.

She applied this non-critical rule to her children. We were not allowed to "get personal" with another sibling. We could compliment another on some accomplishment, but we weren't allowed to mention the times the others had goofed up on some project. We could mention, for instance, a streak of dirt on a face in the interest of getting the face clean, but we couldn't say it was a homely or ugly face. We could say another's hair hadn't been combed so that little matter could be remedied, but we couldn't say the hair color was not pretty. Years later I could hear my mother speaking through me as I instructed my own children, "Don't get personal. If they can't do anything about it, or if they like it but you don't, just don't mention it." It was Mama putting into action "Be ye kind, one to another."[9]

We were never allowed to call anyone dumb, stupid, and never, no never, could we call anyone a fool. In fact, we seldom used that word. I was surprised to discover in my adult years the verse "whosoever shall say, Thou fool, shall be in danger of hell fire."[10]

I don't remember Mama saying "Thou shalt not take the name of the Lord thy God in vain."[11] She and Papa and we children just didn't do it. She believed that "gosh" and "gee" were just abbreviations for "God" and "Jesus," and "darn" was another form of "damn." In a time and place where nearly everyone said, "Good Lord," "My Lord" or "Oh, Lord" to express their frustrations and surprise, we were discouraged from using the name "Lord" in an empty manner. My high school friends told me they were reluctant to say "Dingbust it" around me. We didn't even know any of the scatological terms so prevalent today.

When Mama was helping a woman boarder shut the garage door in a hard, West Texas wind and sandstorm, I overheard Mama say to her, "Do you ever wonder why we live in this damn windy country?" I was shocked.

I never heard Papa take the Lord's name in vain, either. When he was exasperated with us—which I'm sure was often—he might say, "Oh, Pshaw!" Stronger expletives were "Tommyrot!" and "Tarnation!" And then there was "Ta! Ta!" Or even worse, "Ta! Ta! Ta!" As the boys would say, "When Papa gets up to 'Ta! Ta! Ta! Ta!—four 'ta's'—you'd better head for cover."

As Mama rocked her three-year-old grandson, Jimmy, I teased him about being a big baby and having to be rocked like his little sister. Mama said, "You just hush. All little people need lovin'." She practiced "Suffer little children to come unto me"[12] with her children and grandchildren and with countless other children who came under her care through the years.

Mama never told Jesus's story of the king who said, "Verily I say unto you. Inasmuch as ye have done it unto one of the least of these my brethren, ye have done it unto me."[13] She didn't have to tell it, she lived it.

When Mama took Mahaley to be operated on for appendicitis, Mama stayed with her during the operation and for the rest of the day. Mama was assured that someone would be with Mahaley during the night, but when she returned the next morning Mahaley had been moved to the basement, and she told Mama no one had come in to care for her during the night. It was a time and place where black people were treated shamefully by some people. Mama cleaned up Mahaley and her bed, read the riot act to the staff, made arrangements for Grandma to stay with us children, and then settled in to stay in the

Afterword—The Gospel According to Mama

basement with Mahaley night and day until she was able to come home.

Another time, Papa's sister, Aunt Willie, her husband, and their children, wanted to move to Big Spring where we lived. As the saying goes, "We weren't poor, we just didn't have any money," but Aunt Willie's family had even less. Mama and Papa found an old, run-down house to rent—its main attraction being rent of about five dollars a month—and Mama set out to get the old place cleaned up. Mama and I spent a long cold day trying to clean the unheated, barren place. The only water tap was outside, and I'm sure I spent the day griping to high heaven. I asked Mama if she thought Aunt Willie could do as much for Mama. She replied, "I don't know about that, but I do know that not a one of my sisters would be doing this for their sisters-in-law." But Mama did it for some of the least of them.

Mama didn't practice what she believed in one area—that of tithing. She believed in "Bring ye all the tithes into the storehouse."[14] But, she told me in her later years, it was the big regret of her life that they had not tithed. "But we just didn't see how we could do it. Maybe if we had, I reckon we wouldn't have had such a hard row to hoe—financially—all these years."

Mama told me the most money Papa ever made was one hundred and eighty dollars a month, and that was for a very short time right before the Depression. With ten or eleven mouths to feed most of the time, I can certainly understand how they didn't feel able to tithe. However, by the time they distributed nickels, dimes, quarters and half-dollars to all of those kids and cousins to take to Sunday School, the folks may have been tithing, or mighty close to it, without knowing it. But because they didn't make a systematic plan of tithing, Mama felt they missed the blessing of knowing they were completely within God's will in that respect.

She did try to teach her children to tithe as soon as each started making any salary. On some it took, on some it didn't. After Papa died, she sold the old house at 2118 to the Lutheran congregation that had built a lovely building on the lots next door. Mama wanted to tithe the ten thousand-dollar selling price, but she didn't think it was quite right to give that Lutheran money to the Baptist Church, and she returned the one thousand dollars to the Lutheran church. So she *was* tithing by the end of her life, when the children were grown.

Mama said, "My children don't worry whether we can pay the utility bills. They take it for granted that their parents will pay the bills. That's the attitude I should have toward God—He has said He'd take care of our needs, so I ought to quit worryin' about the utility bills." And I think perhaps she did worry a little less when she considered "For your Father knoweth what things ye have need of, before ye ask him."[15] One of her favorite sayings in the dialect of the community was "The Lord do provide," and she proved it over and over again.

Mama and Papa didn't have much of a social life in the middle years of their marriage. I can understand that—they both worked long days and must have been exhausted each evening. Consequently, I was quite surprised when I came in after an evening out and found them with another couple, playing dominoes. They seemed to have a pleasant evening with laughter and congenial conversation. I was in bed before the party broke up, but the next day I asked Mama, "What gives? It's not like you and Papa to have a wild evening of dominoes and fast living."

Mama replied, "Oh, we just thought we'd enjoy an evening with them."

I persisted, "Come on, Mama. You know only something most unusual could keep you and Papa from going to bed by nine o'clock."

I kept after her until she finally answered, "Oh, all right. I'll tell you, but you keep your mouth shut. There's been a lot of talk about Mrs. Smith (another name change) and Mr. (she named a certain man in town). She's so pretty and likeable I'm sure any man could be tempted. But Mr. Smith is such a nice man that I know he must be hurt as all git out by the talk, so I just thought they'd enjoy a night away from gossip. And they seemed to."

I reckon Mama had decided to "let he that is without sin among you, first cast a stone after her."[16] It must have worked. The Smiths were still married fifty years later.

Not all of her efforts to influence relationships were as successful. She once told a young woman who was living with a man without bothering to marry (long before the practice was so prevalent) that they had no business living that way, that they should get married. The young woman told her to bug off, get lost (or that decade's equivalent), that it was none of Mama's business.

One of the rare times I saw Mama cry came about in this manner: A few of Mama's young lady boarders and daughters were having a deep philosophical discussion (translate that to read "a knock-down drag-out argument") about the relative merits of different denominations' roads to heaven, and they called Mama to come upstairs to referee—and to answer some questions. I wasn't upstairs at the time, but I saw Mama come down the narrow stairs, crying, "I feel so guilty—I've had all these young people come through my home, or be under my influence, and I've never told them of Jesus' wonderful love and of how God wants us to live."

Mama, that fine example of agape love, didn't have to tell us. She lived a life that showed us.

SCRIPTURE REFERENCES FROM KING JAMES' VERSION

1. Proverbs 22:6
2. Deuteronomy 6:7
3. Psalms 119:151a
4. Hebrews 10:25a, b
5. Exodus 20:8
6. Psalms 100:2a
7. Ephesians 6:6c-7b
8. I Timothy 5:19a
9. Ephesians 4:32
10. Matthew 5:22c
11. Exodus 20:7a
12. Luke 18:16b
13. Matthew 25:37-40
14. Malachi 3:10
15. Matthew 6:8b
16. John 8:7b

Those Mobberly Girls (1886): from left, Lydia, Daisy (holding Ida), and Jessie.

The Last Family Photograph (1937): from left, Howard, Ida Rule, Beryl, Rosemary, Mama (Ida Mobberly Duff), Lydia Ann, Elsie, Berry N., and Frederick.